FHEasy

A YEAR OF

WEEKLY TEACHINGS
& DAILY DEVOTIONALS

FHEasy

A YEAR OF

WEEKLY TEACHINGS & DAILY DEVOTIONALS

CHRISTINA SHELLEY ALBRECHT

CFI, an imprint of Cedar Fort, Inc.
Springville, Utah

ISBN 13: 978-1-4621-1869-4

Published by CFI, an imprint of Cedar Fort, Inc., 2373 W. 700 S., Springville, UT 84663
Distributed by Cedar Fort, Inc., www.cedarfort.com

LIBRARY OF CONGRESS CATALOGING-IN-PUBLICATION DATA

Names: Albrecht, Christina Shelley, 1980- author.
Title: FHEasy : a year of weekly teachings and daily devotionals / Christina
    Shelley Albrecht.
Other titles: FHE easy
Description: Springville, Utah : CFI, an imprint of Cedar Fort, Inc., [2016]
    | Includes bibliographical references and index.
Identifiers: LCCN 2016038549 (print) | LCCN 2016041627 (ebook) | ISBN
    9781462118694 (perfect bound : alk. paper) | ISBN 9781462126606 (epub,
    pdf, mobi)
Subjects: LCSH: Family home evenings (Mormon Church)--Handbooks, manuals,
    etc. | LCGFT: Handbooks and manuals.
Classification: LCC BX8643.F3 A43 2016 (print) | LCC BX8643.F3 (ebook) | DDC
    249--dc23
LC record available at https://lccn.loc.gov/2016038549

Cover design by Shawnda T. Craig
Cover design © 2016 by Cedar Fort, Inc.
Edited and typeset by Chelsea Holdaway

Printed in the United States of America

10 9 8 7 6 5 4 3 2 1

Printed on acid-free paper

To my three beautiful daughters:
Leia Christina, Hana Rachelle, and Avonlea Shelley.
Thank you for coming to my family.

Contents

Contents

Acknowledgments

Thank you to all who have supported the creation of this book.

First, great appreciation goes to my parents, Monte and Elona Shelley. Mom, I deeply appreciate your persistent encouragement and your generous donation of time and resources. This book would never have been completed without your help. Pop, this book is much cleaner and easier to use thanks to all your work and feedback. Your help is invaluable to me.

Special thanks goes to McKell Parsons, Chelsea Holdaway, and everyone at Cedar Fort, Inc. for all of their excellent work. It has been a pleasure working with you.

Many thanks to my Quantum Leap friends and coaches: Bill and Steve Harrison, Geoffrey Berwind, Martha Bullen, Brian Edmondson, Deb Englander, Raia King, and Tamra Nashman Richardt. More people will benefit from this book because of you.

Finally, thanks to my husband, Ryan Albrecht, for encouraging this book's progress and for participating in our using this book in our home. And to my three beautiful daughters, thank you for participating in *FHEasy* lessons and scriptures. Thank you for giving me real-time feedback from the most important source. You are my treasures.

Introduction
Why Some Parents Give Up
and Why You Don't Need To

Are you tired of scrambling for a family home evening lesson every week? Tired of trying to figure out a way to do family scripture study that will work long term? Are you frustrated with battling wiggly kids or a distracted spouse? Are you so exhausted when FHE or scripture time rolls around that you'd rather not bother?

Well, if you are, you are in good company! Many parents face the same obstacles. Mine did! After years of trying, failing, and Mom fleeing the scene in tears, my parents finally just gave up.*

But I missed it.

I missed having family home evening and family scripture study.

I wanted to have them.

Even as a teenager.

And I wanted to give my children happy home evenings and scripture times that they would enjoy and that would bond us as a family.

This book was designed to meet the challenges that most families with children at home face: busy schedules, tired parents and kids, and short attention spans.

Speaking of busy schedules and short attention spans, how can parents with active, talkative children regularly and successfully teach gospel principles?

Well, this book addresses that too. In fact, this is the only book to date that I know of that combines family home evening and family scripture study in one easy-to-use manual.

May it bless your family in a million ways.

*To read my mother's experiences with family home evening when she had young children at home, along with how her perspective has changed, go to http://elonashelley.com/Articles.html and click on the article "Monday Night Madness."

My Story
Parent and Husband Approved

I was raised in a strong Latter-day Saint family with parents who embraced the lifestyle. From my perspective, we did everything we were "supposed" to do pretty well—except two things. My parents just couldn't seem to master having consistent, harmonious family home evenings or scripture study. They tried various things, but nothing really worked. In the process, we had a *lot* of unpleasant experiences, especially with family home evening.

You see, my mom had the idea that it was her job to prepare a lesson, and my dad's job to cheerfully call us all together (without having to be reminded) every Monday night (no other night was acceptable). We children were supposed to rush to their sides the moment we were called, participate attentively, and never interrupt. The problem was that Dad hadn't caught the vision, and neither had most of us kids.

So what really happened was that Mom would occasionally prepare a lesson with great enthusiasm. While she finished pulling her final materials together, she would tell Dad to round us all up. Eventually, everyone would reluctantly stop what they were doing and gather in the living room. Mom would get upset and scold us. By then, Dad was often already dozing on the couch. We'd run through the whole scene again a couple of times, except that Mom would sometimes nudge Dad awake so he could scold us too. Finally, Mom would jump up and run out of the room in tears. We'd get one last scolding from Dad, and then we'd all slink away feeling pretty *un*harmonious.

Things got harder as we got older and started working and participating in after-school activities. Eventually, Mom and Dad just gave up on having organized family home evenings.

But I always loved the idea because, although we had a lot of rough family home evenings, we also had some great ones. I loved snuggling with my oldest brother during family time. When the lesson was over, my older brothers would wrestle and laugh with my dad while my younger sister and I watched and laughed along with them. I absolutely loved our family trips to a nearby canyon park; exploring and playing with my family in such a beautiful place was heaven for me as a five-year-old.

I also remember some good family scripture times when I was little, though scripture time fizzled out before I graduated from elementary school. I remember loving when my parents read us children's scripture storybooks, and I enjoyed taking turns reading scriptures at an age when I had to be told that *hell* wasn't a swear word in the scriptures and that I could say it in good conscience. In short, I loved relaxing and playing with my family and just being together. I actually really needed that downtime to reconnect with my family no matter how old I was.

I knew I wanted my own family someday, and I knew I wanted us to be happy and close. I knew I would take on the responsibility of teaching my children core values and moral boundaries, but I also yearned for family closeness, love, and fun. I believed family home evening and scripture study were great ways to accomplish this. So, even though we didn't always have them growing up, I definitely planned on having them regularly when I had my own family.

Because of my family's experience, I realized that I might very well have to take the lead when it came to family time. I hoped my future husband would help gather the kids and participate in the discussions and activities, but I kept my expectations low.

When my husband and I were engaged, I asked him what he thought about family home evening and scripture study. He assured me he was planning on having them as a regular part of our family life when we had children. It was a huge relief for me to think I wouldn't be totally on my own.

But after we were married and had our first little girl, my husband was so busy making a living and his schedule was so unpredictable that family home evening and scripture time just didn't happen. When I talked to my husband about it, he told me he couldn't consistently be home for family nights because his work schedule was too random. He also didn't see how a planned family night or planned scripture time would make things any better than they were, since our family already spent quality time together and one of us regularly read scripture stories to our daughter.

He was right, of course, that we did lots of good things as a family, but we weren't reading the scriptures together *as a family*, and we weren't having the kind of thought-out family home evenings I'd dreamed of. There was no routine I could count on and no gospel focus. I knew I wanted to have regular family home evenings and scripture study when my children were teenagers, and I knew we needed to establish the habit while the kids were little. Plus, it sounded like something fun we could all look forward to—if I could figure out how to pull it off, that is.

So I owned my desire and decided to take it to the Lord.

One day while my baby was taking a nap, I felt the time was right. That afternoon, the house was peaceful and quiet. I gathered my scriptures, a notebook, and a pen, and sat in my favorite study spot where the sunlight was shining through the glass door onto our kitchen table. I placed my books and pen on the table, sat down, and gazed at nothing while thinking about my situation. My toddler was like the Tasmanian Devil, speeding around leaving disasters wherever she went—creating messes for me to clean up all day long. My husband was pushing himself hard at work and came home tired and irritable most of the time. The endless housework, yard work, cooking, cleaning, laundry, diapers, and taking care of my energetic child left me exhausted. The only one ever interested in doing *anything* in the evening was my daughter. My husband and I just wanted to fall over somewhere and go to sleep.

But I believed things could change. I didn't get married so I could do mundane chores, cook all the time, and clean up after a little person all day. I got married for the joy of it.

As I sat there, I pondered 1 Nephi 3:7, "I will go and do the things which the Lord hath commanded, for I know that the Lord giveth no commandments unto the children of men, *save he shall prepare a way for them that they may accomplish the thing he commandeth them*" (italics mine). I knew God had commanded parents to raise their children in light and truth. I also knew that family home evening and scripture study were the main strategies Church leaders encouraged parents to use. I believed God would hear and answer my prayers because I was trying to fulfill His commandments and follow the counsel of His servants.

So, I prayed my heart out. When I finished, I opened my eyes, relaxed, and turned to my scriptures. Within seconds, ideas rushed into my brain: "For family home evening, keep it short, play every time, and do it whether your husband is there or not. Use the Gospel Art pictures for lessons and read from the book *Stand a Little Taller* for family scripture time when you are all together for breakfast."

The inspired answers I received came to me over the course of about ten seconds, *but those ten seconds changed my family's life forever.*

I followed my inspiration and immediately found success. I bought *Stand a Little Taller*, which provides a quote by President Hinckley along with a scripture for each day of the year. At breakfast, I read the quote and scripture for the day. Though it was short, it was enjoyable, and I loved knowing we were establishing the habit of family scripture time.

I also bought the Gospel Art Picture Kit, which at that time had stories and information about each picture printed on the back. When family home evening came around, no matter how rough a day it had been, it was easy to grab a picture, read the story, and play with my daughter. When my husband was home, he participated. When he wasn't, we did it anyway. And my daughter ate it up. She became our number one family home evening fan. Her enthusiasm was very encouraging!

We followed that pattern for a few years, and it worked marvelously. But after our second daughter turned two, an interesting thing happened. I noticed that my older daughter was growing up and asking more thoughtful questions. At five, she still had a very short attention span, but I could tell she was thinking more deeply about things.

As I thought about how we could teach her gospel principles at a deeper level but in a practical way, I began to envision exactly what we needed—a resource that introduced a topic during family home evening, accompanied by short scripture verses for each day of the week on that same topic. We could spend some time introducing and discussing the topic at family home evening and then reinforce it with the short scripture verses throughout the week.

I knew it would work perfectly! So I got online to find that perfect resource because I thought, "You can find anything online, right?" Wrong! I was shocked! I couldn't find anything like it.

I couldn't believe it. The Internet had failed me! There were books with family home evening ideas, and there were scripture storybooks, but they were sold separately. I also saw online resources for family home evening, but I knew I'd have to spend hours trying to find even a few that might work for my family. It was overwhelming for me to even think about searching for appropriate family home evening ideas, for who knows how long, when my time was already maxed out. Plus, that didn't give me the correlating scriptures for the week.

Since the book I wanted didn't exist, I realized I would have to create it. At first, I created a book for all ages that simply did not go over well with my kids. They were too young for the long quotes and scriptures I had included. Plus, they missed the lessons from *Behold Your Little Ones*. So I designed a handbook tailored toward families with young children who had super short attention spans, just like my children's. And my kids loved it! In fact, we all loved it. Using my book, I could pull off a great family home evening in a flash *every time*. And we could read the short, accompanying scripture verses while everyone ate breakfast together. It was lovely. Family home evening and scripture study became smooth sailing.

One day while visiting teaching, we started talking about the challenge of having family home evening and scripture study with small children. The friend we were visiting had a four-year-old and a two-year-old, and she was experiencing many of the same frustrations I had. I offered her some lessons from my book, and she gladly accepted. A few weeks later, she came up to me at church and excitedly started telling me how my lessons were transforming her family's experience. She now *loves* family home evening and scripture study with her kids. I was so happy for her!

When I learned that my ideas were making a difference and that more people wanted copies, I decided to expand my book to have adaptations that could work for all families, regardless of the ages of their children. Then when it was published, my book could help as many families as possible transform their experiences with family home evening and scripture study.

But more than wanting to help parents meet their responsibility to teach their children, I want to help families experience love and closeness and have a wonderful time just being together.

I hope this book helps bring an abundance of love, fun, and closeness into your home.

Is This Approach Really Easy?

Yes! Simply choose a topic from the table of contents and flip to the right page. Often, we choose topics based on family needs or the holiday for the week. Some weeks we don't have any specific needs, so we just pick any topic we are interested in.

Key Features of This Book

- Every week is laid out for you on four pages: general FHE ideas on the first page, adaptations for younger children on the second page, adaptations for older children on the third page, and the daily scriptures for the week on the fourth page.

- Each FHE lesson includes a scripture of the week, several quotes, references to Primary songs and church hymns, scripture stories, references to Gospel Art pictures, a Church history section, lessons from Church manuals, and activity ideas—all of which are either/or options. (I never use all the ideas listed in one FHE lesson. Just pick and choose what you want to do and leave the rest.) I also QR codes are included in each lesson for those who are tech savvy. Prep time should never need more than five minutes, and none of the additional resource materials are required.

- For family scripture study, there is a scripture for each day of the week that correlates with the FHE lesson topic. I have included all of the Articles of Faith and almost all of the seminary doctrinal mastery scriptures as scriptures of the week. They are identified so you can emphasize them and help your children become familiar with them. Articles of Faith are marked with this graphic. AF Doctrinal mastery scriptures are marked with this graphic. DM

In Practice

While this manual is easy for parents to use, the bonus is that it's also easy for *kids* to use. Kids love to be involved. My children are now ages ten, seven, and four. One family night, my oldest daughter chose the topic for the week. She read the quote and sang a song off the list. My second daughter chose to show a picture and talk about it for the lesson. Afterward, we played with toys together.

For families with older children, take turns picking a topic and leading the family home evening: selecting from the songs, quotes, scripture stories, and Church history sections, and then adding in appropriate content from the section "Adaptations for Older Children."

For families with children that span both age groups, it's easy to adapt the content to the needs of each age group. As a family, you can sing a song, read a quote, talk about a scripture story, and discuss a

Church history event. After that, everyone could do the younger children's activity together, or you could break off into age-appropriate activities: coloring pages from *Behold Your Little Ones* for younger children and *Personal Progress* or *Duty to God* activities for the older children.

Note that there are a few activities with this symbol beside them: ⏰ . This means that this activity involves some preparation ahead of time. It might be making or buying a pizza or a treat, reviewing a page in the appendix so you are prepared for the activity, or trying out an object lesson so you can do it smoothly when the time comes. Remember that even these activities can be adapted so there's less prep. You can draw the pizza, talk about the object lesson but not do it, or simply skip the activity idea and focus on other things. Whatever works for you!

Where Can I Go to Get Recommended Resources or Access Them Online for Free?

In each lesson, I reference the Primary *Children's Songbook*, the LDS hymnbook, the LDS scriptures, the *Gospel Art Book*, and several Church manuals (details below). I also frequently quote from the "My Gospel Standards" Primary poster. This is a poster for Primary-aged children that lists thirteen standards for gospel living. When it was introduced, the Primary general presidency said, "Primary children have been given [a list of] gospel standards to help them live the gospel of Jesus Christ. . . . During the coming year, find opportunities to teach these standards in family home evening, in the classroom, and in sharing time" ("My Gospel Standards," *Ensign,* September 2000).

You can purchase these resources at any LDS distribution center or at store.lds.org. You might also find them at amazon.com, depending on availability.

Most of these resources are found at LDS.org. From there you may view or download them by using the search bar or by going to the following URLs. Note that the URLS are current as of the date of publication; however URLs can change at any time and shortened URLs may occasionally stop working.

Songs

- *Hymns* table of contents
  https://www.lds.org/music/library/hymns?lang=eng or at https://goo.gl/qrZSui.

- *Children's Songbook* table of contents
  https://www.lds.org/music/library/childrens-songbook?lang=eng or at https://goo.gl
  /tMN7qj.

Scriptures

- At LDS.org, the "Scriptures and Study" tab links to all the standard works, study helps, and the "About the Scriptures" page. The "About the Scriptures" page has additional resources for learning about scriptures, studying scriptures, and watching Bible videos. It also includes information about the newest edition of LDS scriptures.

- LDS View™ is a Church scripture program for Windows computers found at http:// ldsview.wordcruncher.com. LDS View is a version of WordCruncher®, which was developed at Brigham Young University. Both programs have study tools to help students and scholars better understand the scriptures. You can search for words, see how many times they occur in books or chapters, see their common "neighbors," see footnotes and study helps, look up Hebrew and Greek meanings of Bible words, add notes and bookmarks, and highlight text. At www.wordcruncher.com, you can find additional information, resources, and ideas for scripture study. WordCruncher offers a variety of downloads including, the scriptures (in 30+ languages), general conference talks, and some Church manuals.

Pictures

- *Gospel Art Book*
  https://www.lds.org/manual/gospel-art-book/gospel-art-book?lang=eng&query=gospel+art+book+contents or at https://goo.gl/acnvBP

Church History

- LDS.org Gospel Topics
  https://www.lds.org/topics?lang=eng or at https://goo.gl/3fB43i.

- LDS.org Church History website
  https://history.lds.org/?lang=eng or at https://goo.gl/UhRE9e.

- FAIR Mormon website
  http://www.FairMormon.org

  FAIR stands for "Foundation for Apologetic Information and Research." An "apologist" is a person who defends their faith, not someone apologizing for their beliefs. Volunteer church members address issues brought up by church critics or those who have questions. Their slogan is "Critical questions. Faithful answers."

Resources for Younger Children

- "My Gospel Standards" Primary poster
  https://www.lds.org/media-library/images/my-gospel-standards-183289?lang=eng&_r=1 or at http://goo.gl/EGmA8m (for downloading)

  http://media.ldscdn.org/images/media-library/beliefs-practices/my-gospel-standards-183289-print.jpg or at http://goo.gl/C7eGdU (clearer version for viewing online).

  Throughout *FHEasy*, this poster is referred to simply as "My Gospel Standards." However, the full citation is "My Gospel Standards," *Friend*, October 2004, illustrated poster by Del Parson

- *Behold Your Little Ones* table of contents
  https://www.lds.org/manual/behold-your-little-ones-nursery-manual?lang=eng or at https://goo.gl/vYhXHk

- *Faith in God for Girls* pamphlet (An activity book to help young girls ages 8–11 develop faith in God.)
  https://www.lds.org/manual/faith-in-god-for-girls?lang=eng or at https://goo.gl/2fa9L8

- *Faith in God for Boys* pamphlet (An activity book to help young boys ages 8–11 develop faith in God.)
  https://www.lds.org/manual/faith-in-god-for-boys?lang=eng or at https://goo.gl/a9uva4

Resources for Older Children

- *Preach My Gospel* (The Church's official missionary guidebook.)
  https://www.lds.org/manual/preach-my-gospel-a-guide-to-missionary-service?lang=eng or at https://goo.gl/cBvY69

- *Young Women Personal Progress* guidebook (This guidebook and program are for young women ages 12–18.)
  https://www.lds.org/young-women/personal-progress?lang=eng or at https://goo.gl/bKdH3L

- *Fulfilling My Duty to God For Aaronic Priesthood Holders* (This guidebook and program are for young men ages 12–18.)
  https://www.lds.org/young-men/duty-to-god?lang=eng or at https://goo.gl/KttJVz

- *For the Strength of Youth* pamphlet (This pamphlet outlines eighteen standards and guidelines to strengthen, educate, and protect youth.)
  https://www.lds.org/youth/for-the-strength-of-youth?lang=eng or at https://goo.gl/nR2T23

Why Is Scripture Memorization Optional in This Manual?

Elder Richard G. Scott stated,

> Learning, pondering, searching, and memorizing scriptures is like filling a filing cabinet with friends, values, and truths that can be called upon anytime, anywhere in the world. . . . Great power can come from memorizing scriptures. To memorize a scripture is to forge a new friendship. It is like discovering a new individual who can help in time of need, give inspiration and comfort, and be a source of motivation for needed change. ("The Power of Scripture," *Ensign,* November 2011)

Many children love to memorize scriptures. Even young children who do not understand a scripture's full meaning often enjoy memorizing short scriptures. Each week's lesson starts with a scripture. These scriptures are meant for children who like to memorize, and for teens and adults who like to "ponderize" (see Devin G. Durrant, "My Heart Pondereth Them Continually," *Ensign*, November 2015).

Doctrinal Mastery homepage
https://goo.gl/MGeX38

Students share blessings of the SM scriptures (now Doctrinal Masteries). https://goo.gl/SUDcay

Some of the Articles of Faith and seminary doctrinal mastery scriptures can be too long for young children to fully memorize. You can teach the Articles of Faith by singing the songs out of the *Children's Songbook* (122–32), which makes them easier to memorize. For doctrinal mastery scriptures, have older children memorize them in full and give younger children a shortened version of the scripture to memorize.

Go to https://goo.gl/MGeX38 to see the Doctrinal Mastery home page. To watch a short video about the blessings of teenagers memorizing seminary scripture mastery scriptures (now known as doctrinal mastery scriptures), go to https://goo.gl/SUDcay.

If children are interested and ready to memorize scriptures, they will love it. If it is not working, try other approaches or don't worry about it for a while. Scripture study is intended to help you and your family come closer together and closer to God, so if memorizing scriptures helps meet those goals, do it. If it is proving stressful, don't worry about it.

Here are a few ideas for how you could make scripture memorization part of your family.

•   Read the scripture of the week every day and have your children repeat it to you. Then read the scripture for the day.

•   Make a copy of some or all of the scriptures of the week and tape the list somewhere conspicuous, like near the dinner table or your children's beds. If your children can read, they will be more likely to review the scriptures on their own because they see them often. If they can't read yet, you can read the scripture of the week to them during meals, family scripture time, or at night before they go to bed. A list of all the weekly scriptures in this book can be found at http://goo.gl/hu6X1M.

•   Have your children draw pictures that represent the scripture of the week. If your children can read and write, have them write the scripture and its reference on a piece of paper. Then have them draw around or under it. If they are too young for that, do the writing and drawing yourself and let them color or scribble on the paper. This is a great Sunday or FHE activity that helps them focus on what you will be talking about that week.

•   Make scripture memorization fun for your family by putting fun stickers on a chart or rewarding them with a treat when they memorize a new scripture.

FHEasy Lessons and
Daily Scriptures

An Overview of the Articles of Faith

"We believe in God, the Eternal Father, and in His Son, Jesus Christ, and in the Holy Ghost." (Articles of Faith 1:1) 📖

LDS.org video "The Doctrines and Principles Contained in the Articles of Faith" https://goo.gl/x9AT6a

Music from Children's Songbook & Hymns

- Faith (*CS*, 96)
- The Articles of Faith (*CS*, 122–32)
- Praise to the Man (*Hymns*, 27)
- True to the Faith (*Hymns*, 254)

Quote

"What a great blessing it would be if every member of the Church memorized the Articles of Faith and became knowledgeable about the principles contained in each. We would be better prepared to share the gospel with others" (L. Tom Perry, "The Articles of Faith," *Ensign*, May 1998).

Scripture Stories

Joseph Smith was called by God to restore the true Church of Jesus Christ, whose doctrines are described in the Articles of Faith, which are recorded in the Pearl of Great Price. Joseph Smith and his calling as a prophet were revealed to other prophets in earlier times (see 2 Nephi 3:6–15 and Joseph Smith Translation, Genesis 50:30–33, [in the Bible appendix]).

LDS.org article "Sharing Time: The Articles of Faith" goo.gl/ubqWiz

Joseph Smith wrote the Articles of Faith in 1842. The year before that, the Lord commanded the Saints to build the Nauvoo Temple, which was dedicated in 1846. The Lord said that baptisms for the dead would be recognized while the temple was being built, but when the temple was completed, the baptisms would be required to be done in the temple (see D&C 124:22–44; D&C 127). The method of baptism—and even whether or not baptism was really necessary—was highly debated in Joseph Smith's time. In Article of Faith 4, Joseph clearly stated that it was necessary and that God's method was baptism by immersion. In Doctrine and Covenants 124, God also makes it clear that baptisms for the dead need to be performed in His temple when temples are available.

Gospel Art Pictures

- *Brother Joseph* (#87)
- *The First Vision* (#90)
- *Nauvoo Illinois Temple* (#118)
- *Temple Baptismal Font* (#121)

Church History

Why did Joseph Smith write the Articles of Faith? Joseph wrote,

> "March 1, 1842.—At the request of Mr. John Wentworth, editor and proprietor of the *Chicago Democrat,* I have written the following sketch of the rise, progress, persecution, and faith of the Latter-day Saints, of which I have the honor, under God, of being the founder. Mr. Wentworth says that he wishes to furnish Mr. Bastow [Barstow], a friend of his, who is writing the history of New Hampshire, with this document." ("The Wentworth Letter," *Ensign,* July 2002)

LDS.org images "Nauvoo Illinois Temple" https://goo.gl/AgwNX5

A year before Joseph wrote the letter to Mr. Wentworth first outlining the Articles of Faith, the Lord commanded the Saints to build the Nauvoo Temple. The dedication of the original Nauvoo Temple was performed by Elder Orson Hyde. It lasted for three days, from May 1, 1846, to May 3, 1846. In 1848, the temple was burned, and in 1850, a tornado damaged it even more. Nearly 150 years later, on April 4, 1999, President Gordon B. Hinckley announced the rebuilding of the Nauvoo Temple, and on June 27, 2002, he dedicated it.

LDS.org video "Overview of Church History." Filmed before the restored Nauvoo Illinois Temple was built, this video divides Church history into six periods. The third is the Nauvoo period. http://goo.gl/qS6U7a

Adaptations for Younger Children

Quote

"I encourage you to use your bright minds to study and learn the Articles of Faith and the doctrines they teach" (L. Tom Perry, "The Doctrines and Principles Contained in the Articles of Faith," *Ensign,* November 2013).

Lesson from *Behold Your Little Ones*

"I Belong to The Church of Jesus Christ of Latter-day Saints" (Lesson 25, pp. 104–7).

Faith in God

Find the Articles of Faith in the *Faith in God* booklet (p. 16). Review them and have your children pass off any they have memorized. Record any Articles of Faith they pass off (p. 20).

Activity

If your children are very young, draw something to symbolize each Article of Faith, and then let them scribble or color.

If your children are older and have learned some or all of the Articles of Faith, play charades. Get thirteen pieces of paper and put a number on each paper to represent each of the Articles of Faith. Put the pieces of paper in a bag or a hat and let people take turns drawing out a piece of paper. If necessary, help the person who chose the number know which Article of Faith to silently act out. Let everyone try to guess which Article of Faith is being acted out.

Adaptations for Older Children and Teens

Quote

"I encourage you to use your bright minds to study and learn the Articles of Faith and the doctrines they teach. They are among the most important and certainly the most concise statements of doctrine in the Church. If you will use them as a guide to direct your studies of the gospel of Jesus Christ, you will find yourself prepared to declare your witness of the restored truth to the world. You will be able to declare in simple, straightforward, and profound ways the core beliefs you hold dear as a member of The Church of Jesus Christ of Latter-day Saints" (L. Tom Perry, "The Doctrines and Principles Contained in the Articles of Faith," *Ensign,* November 2013).

Preach My Gospel

Look over the introduction to familiarize yourself with how the book is laid out (pp. vii–xi), and then flip through the whole *Preach My Gospel* book. If you have studied it for a while, test yourself and see how many chapter headings and lessons you can remember.

Personal Progress

Look through the *Personal Progress* book; see how it is laid out and what is in it. Read over the introductory pages (pp. 1–10), the value sections (pp. 11–75), and the pages after the value sections (pp. 76–84). Parents, look over the section "Overview for Parents and Leaders" (pp. 86–94). Also, notice that "The Family: A Proclamation to the World" and "The Living Christ: The Testimony of the Apostles" are on pages 101 and 102 for future reference.

Duty to God

Look through the *Duty to God* book; see how it is laid out and what is in it. Read over the introductory pages (pp. 5–11); the sections for deacons, teachers, and priests (pp. 12–89); and the section "To Quorum Presidents" (pp. 90–92). Parents, look over the section "To Quorum Advisers and Parents (pp. 93–102). Read over the appendix, which contains information about Aaronic Priesthood ordinances (pp. 103–5). Also, notice that "The Living Christ: The Testimony of the Apostles" and "The Family: A Proclamation to the World" are on pages 106 and 107 of the *Duty to God* book for future reference.

Activity ⊘

Quickly review all of the Articles of Faith. Get thirteen pieces of paper and put a number on each paper to represent each of the Articles of Faith. Put the pieces of paper in a bag or a hat and let everyone take turns drawing out a piece of paper. As a family, you can either read or recite each Article of Faith as it is drawn, or you can play a speed game. For the game, sit in a tight circle. Have one person pick a paper and start reciting the Article of Faith. Slap one hand in the middle of the circle when you recognize which Article of Faith is being recited. The person whose hand is on the bottom recites the Article of Faith. Don't get too picky about it being recited word for word. As a bonus, see if people can think of a scripture, scripture story, or Church history story that goes along with each Article of Faith.

Daily Scriptures

An Overview of the Articles of Faith

Sunday 📖

"We believe in God, the Eternal Father, and in His Son, Jesus Christ, and in the Holy Ghost. We believe that men will be punished for their own sins, and not for Adam's transgression. We believe that through the Atonement of Christ, all mankind may be saved, by obedience to the laws and ordinances of the Gospel." (Articles of Faith 1:1–3)

Monday 📖

"We believe that the first principles and ordinances of the Gospel are: first, Faith in the Lord Jesus Christ; second, Repentance; third, Baptism by immersion for the remission of sins; fourth, Laying on of hands for the gift of the Holy Ghost. We believe that a man must be called of God, by prophecy, and by the laying on of hands by those who are in authority, to preach the Gospel and administer in the ordinances thereof." (Articles of Faith 1:4–5)

Tuesday 📖

"We believe in the same organization that existed in the Primitive Church, namely, apostles, prophets, pastors, teachers, evangelists, and so forth. We believe in the gift of tongues, prophecy, revelation, visions, healing, interpretation of tongues, and so forth." (Articles of Faith 1:6–7)

Wednesday 📖

"We believe the Bible to be the word of God as far as it is translated correctly; we also believe the Book of Mormon to be the word of God. We believe all that God has revealed, all that He does now reveal, and we believe that He will yet reveal many great and important things pertaining to the Kingdom of God." (Articles of Faith 1:8–9)

Thursday 📖

"We believe in the literal gathering of Israel and in the restoration of the Ten Tribes; that Zion (the New Jerusalem) will be built upon the American continent; that Christ will reign personally upon the earth; and, that the earth will be renewed and receive its paradisiacal glory." (Articles of Faith 1:10)

Friday 📖

"We claim the privilege of worshiping Almighty God according to the dictates of our own conscience, and allow all men the same privilege, let them worship how, where, or what they may. We believe in being subject to kings, presidents, rulers, and magistrates, in obeying, honoring, and sustaining the law." (Articles of Faith 1:11–12)

Saturday 📖

"We believe in being honest, true, chaste, benevolent, virtuous, and in doing good to all men. . . . We believe all things, we hope all things, we have endured many things, and hope to be able to endure all things. If there is anything virtuous, lovely, or of good report or praiseworthy, we seek after these things." (Articles of Faith 1:13)

Article of Faith 1:
The Godhead

"We believe in God, the Eternal Father, and in His Son, Jesus Christ, and in the Holy Ghost." (Articles of Faith 1:1) 📖

Mormon.org article and videos "The Godhead: A Quick Overview" https://goo.gl/cHcMbK

Music from Children's Songbook & Hymns

- This Is My Beloved Son (*CS*, 76)
- The First Article of Faith (*CS*, 122)
- Joseph Smith's First Prayer (*Hymns*, 26)
- Our Savior's Love (*Hymns*, 113)

Quote

"We declare it is self-evident from the scriptures that the Father, the Son, and the Holy Ghost are separate persons, three divine beings, noting such unequivocal illustrations as the Savior's great Intercessory Prayer . . . , His baptism at the hands of John, the experience on the Mount of Transfiguration, and the martyrdom of Stephen" (Jeffrey R. Holland, "The Only True God and Jesus Christ Whom He Hath Sent," *Ensign*, November 2007).

Gospel Topic: Godhead https://goo.gl/cfQSJz

Scripture Stories

Jesus is baptized by John the Baptist. All three members of the Godhead are present and obviously distinct (see Matthew 3:13–17 and Joseph Smith Translation, Matthew 3:43–46 [in Matthew 3:15, footnote *a*]).

When Stephen was martyred, he was full of the Holy Ghost and saw the Father and Jesus Christ together as separate Beings (see Acts 7:55).

Joseph Smith ponders, reads, prays, and receives the First Vision—a visitation from Heavenly Father and Jesus Christ (see Joseph Smith—History 1:14–20).

Gospel Art Pictures

- *John the Baptist Baptizing Jesus* (#35)
- *Stephen Sees Jesus on the Right Hand of God* (#63)
- *The First Vision* (#90)

Church History

Joseph Smith received what he called "the first visitation of angels" in the spring of 1820 when he was fourteen years old. There are several accounts of what we now call "the First Vision" that share details that are different from the official account published in the Pearl of Great Price. To see a graphic visualization of the similarities and differences among the accounts, go to http://goo.gl/txHsVq.

For the text of twelve original accounts of the First Vision, go to LDS.org's gospel topic "First Vision Accounts" at https://goo.gl /qFMWhm. This page also addresses two common concerns people have about the credibility of Joseph Smith's experience: memory and embellishment. It concludes by encouraging people to pray and ask God if He and Jesus Christ came to Joseph Smith and spoke with him.

FairMormon.org page "Joseph Smith's different accounts of the First Vision" http://goo.gl/txHsVq

Gospel Topics: First Vision Accounts https://goo.gl/qFMWhm

Adaptations for Younger Children

Quotes

"I am a child of God. I know Heavenly Father loves me, and I love Him. I can pray to Heavenly Father anytime, anywhere. I am trying to remember and follow Jesus Christ" ("My Gospel Standards").

"I will follow Heavenly Father's plan for me" ("My Gospel Standards").

"I will remember my baptismal covenant and listen to the Holy Ghost" ("My Gospel Standards").

Lessons from *Behold Your Little Ones*

"The Holy Ghost Helps Me" (Lesson 6, pp. 28–31) and "Joseph Smith Saw Heavenly Father and Jesus Christ" (Lesson 21, pp. 88–91).

Faith in God

Help your children memorize and pass off the first article of faith this week. Recite this Article of Faith or sing the primary song daily as part of your family scripture study (*Children's Songbook*, 122). For Article of Faith 1, the memory trick is the rhyme "One" and "Son." We believe in the Father, the Son, and the Holy Ghost. See page 230 in this book for the full list of memory helps. On a piece of paper, have your children write the first article of faith, draw a picture that represents it, and then tape it in a prominent place (*Faith in God*, pp. 16, 20).

Activity ☉

Get a pen, pencil, crayon, and rubber band. Put the rubber band around the pen, pencil, and crayon to tie them together. Explain that they represent the Father, the Son, and the Holy Ghost. They have similarities, but they are different. They are distinct, yet unified. After the lesson, draw or color.

Adaptations for Older Children and Teens

Quote

"I am not worried that the Prophet Joseph Smith gave a number of versions of the first vision anymore than I am worried that there are four different writers of the gospels in the New Testament, each with his own perceptions, each telling the events to meet his own purpose for writing at the time. I am more concerned with the fact that God has revealed in this dispensation a great and marvelous and beautiful plan that motivates men and women to love their Creator and their Redeemer, to appreciate and serve one another, to walk in faith on the road that leads to immortality and eternal life" (Gordon B. Hinckley, "God Hath Not Given Us the Spirit of Fear," *Ensign*, October 1984).

Preach My Gospel

"God Is Our Loving Heavenly Father," pp. 31–32; "Through Christ We Can Be Cleansed from Sin," pp. 60–61; "Faith in Jesus Christ," pp. 61–62; "The Holy Ghost," pp. 90–92.

Personal Progress

Individual Worth #1—Read the listed scriptures and write about what you learn about Heavenly Father in your journal (p. 30). As a daughter of God, you have great individual worth. Review the section on "Individual Worth." See what you've done and what you haven't done. Review value project ideas (pp. 29–36).

Choice and Accountability #5—Learn about the Holy Ghost by reading the suggested scriptures, discussing them with another person, and writing about them in your journal (p. 47).

Integrity #3—Learn about the Savior and His integrity. Write about examples of people showing integrity and think of times when you have acted with integrity (p. 63).

Duty to God

Study the doctrinal topic of "The Godhead." Record what you learn and share what you learned with your parents or a priesthood leader (see pp. 18–21, 42–45, 66–69).

Activity 📖

Look on pages 232–33 in the appendix for a brief comparison of the four accounts of the First Vision. Discuss the various things mentioned in different accounts of the First Vision. For members of the Church, the details are not the most important thing. The most important thing is to discover for ourselves through prayer and personal revelation if Heavenly Father and Jesus Christ appeared to Joseph Smith and began the events that led to the Restoration of Christ's Church. Share your thoughts and testimonies about the First Vision.

Daily Scriptures

Article of Faith 1: The Godhead

Sunday 📖

"We believe in God, the Eternal Father, and in His Son, Jesus Christ, and in the Holy Ghost." (Articles of Faith 1:1)

Monday 📖

"The Father has a body of flesh and bones as tangible as man's; the Son also; but the Holy Ghost has not a body of flesh and bones, but is a personage of Spirit. Were it not so, the Holy Ghost could not dwell in us. A man may receive the Holy Ghost, and it may descend upon him and not tarry with him." (D&C 130:22–23)

Tuesday 📖

"I saw a pillar of light exactly over my head, above the brightness of the sun, which descended gradually until it fell upon me. . . . When the light rested upon me I saw two Personages, whose brightness and glory defy all description, standing above me in the air. One of them spake unto me, calling me by name and said, pointing to the other—This is My Beloved Son. Hear Him!" (Joseph Smith—History 1:16–17)

Wednesday

"Jesus saith unto him, I am the way, the truth, and the life: no man cometh unto the Father, but by me. The Holy Ghost, whom the Father will send in my name, he shall teach you all things, and bring all things to your remembrance, whatsoever I have said unto you." (John 14:6, 26)

Thursday 📖

"For behold, this is my work and my glory— to bring to pass the immortality and eternal life of man." (Moses 1:39)

Friday 📖

"For if ye would hearken unto the Spirit which teacheth a man to pray, ye would know that ye must pray; for the evil spirit teacheth not a man to pray, but teacheth him that he must not pray. But behold, I say unto you that ye must pray always, and not faint; that ye must not perform any thing unto the Lord save in the first place ye shall pray unto the Father in the name of Christ, that he will consecrate thy performance unto thee, that thy performance may be for the welfare of thy soul." (2 Nephi 32:8–9)

Saturday

"Put your trust in that Spirit which leadeth to do good—yea, to do justly, to walk humbly, to judge righteously; and this is my Spirit. Verily, verily, I say unto you, I will impart unto you of my Spirit, which shall enlighten your mind, which shall fill your soul with joy." (D&C 11:12–13)

Article of Faith 2:
The Creation and the Fall of Adam

"We believe that men will be punished for their own sins, and not for Adam's transgression." (Articles of Faith 1:2) 📖

Music from Children's Songbook & Hymns

- The Second Article of Faith (*CS*, 122)
- My Heavenly Father Loves Me (*CS*, 228)
- Adam-ondi-Ahman (*Hymns*, 49)
- How Great Thou Art (*Hymns*, 86)

MormonChannel.org video
"The World Around Us:
Our Home, The Earth."
http://goo.gl/qqRPOj

Quote

"Grand as it is, planet Earth is part of something even grander—that great plan of God. Simply summarized, the earth was created that families might be" (Russell M. Nelson, "The Creation," *Ensign*, May 2000).

Scripture Stories

God creates the world and everything in it. He creates the Earth, light and darkness, land and water, plants and animals, and finally, Adam and Eve. He places them in the Garden of Eden.

God tells Adam and Eve they can eat any fruit, except the fruit from the tree of knowledge of good and evil. If they do, they will become mortal and die. God also tells them they can choose for themselves. When they eat the fruit, the consequence is that they must leave the Garden of Eden, but now they can have children (see Moses 3:1–9, 15–25; 4:7–31; 2 Nephi 2:22–23).

Lehi teaches about God, the Creation, agency, the Fall of Adam, the consequences of Adam and Eve's choices, and the Atonement of Jesus Christ (see 2 Nephi 2:14–30).

Gospel Art Pictures

- *The Lord Created All Things* (#2)
- *The Earth* (#3)
- *Adam and Eve Kneeling at an Altar* (#4)
- *Adam and Eve Teaching Their Children* (#5)

Church History

Some people believe that Adam and Eve made a big mistake by eating the fruit of the tree of knowledge of good and evil. They believe that if Adam and Eve had not done so, all people would be born as immortals into a glorious garden where no pain or suffering exists. The Book of Mormon and the Pearl of Great Price clearly teach that Adam and Eve would have had no children had they not fallen (see 2 Nephi 2:22–23; Moses 5:11).

Throughout the Church's history, leaders have taught that we should honor Adam and Eve and be grateful for their choice to become mortal, thereby allowing the family of mankind to come to earth. President Harold B. Lee taught, "We [should], with Eve, rejoice in the Fall, which permitted the coming of the knowledge of good and evil, which permitted the coming of children into mortality, which permitted the receiving of joy of redemption and the eternal life which God gives to all" (*Teachings of Presidents of the Church: Harold B. Lee*, 21).

See the topic "Fall of Adam" on LDS.org here: https://goo.gl/7jvjDH. See also http://goo.gl/hfLsrU for differing views on the Fall of Adam and faithful responses to those views.

This LDS.org video titled "The Atonement" shows children talking about the Atonement in their own words. https://goo.gl/gMqbMp

LDS.org video, "We Become." In this video, young men and young women talk about how the program "Come Follow Me" has helped them become converted and use the Atonement more. https://goo.gl/DZ3GXf

Adaptations for Younger Children

Quote

"I will choose the right. I know I can repent when I make a mistake" ("My Gospel Standards").

Lessons from *Behold Your Little Ones*

"Jesus Christ Created the World for Me" (Lesson 7, pp. 32–35) and "I Love the Scriptures" (Lesson 23, pp. 96–99). Tell the story of the Creation from lesson 7 and include Adam and Eve. Use the puppet activity from Lesson 23.

Faith in God 🔳

Help your children memorize and pass off the second article of faith this week. Recite it or sing it every day during family scripture study (*Children's Songbook*, 122). For Article of Faith 2, the memory trick is "two" and "too." "Two" refers to the first two people, Adam and Eve. "Too" refers to the choices that come with consequences "too." See page 230 in this book for the full list of memory helps. On a piece of paper, have your children write the second article of faith, draw a picture that represents it, and then tape it in a prominent place (*Faith in God*, pp. 16, 20).

Activity

Get a pencil or stick and show the children that when you pick up one end of the stick, the other end comes up too. Explain that one end represents choices and one end represents consequences. When we make choices, we get the consequences attached to those choices. You can choose your choices, but not your consequences. Some choices have positive consequences, and some have negative consequences. Discuss some choices and their consequences.

Adaptations for Older Children and Teens

Quote

"From the moment those first parents stepped out of the Garden of Eden, the God and Father of us all, anticipating Adam and Eve's decision, dispatched the very angels of heaven to declare to them—and down through time to us—that this entire sequence was designed for our eternal happiness. It was part of His divine plan, which provided for a Savior, . . . who would come in the meridian of time to atone for the first Adam's transgression. That Atonement would achieve complete victory over physical death, unconditionally granting resurrection to every person who has been born or ever will be born into this world. Mercifully it would also provide forgiveness for the personal sins of all, from Adam to the end of the world, conditioned upon repentance and obedience to divine commandments" (Jeffrey R. Holland, "Where Justice, Love, and Mercy Meet," *Ensign*, May 2015).

Preach My Gospel

Lesson 2: "The Plan of Salvation," pp. 47–59; "Agency and the Fall of Adam and Eve," pp. 49–50.

Personal Progress

Choice and Accountability #3—Discuss the blessing of agency and the responsibility we have to accept consequences for the choices we make. The guidelines and standards taught at church can help us if we choose to live them, but they do us no good unless we *choose* to follow them. What guidelines, standards, and commandments do you feel are mocked in our world today? Which ones do you feel help you the most? Which ones could you embrace more fully? (p. 47).

Duty to God

Study the doctrinal topic of "The Plan of Salvation." Record what you learn and share what you learned with your parents or a priesthood leader (see pp. 18–21, 42–45, 66–69).

Activity

Get a pencil or stick and have someone pick it up by one end. Point out that when you pick up one end of the stick, the other end comes up too. Explain that one end represents choices and one end represents consequences. When we make choices, we get the consequences attached to those choices. Some choices have positive consequences, and some have negative consequences. Media messages often portray inaccurate consequences for choices, making good choices appear to have dull and boring consequences, while evil choices are made to produce magnificent and exciting consequences. It is essential that we develop discernment so we are not seduced by lies, act on false advertising, and then reap the bitter consequences. Discuss some choices and consequences, both how they are portrayed falsely by media outlets and how they are in real life.

Daily Scriptures

Article of Faith 2: The Creation and the Fall of Adam

Sunday 📖

"We believe that men will be punished for their own sins, and not for Adam's transgression." (Articles of Faith 1:2)

Monday

"The Son of God hath atoned for original guilt, wherein the sins of the parents cannot be answered upon the heads of the children, for they are whole from the foundation of the world." (Moses 6:54)

Tuesday 📖

"Behold, if Adam had not transgressed he would not have fallen, but he would have remained in the garden of Eden. . . . [Adam and Eve] would have had no children; wherefore they would have remained in a state of innocence, having no joy, for they knew no misery; doing no good, for they knew no sin. But behold, all things have been done in the wisdom of him who knoweth all things. Adam fell that men might be; and men are, that they might have joy." (2 Nephi 2:22–25)

Wednesday 📖

"And the Messiah cometh in the fulness of time, that he may redeem the children of men from the fall. . . . Wherefore, men are free according to the flesh; and all things are given them which are expedient unto man. And they are free to choose liberty and eternal life, through the great Mediator of all men, or to choose captivity and death, according to the captivity and power of the devil; for he seeketh that all men might be miserable like unto himself." (2 Nephi 2:26–27)

Thursday 📖

"Adam blessed God and was filled, . . . saying: Blessed be the name of God, for because of my transgression my eyes are opened, and in this life I shall have joy, and again in the flesh I shall see God." (Moses 5:10)

Friday

"Eve . . . was glad, saying: Were it not for our transgression we never should have had seed, and never should have known good and evil, and the joy of our redemption, and the eternal life which God giveth unto all the obedient. And Adam and Eve blessed the name of God, and they made all things known unto their sons and their daughters." (Moses 5:11–12; "seed" means children)

Saturday 📖

"And I saw the dead, small and great, stand before God; and the books were opened: and another book was opened, which is the book of life: and the dead were judged out of those things which were written in the books, according to their works." (Revelation 20:12)

Article of Faith 3:
The Atonement, Sacrament, and Salvation

"We believe that through the Atonement of Christ, all mankind may be saved, by obedience to the laws and ordinances of the Gospel." (Articles of Faith 1:3) 🔖

Music from *Children's Songbook* & *Hymns*

Mormonads—Christ
https://goo.gl/xXZuCd

- I Lived in Heaven (*CS*, 4)
- He Sent His Son (*CS*, 34)
- The Third Article of Faith (*CS*, 123)
- I Will Follow God's Plan (*CS*, 164)
- *Children's Songbook* songs about the sacrament (*CS*, 71–73)
- I Believe in Christ (*Hymns*, 134)
- I Stand All Amazed (*Hymns*, 193)
- Sacrament hymns (*Hymns*, 169–96)

Quote

"We often speak of the Savior's Atonement—and rightly so! . . . But as 'we talk of Christ, . . . rejoice in Christ, . . . preach of Christ, [and] prophesy of Christ' at every opportunity, we must never lose our sense of awe and profound gratitude for the eternal sacrifice of the Son of God. The Savior's Atonement cannot become commonplace in our teaching, in our conversation, or in our hearts. It is sacred and holy, for it was through this 'great and last sacrifice' that Jesus the Christ brought 'salvation to all those who shall believe on his name'" (Dieter F. Uchtdorf, "The Gift of Grace," *Ensign*, May 2015).

Scripture Stories

Jesus introduces the sacrament to His Apostles in Jerusalem during the Last Supper (see Matthew 26:17–19, 26–30).

Jesus prays that Heavenly Father will spare Him the agony of going through the Atonement, but adds, "Nevertheless not my will, but thine, be done" (Luke 22:42) (see also Luke 22:39–44).

Jesus institutes the sacrament among the Nephites (see 3 Nephi 18:1–11).

These scriptures contain the sacrament prayers (see Moroni 4–5; D&C 20:75–79).

Gospel Art Pictures

- *The Last Supper* (#54)
- *Jesus Praying in Gethsemane* (#56)
- *Blessing the Sacrament* (#107)
- *Passing the Sacrament* (#108)

Church History

When and why did members of the Church start using liquids other than wine for the sacrament? When and why did the Church officially begin using only water for the sacrament ordinance?

In August 1830, the Lord warned the Saints not to buy wine from their enemies. He also told them it didn't matter what they used for the sacrament ordinance; what mattered was that they participated in the ordinance sincerely (see D&C 27:1–4). On July 5, 1906, the Church leaders began using only water in sacrament meetings, presumably due to a desire to adhere to the Word of Wisdom (see FairMormon's page "Question: How was enforcement of the Word of Wisdom phased in over time?," at http://goo.gl/r8P4c3).

LDS.org video "The Emblems of the Sacrament" with Elder Holland
https://goo.gl/PsEnEE

For more information about the history of using water and wine for sacrament ordinances, see FairMormon's page "Why do Mormons use water instead of wine for its sacrament service?" at http://goo.gl/jdvnvM.

Adaptations for Younger Children

Quote

"I am a child of God. I know Heavenly Father loves me, and I love Him. I can pray to Heavenly Father anytime, anywhere. I am trying to remember and follow Jesus Christ" ("My Gospel Standards").

Lessons from *Behold Your Little Ones*

"Heavenly Father Has a Plan for Me" (Lesson 2, pp. 12–15) and "The Sacrament Helps Me Think about Jesus Christ" (Lesson 27, pp. 112–15).

Faith in God

Help your children memorize and pass off the third article of faith this week. Recite it or sing it every day during family scripture study (*Children's Songbook*, 123). For Article of Faith 3, the memory trick is "tree, free, obee." "Tree" refers to the cross Jesus died on while atoning for us. "Free" reminds us that salvation is free. "Obee" is the start of "obedience." See page 230 in this book for the full list of memory helps. On a piece of paper, have your children write the third article of faith, draw a picture that represents it, and then tape it in a prominent place (*Faith in God*, pp. 16, 20).

Activity

Symbols are things that represent and remind us of other things. Think of common symbols like a heart, a smiley face, and an arrow. A heart often symbolizes love. Smiley faces symbolize happiness. An arrow shows you which way to go. If you have some bread and a small cup of water on hand, show them to the kids. The symbols of the sacrament are bread, which represents Jesus's body, and water, which represents His blood. Both remind us of His Atonement and His love for us.

Adaptations for Older Children and Teens

Quote

"What do we say when someone asks us, 'Have you been saved?' . . . As I understand what is meant by the good Christians who speak in these terms, we are 'saved' when we sincerely declare or confess that we have accepted Jesus Christ as our personal Lord and Savior. . . . Every sincere Latter-day Saint is 'saved' according to this meaning. We have been converted to the restored gospel of Jesus Christ, we have experienced repentance and baptism, and we are renewing our covenants of baptism by partaking of the sacrament. . . . The short answer to the question of whether a faithful member of The Church of Jesus Christ of Latter-day Saints has been saved or born again must be a fervent 'yes.' Our covenant relationship with our Savior puts us in that 'saved' or 'born again' condition meant by those who ask this question" (Dallin H. Oaks, "Have You Been Saved?," *Ensign*, May 1998).

Preach My Gospel

"The Atonement," pp. 51–52; "Through Christ We Can Be Cleansed from Sin," pp. 60–61; Lesson 5: "Laws and Ordinances," pp. 82–88.

Personal Progress

Faith #5—Read scriptures about the Atonement, the sacrament, and the sacrament prayers. Decide how you will make taking the sacrament a sacred experience for you, and then make a habit of following your plan (p. 16).

Duty to God

Look over the sections titled "Administer Priesthood Ordinances." Read scriptures about the sacrament and the sacrament prayers. Talk to your family about their feelings on the sacrament. Ask them what they appreciate in those who help with the sacrament. Decide what you can do to bring a greater spirit to the sacrament portion of sacrament meeting (see pp. 24–25, 48–49, 72–73).

Study the doctrinal topic of "The Atonement of Jesus Christ." Record what you learn and share what you learned with your parents or a priesthood leader (see pp. 18–21, 42–45, 66–69).

Activity ☺

Give everyone a small bag of sugar. Tell them that every person on earth receives the sweet gift of resurrection thanks to Jesus's Atonement. However, people who use the Savior's Atonement to become sanctified can receive an even sweeter gift—eternal life: "which gift is the greatest of all the gifts of God" (D&C 14:7). Tell everyone you will share a treat with them that's nicer than straight sugar. Then give everyone a sweet treat like cookies, cake, pie, or ice cream.

Daily Scriptures

Article of Faith 3: The Atonement, Sacrament, and Salvation

Sunday

"We believe that through the Atonement of Christ, all mankind may be saved, by obedience to the laws and ordinances of the Gospel." (Articles of Faith 1:3)

Monday

"[Jesus] is despised and rejected of men; a man of sorrows, and acquainted with grief. . . . Surely he hath borne our griefs, and carried our sorrows. . . . He was wounded for our transgressions, he was bruised for our iniquities: the chastisement of our peace was upon him; and with his stripes we are healed." (Isaiah 53:3–5)

Tuesday

"For God so loved the world, that he gave his only begotten Son, that whosoever believeth in him should not perish, but have everlasting life. For God sent not his Son into the world to condemn the world; but that the world through him might be saved." (John 3:16–17)

Wednesday

"I, God, have suffered these things for all, that they might not suffer if they would repent; But if they would not repent they must suffer even as I; Which suffering caused myself, even God, the greatest of all, to tremble because of pain, and to bleed at every pore, and to suffer both body and spirit—and would that I might not drink the bitter cup, and shrink—Nevertheless, glory be to the Father, and I partook and finished my preparations unto the children of men." (D&C 19:16–19)

Thursday

"I will testify unto you of myself that these things are true. . . . Christ shall come among the children of men, to take upon him the transgressions of his people, and that he shall atone for the sins of the world. . . . For it is expedient that an atonement should be made; for according to the great plan of the Eternal God there must be an atonement made, or else all mankind must unavoidably perish . . . but it must be an infinite and eternal sacrifice." (Alma 34:8–10)

Friday

"Behold, I am Jesus Christ, whom the prophets testified shall come into the world. And behold, I am the light and the life of the world; and I have drunk out of that bitter cup which the Father hath given me, and have glorified the Father in taking upon me the sins of the world, in the which I have suffered the will of the Father in all things from the beginning. . . . Arise and come forth unto me . . . that ye may know that I am the God of Israel, and the God of the whole earth, and have been slain for the sins of the world." (3 Nephi 11:10–11, 14)

Saturday

"In the ordinances [of the gospel], the power of godliness is manifest." (D&C 84:20)

Article of Faith 4:
The First Principles and Ordinances of the Gospel

(Note: This lesson focuses mostly on faith.)

"We believe that the first principles and ordinances of the Gospel are: first, Faith in the Lord Jesus Christ; second, Repentance; third, Baptism by immersion for the remission of sins; fourth, Laying on of hands for the gift of the Holy Ghost." (Articles of Faith 1:4) 🅰🅵

YouTube video "I Know That My Savior Loves Me" posted by Cheri Dennet. This video shows related pictures as children sing the song. http://goo.gl/qzmnFo

Music from Children's Songbook & Hymns

- Faith (*CS*, 96)
- The Fourth Article of Faith (*CS*, 124)
- I Believe in Christ (*Hymns*, 134)
- I Know That My Redeemer Lives (*Hymns*, 136)

Quote

"Faith, this gift from God . . . is still the strength of this work and the quiet vibrancy of its message. Faith underlies it all. Faith is the substance of it all. Whether it be going into the mission field, living the Word of Wisdom, paying one's tithing, it is all the same. It is the faith within us that is evidenced in all we do" (Gordon B. Hinckley, "The Miracle of Faith," *Ensign*, May 2001).

Scripture Stories

Nephi teaches that the Holy Ghost will show people what to do (see 2 Nephi 32:5).

Alma teaches and baptizes in the waters of Mormon (see Mosiah 18:7–17).

Alma the Younger and the four sons of Mosiah fight against the Church. They are stopped by an angel, who tells them to repent. Alma is unconscious for several days. He has faith in Jesus Christ, repents, and becomes a missionary (see Mosiah 27:8–37; Alma 36:3–24).

Alma teaches that faith is not knowledge. He compares the word to a seed and shows how we use faith to test it. If you have a good seed and you take good care of it, it will grow and produce fruit (see Alma 32:26–43).

Gospel Art Pictures

- *Conversion of Alma the Younger* (#77)
- *Young Man Being Baptized* (#103)
- *Girl Being Baptized* (#104)
- *The Gift of the Holy Ghost* (#105)

Church History

David O. McKay became the President of the Church in 1951 and continued to lead the Church until January 1970. About the first principles and ordinances of the gospel, he taught,

"An unwavering faith in Christ is the most important need of the world today. . . . Faith in God cannot of course be other than personal. It must be yours; it must be mine; and, to be effective, must spring from the mind and heart. . . . The message of [missionaries] who are going in all parts of the world, the message of the Church to all the world is: Repent of those things which contribute to the superiority of the physical senses over our love for spirituality. That is why they cry repentance! What does repentance mean? A change of life, a change of thought, a change of action. . . . The ordinance of baptism is a law of God, obedience to which, in sincerity, in purity, in simplicity, brings inevitably the promised blessing of the Comforter, a divine Guide. (*Teachings of Presidents of the Church: David O. McKay*, 196, 198, 201; brackets in the original)

David O. McKay: Documentary
https://goo.gl/Bm8cwv

Adaptations for Younger Children

Quote

"I will remember my baptismal covenant and listen to the Holy Ghost" ("My Gospel Standards").

Lessons from *Behold Your Little Ones*

"Heavenly Father and Jesus Christ Love Me" (Lesson 4, pp. 20–23), "I Will Say 'I'm Sorry'" (Lesson 16, pp. 68–71), and "I Will Be Baptized and Confirmed" (Lesson 26, pp. 108–11).

Faith in God

Help your children memorize and pass off the fourth article of faith this week. Recite it or sing it every day during family scripture study (*Children's Songbook*, 124). For Article of Faith 4, the memory trick is "four" for the first four principles and ordinances of the gospel. See page 230 in this book for the full list of memory helps. On a piece of paper, have your children write the fourth article of faith, draw a picture that represents it, and then tape it in a prominent place (*Faith in God*, pp. 16, 20).

Activity

Faith is both an internal experience, as well as something we demonstrate through our actions. Talk about ways we develop the internal feeling of faith, which is belief. We hear faith-promoting stories that increase our own faith. We pray and read scriptures to increase our faith. We feel the Holy Ghost, which increases our faith. Talk about faithful actions we do that show our faith, such as going to church, praying, obeying the commandments, and following promptings. Draw or act out the things people say.

Adaptations for Older Children and Teens

Quotes

"We must take time to actively exercise our faith. Such exercise invites the positive, faith-filled power of the Atonement of Jesus Christ into our lives. Our Father in Heaven has given us tools to help us come unto Christ and exercise faith in His Atonement. When these tools become fundamental habits, they provide the easiest way to find peace in the challenges of mortality" (Richard G. Scott, "Make the Exercise of Faith Your First Priority," *Ensign*, November 2014).

"I testify to you that our promised blessings are beyond measure. Though the storm clouds may gather, though the rains may pour down upon us, our knowledge of the gospel and our love of our Heavenly Father and of our Savior will comfort and sustain us and bring joy to our hearts as we walk uprightly and keep the commandments. There will be nothing in this world that can defeat us. My beloved brothers and sisters, fear not. Be of good cheer. The future is as bright as your faith" (Thomas S. Monson, "Be of Good Cheer," *Ensign*, May 2009).

"Spiritual strength is like physical strength; it is like the muscle of my arm. It grows only as it is nourished and exercised. As you exercise your time and talents in service, your faith will grow and your doubts will wane" (Gordon B. Hinckley, "He Is Risen, As He Said," *Ensign*, April 1983).

Preach My Gospel

Lesson 3: "The Gospel of Jesus Christ," pp. 60–70.

Personal Progress

Faith #1—Learn about faith by reading scriptures and conference talks on faith, praying regularly for three weeks, talking about faith and prayer with others, and writing about it in your journal (p. 14).

Duty to God

Study the doctrinal topic of "Faith." Record what you learn and share what you learned with your parents or a priesthood leader (see pp. 18–21, 42–45, 66–69).

Activity

Invite each person to share a faith-promoting story or experience they have recently had. This could be an experience with prayer, scripture reading, a prompting from the Holy Ghost, something they read in a church magazine, or something they heard at church or general conference. Then invite each person to share things they've noticed that show the faith of family members. For example, one person may have seen another family member in personal prayer or scripture reading. One person may have noticed someone's cheerful service. Another person may have heard someone mention something that the Holy Ghost prompted them to do. The point is to share two sides of faith—the internal belief and the external actions.

Daily Scriptures

Article of Faith 4: The First Principles and Ordinances of the Gospel

Sunday 📖

"We believe that the first principles and ordinances of the Gospel are: first, Faith in the Lord Jesus Christ; second, Repentance; third, Baptism by immersion for the remission of sins; fourth, Laying on of hands for the gift of the Holy Ghost." (Articles of Faith 1:4)

Monday 📖

"Even so faith, if it hath not works, is dead, being alone. Yea, a man may say, Thou hast faith, and I have works: shew me thy faith without thy works, and I will shew thee my faith by my works." (James 2:17–18)

Tuesday 📖

"I will go and do the things which the Lord hath commanded, for I know that the Lord giveth no commandments unto the children of men, save he shall prepare a way for them that they may accomplish the thing which he commandeth them." (1 Nephi 3:7)

Wednesday

"By the ministering of angels, and by every word which proceeded forth out of the mouth of God, men began to exercise faith in Christ; and thus by faith, they did lay hold upon every good thing; and thus it was until the coming of Christ. And after that he came men also were saved by faith in his name; and by faith, they become the sons of God." (Moroni 7:25–26)

Thursday 📖

"And now, I, Moroni, would speak somewhat concerning these things; I would show unto the world that faith is things which are hoped for and not seen; wherefore, dispute not because ye see not, for ye receive no witness until after the trial of your faith." (Ether 12:6)

Friday 📖

"Trust in the Lord with all thine heart; and lean not unto thine own understanding. In all thy ways acknowledge him, and he shall direct thy paths." (Proverbs 3:5–6)

Saturday

"And now as I said concerning faith—faith is not to have a perfect knowledge of things; therefore if ye have faith ye hope for things which are not seen, which are true." (Alma 32:21)

Article of Faith 5: Missionary Work

"We believe that a man must be called of God, by prophecy, and by the laying on of hands by those who are in authority, to preach the Gospel and administer in the ordinances thereof." (Articles of Faith 1:5)

Mormonads—Missionary Work
https://goo.gl/LdBbYv

Music from Children's Songbook & Hymns

- The Fifth Article of Faith (*CS*, 125)
- I Hope They Call Me on a Mission (*CS*, 169)
- *Children's Songbook* songs about missionary work (*CS*, 168–74)
- Called to Serve (*CS*, 174; *Hymns*, 249)
- I'll Go Where You Want Me to Go (*Hymns*, 270)

Quote

"[Missionaries] serve with the sole hope of making life better for other people. [Serving] a mission will shape the spiritual destiny of the missionary, his or her spouse, and their posterity" (Russell M. Nelson, "Ask the Missionaries! They Can Help You!," *Ensign*, November 2012).

Scripture Stories

The Pharisees criticize Jesus for eating with sinners and tax collectors. In response, Jesus tells the parable of the lost sheep. He says, "Rejoice with me; for I have found my sheep which was lost. . . . Joy shall be in heaven over one sinner that repenteth" (Luke 15:6–7) (see also Luke 15:1–10).

Ammon serves King Lamoni and later teaches him about God. Lamoni then teaches his people and many are baptized (see Alma 17:20–Alma 19).

Joseph F. Smith shares that he was pondering on the love of Christ, his Atonement, and how Peter talked about the gospel being preached to the dead. He shares a vision of the spirit world, including missionary work done there (see D&C 138).

Gospel Art Pictures

- *Jesus Carrying a Lost Lamb* (#64)
- *Ammon Defends the Flocks of King Lamoni* (#78)
- *Missionaries: Elders* (#109)
- *Missionaries: Sisters* (#110)

Church History

Who was the first officially called, full-time missionary? *Samuel Smith, Joseph Smith's younger brother.* At twenty-two years old, he went on a mission alone with only a few recently printed copies of the Book of Mormon. Before he returned, his efforts had helped bring Brigham Young and Heber C. Kimball, future Apostles and the next president, into the Church (see Ryan Carr, "The First Latter-day Saint Missionary, "*New Era,* September 2004 at https://goo.gl/fH2f3S).

Joseph F. Smith: Documentary
https://goo.gl/3UtvMj

Who was likely the youngest missionary called in the latter days? *Joseph F. Smith, who was called to a mission in Hawaii when he was fifteen years old.* To read an article about him and his mission in Hawaii, see the *Nauvoo Times* article "The Youngest Missionary," by James B. Allen (http://goo.gl/XBj7qQ).

When did President McKay first start saying "Every member a missionary"? *1959* (see David O. McKay, "Closing Address," *Conference Report,* April 1959 at http://scriptures.byu.edu/gettalk.php?ID=1017 or http://goo.gl/vLdLv5. See also Richard G. Scott, "Why Every Member a Missionary?," *Ensign,* November 1997).

When was the Church missionary handbook *Preach My Gospel* introduced? *Elder Scott introduced it in the April 2005 general conference in a talk titled,* "The Power of Preach My Gospel."

Adaptations for Younger Children

Quote

"We can all participate in missionary work. This is the Lord's work, and He will help us do it" (Silvia H. Allred, "Go Ye Therefore," *Ensign,* November 2008).

Lesson from *Behold Your Little Ones*

"Heavenly Father Blesses Me through the Priesthood" (Lesson 28, pp. 116–19). Focus on being called and set apart as a missionary so others can be blessed.

Faith in God

Memorize and pass off the fifth article of faith this week. Recite it or sing it every day during family scripture study (*Children's Songbook,* 125). For Article of Faith 5, the memory trick is the rhyme "thrive." We are called of God to thrive and share the gospel so others can thrive too. See page 230 in this book for the full list of memory helps. On a piece of paper, have your children write the fifth article of faith, draw a picture that represents it, and then tape it in a prominent place (*Faith in God,* pp. 16, 20).

Activity ☉

Invite the missionaries over for family home evening. Have them share a lesson and some stories. Tell missionary stories, especially the story of how your family came to accept the gospel. Show pictures of your mission or of missionaries that have made a difference in your life.

Have one person go out of the room, and then give everyone else a treat. Tell them that there is a treat for the person who is out of the room and ask how that person will get their treat. They can try yelling, throwing the treat, or anything else. They will soon realize that the only way the person will get their treat is if someone takes it to them. Send a couple of "missionaries" to tell the person outside the room that there is a treat for them and invite them to get it.

Adaptations for Older Children and Teens

LDS.org video of Elder Rasband's conference talk "The Divine Call of a Missionary." https://goo.gl/Z55Yqi

Quotes

"Elder Eyring was assigning missionaries to their fields of labor, and as part of my training, I was invited to observe. . . . I had a further witness that morning that every missionary called in this Church, and assigned or reassigned to a particular mission, is called by revelation from the Lord God Almighty through one of these, His servants" (Ronald A. Rasband, "The Divine Call of a Missionary," *Ensign*, May 2010).

"Upon my return home [from my mission], it became increasingly apparent that even though I had left my mission, my mission didn't leave me. In fact, even after all these years, I still feel that my mission was the best two years *for* my life" (Matthew O. Richardson, "Teaching after the Manner of the Spirit," *Ensign*, November 2011; italics in original).

Preach My Gospel

Chapter 1: "What Is My Purpose as a Missionary?," pp. 1–16; Chapter 3: "What Do I Study and Teach?," pp. 29–88; "[Member] Missionary Work," p. 84.

Personal Progress

Good Works #7—Because of your good works, people may become interested in the gospel. "Pray for a missionary experience" (p. 56).

Duty to God

Look over the sections titled "Invite All to Come unto Christ" (pp. 28, 52, 76). Work on the one for your age group.

"Find examples of missionaries in the scriptures. . . . Practice teaching some of the lessons in chapter 3 of *Preach My Gospel*. . . . Interview three returned missionaries" (p. 87).

Activity ⏱

Get some food you can either serve beautifully or mangled: cake, ice cream, bread, soup, and so on Find something you already have that would appeal to your family if served nicely. Ask everyone who would like some of the food or dessert. Then mangle the food onto a serving dish. If it's cake or bread, grab a piece with your hand and slap it onto a plate. If it's ice cream or soup, scoop it out with your fingers, lick them, and scoop out a little more. Go big with this, so your family will be shocked. Tell your family that the gospel is more attractive to people depending on how it is "served." Then serve the food nicely and normally. Talk about different ways people "serve" the gospel to people. What ways are appealing, and what ways are offensive? It matters how we dress, what we do, what we say, and how honest we are, because we are "serving up" the church at *all* times, even when we aren't thinking about it.

Daily Scriptures

Article of Faith 5: Missionary Work

Sunday 📖

"We believe that a man must be called of God, by prophecy, and by the laying on of hands by those who are in authority, to preach the Gospel and administer in the ordinances thereof." (Articles of Faith 1:5)

Monday 📖

"Again I say unto you, that it shall not be given to any one to go forth to preach my gospel, or to build up my church, except he be ordained by some one who has authority, and it is known to the church that he has authority and has been regularly ordained by the heads of the church." (D&C 42:11)

Tuesday 📖

"Wherefore the Lord said, Forasmuch as this people draw near me with their mouth, and with their lips do honour me, but have removed their heart far from me, and their fear toward me is taught by the precept of men: Therefore, behold, I will proceed to do a marvellous work among this people, even a marvellous work and a wonder: for the wisdom of their wise men shall perish, and the understanding of their prudent men shall be hid." (Isaiah 29:13–14)

Wednesday

"[The sons of Mosiah] had searched the scriptures diligently, that they might know the word of God. But this is not all; they had given themselves to much prayer, and fasting; therefore they had the spirit of prophecy, and the spirit of revelation, and when they taught, they taught with power and authority of God." (Alma 17:2–3)

Thursday

"Go ye therefore, and teach all nations, baptizing them in the name of the Father, and of the Son, and of the Holy Ghost: Teaching them to observe all things whatsoever I have commanded you: and, lo, I am with you alway, even unto the end of the world. Amen." (Matthew 28:19–20)

Friday

"Then [Jesus] called his twelve disciples together, and gave them power and authority. . . . And he sent them to preach the kingdom of God." (Luke 9:1–2)

Saturday 📖

"And if it so be that you should labor all your days in crying repentance unto this people, and bring, save it be one soul unto me, how great shall be your joy with him in the kingdom of my Father! And now, if your joy will be great with one soul that you have brought unto me into the kingdom of my Father, how great will be your joy if you should bring many souls unto me!" (D&C 18:15–16)

Article of Faith 6:
The Organization of the Church

"We believe in the same organization that existed in the Primitive Church, namely, apostles, prophets, pastors, teachers, evangelists, and so forth." (Articles of Faith 1:6) 🖼️

LDS.org video "How the Church is Organized" https://goo.gl/PBjL7B

Organization of the Church of Jesus Christ http://goo.gl/29mpo4

Music from Children's Songbook & Hymns

- Follow the Prophet (*CS*, 110)
- The Sixth Article of Faith (*CS*, 126)
- Latter-day Prophets (*CS*, 134)
- We Thank Thee, O God, for a Prophet (*Hymns*, 19)

Quotes

"The Bible helps us understand that Jesus organized His Church with apostles, prophets, pastors, teachers, and other Church officials who held the priesthood, which is the authority to act in God's name. . . . Joseph [Smith] received the priesthood of God, giving him the authority to organize the Church once again" (John B. Dickson, "A Brief Introduction to the Church," *Ensign*, May 2000).

"The growing question of today is clear: are you standing with the leaders of the Church in a darkening world so that you might spread the Light of Christ?" (Ronald A. Rasband, "Standing with the Leaders of the Church," *Ensign*, May 2016).

Scripture Stories

Aaron and his sons are washed and anointed to be priests (see Exodus 40:12–16; Hebrews 5:4).

Jesus calls and ordains His Twelve Apostles (see Matthew 4:18–22; Matthew 10:1–4).

Jesus calls and ordains His twelve Nephite Apostles. He tells the people they will be blessed if they follow His twelve ordained ministers and servants (see 3 Nephi 11:16–22; 3 Nephi 12:1).

Gospel Art Pictures

- *Moses Gives Aaron the Priesthood* (#15)
- *Calling of the Fisherman and Christ Ordaining the Apostles* (#37–38)
- *Jesus Teaching in the Western Hemisphere* (#82)
- *John the Baptist Conferring the Aaronic Priesthood* (#93)
- *Melchizedek Priesthood Restoration* (#94)
- *The Foundation of the Relief Society* (#98)
- *Ordination to the Priesthood* (#106)
- *Latter-day Prophets* (#122–37)

Church History

After the martyrdom of Joseph Smith in the summer of 1844, the Saints had to decide who to follow. Sidney Rigdon claimed to be the next leader, but the Twelve Apostles claimed Joseph had given the keys of the kingdom to them; therefore, they had the right to receive revelation on who was to be the next leader of the Church. Most of the Saints followed the Twelve, and Brigham Young became the second prophet and President of the Church. To learn more this, and also about the succession of the presidency in general, go to https://goo.gl/Xm5Hsb.

Throughout Church history, new leaders have been called. Go to LDS.org's page "Calling an Apostle of God" at https://goo.gl/uaRH9M for information and videos explaining how this is done and what the roles of the Apostles are today.

LDS.org video "Elder Bednar Speaks on Apostles Role" https://goo.gl/VjUxun

Adaptations for Younger Children
Quote

"Our Father in Heaven loves all of His children and desires that they know and understand His plan of happiness. Therefore, He calls prophets. . . . They are messengers of righteousness, witnesses of Jesus Christ and the infinite power of His Atonement" (Carol F. McConkie, "Live according to the Words of the Prophets," *Ensign*, November 2014).

LDS.org video "Apostle Testimony Montage". This video shows the first testimonies of the First Presidency and Quorum of the Twelve Apostles (2016) after being called as Apostles. https://goo.gl/aDBHK5

Lesson from *Behold Your Little Ones*

"I Will Follow the Prophet" (Lesson 24, pp. 100–103).

Faith in God

Memorize and pass off the sixth article of faith this week. Recite or sing it daily during family scripture study (*Children's Songbook*, 126). For Article of Faith 6, the memory trick is the word 'ex-six-ted.' "We believe in the same organization that 'ex-six-ted' in the primitive church." See page 230 in this book for the full list of memory helps. On a piece of paper, have your children write the sixth article of faith, draw a picture that represents it, and then tape it in a prominent place (*Faith in God*, pp. 16, 20)

Talk about the purpose and importance of the Young Men and Young Women organizations (see *Faith in God for Girls*, p. 12). Learn about the restoration of the Aaronic Priesthood by reading Doctrine and Covenants 13, Doctrine and Covenants 107:20, and Joseph Smith—History 1:68–73 (see *Faith in God for Boys*, p. 12).

Activity ⏱

Get a cutting board or a piece of cardstock. This represents the foundation of the Church—Jesus Christ and His ordained Apostles. Get some blocks or non-breakable cups. These represent the Quorum of the Seventy, mission and area presidents, stake presidents, patriarchs, bishoprics, Relief Society presidencies, Young Women and Primary presidencies, along with all the members of all the stakes, wards, and branches in the Church. "Build" the Church organization on the cutting board. Then pull out the "foundation," and watch everything fall apart. Without our foundation, the Church would be on unstable ground and would fall apart. Rebuild the "Church" and show that because we are founded on Christ, we are on stable ground.

Adaptations for Older Children and Teens

Quote

"The most precious thing lost in the Apostasy was the authority held by the Twelve—the priesthood keys. For the Church to be *His* Church, there must be a Quorum of the Twelve who hold the keys and confer them on others. In time came the First Vision and the restoration of the Melchizedek Priesthood by Peter, James, and John. . . . [Since then] there has been an unbroken line of authority. The priesthood keys given to the Apostles have always been held by members of the First Presidency and Quorum of the Twelve" (Boyd K. Packer, "The Twelve," *Ensign*, May 2008).

Preach My Gospel

Lesson 1: "The Message of the Restoration of the Gospel of Jesus Christ," pp. 31–46; Chapter 13: "How Do I Work with Stake and Ward Leaders?," pp. 213–24.

Personal Progress

Integrity #5—Apostles are called to be special witnesses of Jesus. When we are baptized, we covenant to be witnesses of God in our daily lives (see Mosiah 18:9). Learn about what that means and think of something you would like to change in order to become a better example of a Christian. Record your experience (p. 64).

Duty to God

Study the doctrinal topic of "Prophets." Record what you learn and share what you learned with your parents or a priesthood leader (see pp. 18–21, 42–45, 66–69).

Study the doctrinal topics of "The Restoration of the Priesthood" and "The Priesthood and Priesthood Keys." Record what you learn and share what you learned with your parents or a priesthood leader (see pp. 18–21, 42–45, 66–69).

Look over the section "Preparing to Receive the Melchizedek Priesthood" (pp. 84–89). Work on it, or review what you did if you are already a priest. Also, review page 105, titled "Conferring the Aaronic Priesthood and Ordaining to an Office."

Activity

Get a clear plastic bag and fill it with puzzle pieces, or anything that can be put together in an orderly way. Seal the bag. Have someone take the bag. Instruct the person to assemble the puzzle by shaking the bag. No opening allowed. Ask if it is possible. Have everyone think about the earth and ask if they think it would be possible for the earth to have just fallen into place in such an orderly way without God's work, purpose, and order. Have everyone think about the order of the Church. God is a God of order. He created the Earth in an orderly way, and He created His Church in an orderly way to bless our lives. (Adapted from Richard R. Eubank, *Is There an Object to Your Lesson?*, 47.)

Daily Scriptures

Article of Faith 6: The Organization of the Church

Sunday

"We believe in the same organization that existed in the Primitive Church, namely, apostles, prophets, pastors, teachers, evangelists, and so forth." (Articles of Faith 1:6)

Monday

"[Jesus] went out into a mountain to pray, and continued all night in prayer to God. And when it was day, he called unto him his disciples: and of them he chose twelve, whom also he named apostles." (Luke 6:12–13)

Tuesday

"[Jesus] came and preached peace to you which were afar off, and to them that were nigh. For through him we both have access by one Spirit unto the Father. Now therefore ye are no more strangers and foreigners, but fellowcitizens with the saints, and of the household of God; And are built upon the foundation of the apostles and prophets, Jesus Christ himself being the chief corner stone." (Ephesians 2:17–20)

Wednesday

"And he gave some, apostles; and some, prophets; and some, evangelists; and some, pastors and teachers; For the perfecting of the saints, for the work of the ministry, for the edifying of the body of Christ: . . . . That we henceforth be no more children, tossed to and fro, and carried about with every wind of doctrine, by the sleight of men, and cunning craftiness, whereby they lie in wait to deceive." (Ephesians 4:11–14)

Thursday

"Upon you my fellow servants, in the name of Messiah I confer the Priesthood of Aaron, which holds the keys of the ministering of angels, and of the gospel of repentance, and of baptism by immersion for the remission of sins; and this shall never be taken again from the earth." (D&C 13:1)

Friday

"The Melchizedek Priesthood holds the right of presidency, and has power and authority . . . to administer in spiritual things. The twelve traveling councilors are called to be the Twelve Apostles, or special witnesses of the name of Christ in all the world. The Seventy are also called to preach the gospel, and to be especial witnesses unto the Gentiles and in all the world." (D&C 107:8, 23, 25)

Saturday

"The rights of the priesthood are inseparably connected with the powers of heaven, and that the powers of heaven cannot be controlled nor handled only upon the principles of righteousness. No power or influence can or ought to be maintained by virtue of the priesthood, only by persuasion, by long-suffering, by gentleness and meekness, and by love unfeigned; By kindness, and pure knowledge, which shall greatly enlarge the soul without hypocrisy, and without guile." (D&C 121:36, 41–42)

Article of Faith 7:
The Holy Ghost and the Gifts of the Spirit

"We believe in the gift of tongues, prophecy, revelation, visions, healing, interpretation of tongues, and so forth." (Articles of Faith 1:7) 📖

Gospel Topics: Spiritual Gifts
https://goo.gl/H3ngjL

Music from Children's Songbook & Hymns

- The Holy Ghost (*CS*, 105)
- The Seventh Article of Faith (*CS*, 126)
- Testimony (*Hymns*, 137)
- Let the Holy Spirit Guide (*Hymns*, 143)

Quote

"Stay close to the Church if you want your faith in God to grow. And as it grows, so will your ability to claim the promise you were given that you can receive the gifts of the Spirit" (Henry B. Eyring, "Gifts of the Spirit for Hard Times," *Ensign*, June 2007).

Scripture Stories

Jesus heals people in Jerusalem, and later he heals any of the Nephites that need it. The gift of healing and having the faith to be healed are gifts of the Spirit (see Matthew 9:18–19, 23–25; 3 Nephi 7:5–10; D&C 46:19–20).

Lehi sees visions and prophesies to the people of Jerusalem. Visions and prophesies are gifts of the Spirit (see 1 Nephi 1:4–18).

Paul tells the Corinthians about various gifts of the Spirit. He explains how important it is that we all join our gifts together and work together how like the body, with all its different parts, works together (see 1 Corinthians 12).

Moroni writes to the Lamanites about the power of the Holy Ghost, gifts of the Spirit, and faith (see Moroni 10:1–25).

The Lord gives information and instructions about seeking gifts of the Spirit. He says everyone is given spiritual gifts for the benefit of the whole (see D&C 46:7–33).

Gospel Art Pictures

- *Daniel Interprets Nebuchadnezzar's Dream* (#24)
- *Lehi Prophesying to the People of Jerusalem* (#67)
- *Jesus Healing the Nephites* (#83)
- *Moroni Hides the Plates in the Hill Cumorah* (#86)
- *The Gift of the Holy Ghost* (#105)

Church History

In 1839, many of the early Saints gathered in Nauvoo. At that time, part of Nauvoo was a swamp with mosquitoes carrying malaria. People became very sick. On July 22, 1839, Joseph Smith got up from his own sickbed and began healing people. He gave a red silk handkerchief to Wilford Woodruff and told him to bless the sick and then wipe their faces with the handkerchief and the people would be healed. Wilford Woodruff did as he was instructed, and people were miraculously healed. He kept the handkerchief, which is now in the Church History Museum in Salt Lake City, Utah. For more details about this day, and to see a picture of the red handkerchief, see https://goo.gl/HzYtFw.

LDS.org page "A Day of God's Power." This page has a picture of and the story behind the handkerchief Joseph Smith gave to Wilford Woodruff. https://goo.gl/HzYtFw

Adaptations for Younger Children

Quote

"I will . . . listen to the Holy Ghost" ("My Gospel Standards").

Lessons from Behold Your Little Ones

"The Holy Ghost Helps Me" (Lesson 6, pp. 28–31) and "I Will Share" (Lesson 17, pp. 72–75). Talk about how important it is to share our strengths, talents, and spiritual gifts.

Faith in God

Memorize and pass off the seventh article of faith this week. Recite it or sing it every day during family scripture study (*Children's Songbook*, 126). For Article of Faith 7, the memory trick is "seven, heaven." Heaven is filled with the Spirit of God; the gifts of the Spirit come from heaven; and life is heavenly when people share the gifts of the Spirit. See page 230 in this book for the full list of memory helps. On a piece of paper, have your children write the seventh article of faith draw a picture that represents it, and then tape it in a prominent place (*Faith in God*, pp. 16, 20).

Activity ⏲

Wrap some small gifts for your kids. They could be candies, little toys, stickers, or anything your kids would like. Have the children open the gifts. We all love giving and receiving gifts. We all have natural gifts and talents. Take turns talking about the gifts and talents you see in your family members. Act them out where possible. Appropriately share stories about people and their spiritual gifts: for example, great faith, learning another language, healing, or being healed.

Play a "still, small voice" game. Have your kids close their eyes, then whisper instructions to them and see if they can hear you and do what you tell them to do. Set up an obstacle course. Blindfold them or have them close their eyes. Whisper directions to them to navigate the obstacle course safely. If you want someone to play the devil, you can have that person whisper, talk, and yell directions that will make the blindfolded person bump into stuff. The point is to practice identifying and listening to the voice that is trying to help. If the kids are old enough, you can ask them what kinds of things the Spirit invites them to do and what things Satan invites them to do.

Adaptations for Older Children and Teens

Quote

"It is not unusual for one to have received the gift [of the Holy Ghost] and not really know it. I fear this supernal gift is being obscured by programs and activities and schedules and so many meetings. There are so many places to go, so many things to do in this noisy world. We can be too busy to pay attention to the promptings of the Spirit. The voice of the Spirit is a still, small voice—a voice that is *felt* rather than heard. It is a spiritual voice that comes into the mind as a thought put into your heart. . . . It is awakened with prayer and cultivated 'by obedience to the laws and ordinances of the Gospel.' It can be smothered through transgression and neglect. . . . We can learn to sort out the promptings from the temptations and follow the inspiration of the Holy Ghost" (Boyd K. Packer, "The Cloven Tongues of Fire," *Ensign*, May 2000; italics in original).

Preach My Gospel

"The Holy Ghost: Gifts of the Spirit," p. 91; "The Gift of Tongues," p. 133; Chapter 7: "How Can I Better Learn My Mission Language?," pp. 127–36.

Personal Progress

Divine Nature or Individual Worth #8 or #9: Personalized Value Experience—You came to earth with divine qualities and gifts. Ask your parents and leaders to help you identify some of these. Read Doctrine and Covenants 46 and pray to know something about your spiritual gifts. Write what you learn in your journal (pp. 25, 33).

Duty to God

Study the doctrinal topic of "The Gift of the Holy Ghost." Record what you learn and share what you learned with your parents or a priesthood leader (see pp. 18–21, 42–45, 66–69).

Activity

Blindfold someone, or have them close their eyes if you don't have a blindfold handy. Choose someone to represent the Holy Ghost. Guide the blindfolded person to a nearby room and then have the Holy Ghost (still in the original room) say, "Can you hear me?" at different volumes until the blindfolded person says yes. Then, guide the blindfolded person into the same room as the person representing Holy Ghost, but keep them as far apart as the room allows. Have the Holy Ghost say, "Can you hear me?" at different volumes until the blindfolded person says yes. Guide the blindfolded person to stand right next to the Holy Ghost. Have the Holy Ghost whisper, "Can you hear me?" and the blindfolded person should say yes immediately. Share that the closer we are to God and the Holy Ghost, the quieter and clearer the promptings can be. Talk about what things help you stay close to the Holy Ghost and which things separate you. If you feel comfortable discussing your personal gifts of the Spirit and the gifts of those in your family, do so.

Daily Scriptures

Article of Faith 7: The Holy Ghost and the Gifts of the Spirit

Sunday 📖

"We believe in the gift of tongues, prophecy, revelation, visions, healing, interpretation of tongues, and so forth." (Articles of Faith 1:7)

Monday

"Come unto God, the Holy One of Israel, and believe in prophesying, and in revelations, and in the ministering of angels, and in the gift of speaking with tongues, and in the gift of interpreting languages, and in all things which are good; for there is nothing which is good save it comes from the Lord." (Omni 1:25)

Tuesday

"The fruit of the Spirit is love, joy, peace, longsuffering, gentleness, goodness, faith, Meekness, temperance: against such there is no law." (Galatians 5:22–23)

Wednesday

"Seek ye earnestly the best gifts, always remembering for what they are given; For verily I say unto you, they are given for the benefit of those who love me and keep all my commandments, and him that seeketh so to do. . . . For all have not every gift given unto them; for there are many gifts, and to every man is given a gift by the Spirit of God. To some is given one, and to some is given another, that all may be profited thereby." (D&C 46:8–9, 11–12)

Thursday 📖

"To some it is given by the Holy Ghost to know that Jesus Christ is the Son of God. . . . To others it is given to believe on their words. To some is given, by the Spirit of God, the word of wisdom. To another is given the word of knowledge. . . . To some it is given to have faith to be healed; And to others it is given to have faith to heal. And again, to some is given the working of miracles; And to others it is given to prophesy; And to others the discerning of spirits. And again, it is given to some to speak with tongues; And to another is given the interpretation of tongues. And all these gifts come from God, for the benefit of the children of God." (D&C 46:13–14, 17–26)

Friday 📖

"When ye shall receive these things, I would exhort you that ye would ask God, the Eternal Father, in the name of Christ, if these things are not true; and if ye shall ask with a sincere heart, with real intent, having faith in Christ, he will manifest the truth of it unto you, by the power of the Holy Ghost. And by the power of the Holy Ghost ye may know the truth of all things." (Moroni 10:4–5)

Saturday

"If ye will enter in by the way, and receive the Holy Ghost, it will show unto you all things what ye should do." (2 Nephi 32:5)

Article of Faith 8:
The Bible and the Book of Mormon

"We believe the Bible to be the word of God as far as it is translated correctly; we also believe the Book of Mormon to be the word of God." (Articles of Faith 1:8) 📖

LDS.org video "Bible and Book of Mormon." Elder Nelson talks about the Bible and the Book of Mormon as witnesses of Jesus Christ.
https://goo.gl/34gFwP

Music from Children's Songbook & Hymns

- Search, Ponder, and Pray *(CS,* 109)
- The Books in the Old Testament (*CS,* 114)
- The Books in the New Testament (*CS,* 116)
- Book of Mormon Stories (*CS,* 118)
- The Books in the Book of Mormon (*CS,* 119)
- The Eighth Article of Faith (*CS,* 127)
- The Iron Rod (*Hymns,* 274)

Quote

Mormonads—Scriptures and Seminary
https://goo.gl/Qpzfqq

"We believe, revere, and love the Holy Bible. We do have additional sacred scripture, including the Book of Mormon, but it supports the Bible, never substituting for it" (M. Russell Ballard, "The Miracle of the Holy Bible," *Ensign,* May 2007).

Scripture Stories

Lehi tells his family about a dream he had in which he saw a beautiful tree with delicious fruit that makes people happy. A rod of iron led to the tree. Nephi later learns that the tree represents the love of God and the iron rod represents the word of God (see 1 Nephi 8, 11–12).

Alma teaches that the scriptures are like the Liahona. They will guide people in their lives like the Liahona guided Lehi's family to the promised land (see 1 Nephi 16:10, 26–29; Alma 37:38–47).

Before Moroni seals up the plates, he invites readers to ask God if the writings are true. He promises that the Holy Ghost will testify that the Book of Mormon is true (see Moroni 10:1–5).

Joseph Smith ponders on James 1:5 and determines to follow the scriptural advice and pray for the wisdom he needs to know which church to join (see Joseph Smith—History 1:5–13).

Gospel Art Pictures

- *The Liahona* (#68)
- *Lehi's Dream* (#69)
- *Moroni Hides the Plates in the Hill Cumorah* (#86)
- *Joseph Smith Seeks Wisdom in the Bible* (#89)

Church History

Joseph Smith worked as a gold digger; he tried to find gold by looking into special stones. "When Joseph was 16, the *Palmyra Herald* printed [this remark]: 'digging for money hid in the earth is a very common thing and in this state it is even considered as honorable and profitable employment'" (see FairMormon.org's page "Joseph Smith's money digging activities and how it relates to his character?" at http://goo.gl/GyTCgh). When Joseph received the plates on September 22, 1827, people believed he had found gold (see Joseph Smith—History 1:59–60).

Between 1827 and 1829, Joseph Smith translated the Book of Mormon through the use of the Urim and Thummim as well as by looking at a stone and reading the words that appeared on it. Contrary to some artists' depictions (see Gospel Art #92), Joseph did not look at the writings and then dictate the English translation for his scribe. The plates were often not even in the room (see LDS.org's gospel topic "Book of Mormon Translation" at https://goo.gl/guU5mF or FairMormon.org's page "Why did Joseph use the same stone for translating that he used for 'money digging'" at http://goo.gl/LS73kn).

Gospel Topic: Book of Mormon Translation
https://goo.gl/guU5mF

LDS.org video "Book of Mormon Introduction." Elder Holland introduces the Book of Mormon and talks about it being a companion to the Holy Bible.
https://goo.gl/z7EXAW

Adaptations for Younger Children

Quote

"How pleased I am to hear of your love for the Book of Mormon. *I* love it too. . . . It's Heavenly Father's special gift to you. . . . I also hope your parents and leaders will give you opportunities to learn from the Doctrine and Covenants, the Pearl of Great Price, and the Bible as well" (Ezra Taft Benson, "To The Children of the Church," *The Friend*, June 1989; italics in original).

Lessons from *Behold Your Little Ones*

"The Book of Mormon Teaches Me about Jesus Christ" (Lesson 22, pp. 92–95) and "I Love the Scriptures" (Lesson 23, pp. 96–99).

Faith in God

"Read the scriptures daily" (p. 4).

Memorize and pass off the eighth article of faith this week. Recite it or sing it every day during family scripture study (*Children's Songbook*, 127). For Article of Faith 8, the memory trick is the rhyme "gate," a gate made of iron rods. These iron rods represent the word of God in the Bible and the Book of Mormon. See page 230 in this book for the full list of memory helps. On a piece of paper, have your children write the eighth article of faith, draw a picture that represents it, and then tape it in a prominent place (*Faith in God*, pp. 16, 20).

Activity ☺

Wrap a set of scriptures and several candies into a single gift. Have the kids open the gift. Read Alma 32:28, "The word is good. . . . Yea, it beginneth to enlighten my understanding, yea, it beginneth to be delicious to me." Take turns sharing favorite scriptures or scripture stories as you enjoy the candy.

Adaptations for Older Children and Teens

Quote

"We love and revere the Bible. . . . The Bible is the word of God. It is always identified first in our canon, our 'standard works.' . . . One of the great purposes of continuing revelation through living prophets is to declare to the world through additional witnesses that the Bible is true. '*This* is written,' an ancient prophet said, speaking of the Book of Mormon, 'for the intent that ye may believe *that*,' speaking of the Bible. In one of the earliest revelations received by Joseph Smith, the Lord said, 'Behold, I do not bring [the Book of Mormon forth] to destroy [the Bible] but to build it up' " (Jeffrey R. Holland, "My Words . . . Never Cease," *Ensign*, May 2008; italics in original).

Preach My Gospel

"The Book of Mormon: Another Testament of Jesus Christ," pp. 38–39; "Pray to Know the Truth through the Holy Ghost," pp. 39–40; "Study the Scriptures," pp. 73–74; Chapter 5: "What Is the Role of the Book of Mormon," pp. 103–14; "The Book of Mormon and the Bible Support Each Other," p. 106; "Use the Scriptures," pp. 180–82.

Personal Progress

Virtue Value Project—Read the entire Book of Mormon prayerfully, and apply the principles you read about into your own life. Write regularly in your journal about your thoughts on what you are reading, and how you feel about the Book of Mormon (p. 72).

Duty to God

Look over the sections titled "Pray and Study the Scriptures" (pp. 14, 38, 62). Work on the one for your age group. *Preach My Gospel* teaches missionaries to pray for the Spirit at the beginning of each session of scripture study (p. 17). In the *Duty to God* pamphlet it says, "Each time you study the scriptures, ask Heavenly Father in prayer to help you understand what you read" (p. 15).

Activity

Get a compass or a phone that has a compass or GPS system on it. If neither are available, just talk about the concept of a compass. Talk about how good it looks and what a great tool it is. Tell everyone that you appreciate this compass so much that you look at it every day, if only for a few seconds. Show everyone your cool device, but do not activate it or check the direction it is pointing. Ask what the purpose of a compass is. *To get directions and follow them so you can go to a desired destination.* Ask if just looking at your compass or phone without checking the directions they are giving will get you where you want to go. *No.* The scriptures are meant to be our personal compass by helping us connect to God's Spirit. By praying before we read, having specific questions, exercising faith, and writing down impressions we receive, the scriptures can become our personal compass.

Daily Scriptures

Article of Faith 8: The Bible and the Book of Mormon

Sunday 📖

"We believe the Bible to be the word of God as far as it is translated correctly; we also believe the Book of Mormon to be the word of God." (Articles of Faith 1:8)

Monday

"The fruit of thy loins shall write [the Book of Mormon]; and the fruit of the loins of Judah shall write [the Bible]; and [they] . . . shall grow together, unto the confounding of false doctrines and laying down of contentions, and establishing peace." (2 Nephi 3:12)

Tuesday 📖

"The word of the Lord came again unto me, saying, Moreover, thou son of man, take thee one stick, and write upon it, For Judah, and for the children of Israel his companions: then take another stick, and write upon it, For Joseph, the stick of Ephraim, and for all the house of Israel his companions: And join them one to another into one stick; and they shall become one in thine hand." (Ezekiel 37:15–17; "The stick of Judah" refers to the Bible and "the stick of Joseph" refers to the Book of Mormon. They join together to testify of Christ).

Wednesday 📖

"And I [Moroni] said unto him: Lord, the Gentiles will mock at these things, because of our weakness in writing; for Lord thou hast made us mighty in word by faith, but thou hast not made us mighty in writing. . . . And when I had said this, the Lord spake unto me, saying: Fools mock, but they shall mourn; and my grace is sufficient for the meek, that they shall take no advantage of your weakness; And if men come unto me I will show unto them their weakness. I give unto men weakness that they may be humble; and my grace is sufficient for all men that humble themselves before me; for if they humble themselves before me, and have faith in me, then will I make weak things become strong unto them." (Ether 12:23, 26–27)

Thursday

"Learn of me, and listen to my words; walk in the meekness of my Spirit, and you shall have peace in me." (D&C 19:23)

Friday

"Thy word is a lamp unto my feet, and a light unto my path." (Psalm 119:105)

Saturday 📖

"And that from a child thou hast known the holy scriptures, which are able to make thee wise unto salvation through faith which is in Christ Jesus. All scripture is given by inspiration of God, and is profitable for doctrine, for reproof, for correction, for instruction in righteousness: That the man of God may be perfect, throughly furnished unto all good works." (2 Timothy 3:15–17)

Article of Faith 9:
Revelation—Prophetic and Personal

"We believe all that God has revealed, all that He does now reveal, and we believe that He will yet reveal many great and important things pertaining to the Kingdom of God." (Articles of Faith 1:9) 📖

LDS.org video of Elder Oaks's conference talk "Two Lines of Communication."
https://goo.gl/AAYC5H

Music from Children's Songbook & Hymns

- A Child's Prayer (*CS*, 12)
- Follow the Prophet (*CS*, 110)
- The Ninth Article of Faith (*CS*, 128)
- Latter-day Prophets (*CS*, 134)
- We Thank Thee, O God, for a Prophet (*Hymns*, 19)

Quote

"Our Heavenly Father has given His children two lines of communication with Him—what we may call the personal line and the priesthood line. All should understand and be guided by both of these essential lines of communication" (Dallin H. Oaks, "Two Lines of Communication," *Ensign*, November 2010).

Scripture Stories

Lehi finds the Liahona. His family discovers that it will reveal to them the way through the wilderness and to the promised land, if they have faith and obey what it tells them to do. Alma likens the scriptures to the Liahona, which can be a tool for personal revelation if we have faith and obey what we are told through the Spirit when we read them (see 1 Nephi 16:10, 26; Alma 37:38–46).

The Doctrine and Covenants is a compilation of revelations Joseph Smith received after earnestly asking God questions. One example of this is when Joseph Smith was in Liberty Jail. He prayed for the Lord to help the Saints, who were being persecuted. He received reassurance as well as instruction about how the priesthood should be exercised righteously (see D&C 121–23).

Gospel Art Pictures

- *The Liahona* (#68)
- *Joseph Smith in Liberty Jail* (#97)
- *The Gift of the Holy Ghost* (#105)
- *Young Boy Praying* (#111)

Church History

In July 1833, several handwritten revelations were gathered and sent to print, publish, and distribute among the Saints as The Book of Commandments. However, a mob broke into W. W. Phelps's home and print shop where the revelations were. They ransacked the house, threw the expensive printing press out the second-story window, and tossed piles of printed pages out the window as well. Two girls, Mary Elizabeth and Caroline Robbins, waited for an opportunity to save some of the pages. When the time was right, they raced to the pages and grabbed as many as they could before the mob saw them and ran after them. They hid in a nearby cornfield and were not found. The revelations they saved are now included in the Doctrine and Covenants. (For more details, see Steven E. Snow, "Treasuring the Doctrine and Covenants," *Ensign*, January 2009 at https://goo.gl/UNzXnA). The Doctrine and Covenants were officially canonized on August 17, 1835, in Kirtland, Ohio (see the Church History timeline at https://goo.gl/KkHxsE).

Painting of the girls saving the Book of Commandments. https://goo.gl/9bjWav

In "Why Study the Doctrine and Covenants," Elder Bednar teaches the importance of studying the Doctrine and Covenants and Church history. https://goo.gl/3pSm5s

Adaptations for Younger Children

Quote

"I will remember my baptismal covenant and listen to the Holy Ghost" ("My Gospel Standards").

Lesson from *Behold Your Little Ones*

"I Belong to the Church of Jesus Christ of Latter-day Saints" (Lesson 25, pp. 104–7). Explain that our church is led by revelation. Revelation is when God talks to His children. He speaks to the leaders of the Church and individual members about many things. We listen to what He reveals and follow it the best we can.

Faith in God

Memorize and pass off the ninth article of faith this week. Recite it or sing it every day during family scripture study (*Children's Songbook*, 128). For Article of Faith 9, the memory trick is the word "line," reminding us of two lines of revelation: personal and prophetic. See page 230 in this book for the full list of memory helps. On a piece of paper, have your children write the ninth article of faith, draw a picture that represents it, and then tape it in a prominent place (*Faith in God*, pp. 16, 20).

Activity

Play Follow-the-Leader or Simon Says. Talk about how the leader shows us an example of what to do and then everyone else does it. Jesus is our example, and we follow Him. He calls prophets and leaders and inspires them, and then asks us to follow them. In Simon Says, you can talk about paying attention and following "Simon" and doing what he says to do. We want to follow Jesus and His Apostles, not Satan and his followers. You can then play "Jesus Says" or "The Prophet Says." The leader would say something like "Jesus says hug your sister," and everyone would pretend to hug each other. Then, "Hit your friends when you are angry" and everyone would stand and do nothing because the instruction was negative and not prefaced with "Jesus says."

Adaptations for Older Children and Teens

Quotes

"When the First Presidency and the Quorum of the Twelve speak with a united voice, it is the voice of the Lord for that time. The Lord reminds us, 'Whether by mine own voice or by the voice of my servants, it is the same' [D&C 1:38]" (M. Russell Ballard, "Stay in the Boat and Hold On!," *Ensign*, November 2014).

"There has been and still persists some confusion about our doctrine and how it is established. That is the subject I wish to address today. . . . In the Church today, just as anciently, establishing the doctrine of Christ or correcting doctrinal deviations is a matter of divine revelation to those the Lord endows with apostolic authority. . . . The President of the Church may announce or interpret doctrines based on revelation to him (see, for example, D&C 138). Doctrinal exposition may also come through the combined council of the First Presidency and Quorum of the Twelve Apostles (see, for example, Official Declaration 2). . . . At the same time it should be remembered that *not every statement made by a Church leader, past or present, necessarily constitutes doctrine.* It is commonly understood in the Church that a statement made by one leader on a single occasion often represents a personal, though well-considered, opinion, *not meant to be official or binding for the whole Church*" (D. Todd Christofferson, "The Doctrine of Christ," *Ensign*, May 2012; italics added).

Preach My Gospel

Chapter 4: "How Do I Recognize and Understand the Spirit?," pp. 89–102; "Personal Revelation," pp. 89–90.

Personal Progress

Choice and Accountability #5—Study the scriptures on the topic of the "Holy Ghost" and "Revelation." Discuss what you learn with someone, and write about what you learn in your journal (p. 47).

Duty to God

Study the doctrinal topic of "Prayer and Personal Revelation." Record what you learn and share what you learned with your parents or a priesthood leader (see pp. 18–21, 42–45, 66–69).

Activity ☺

Get about five objects that can be dropped on a table without breaking. For example, get a paper clip, a pen, a lid to a bottle, a spoon, and a book. Cover up the objects so they can't be seen. Have everyone get a paper and a pencil. Then have them close their eyes as you drop each item on the table. After each item, have everyone silently write what each thing might be. When you're done, reveal the items and see if anyone guessed correctly. Learning to listen to the Spirit takes effort and it's well worth it. Have everyone share times they've felt the Spirit.

Daily Scriptures

Article of Faith 9: Revelation—Prophetic and Personal

Sunday 📖

"We believe all that God has revealed, all that He does now reveal, and we believe that He will yet reveal many great and important things pertaining to the Kingdom of God." (Articles of Faith 1:9)

Monday 📖

"Search these commandments, for they are true and faithful, and the prophecies and promises which are in them shall all be fulfilled. What I the Lord have spoken, I have spoken, and I excuse not myself; and though the heavens and the earth pass away, my word shall not pass away, but shall all be fulfilled, whether by mine own voice or by the voice of my servants, it is the same." (D&C 1:37–38)

Tuesday 📖

"Surely the Lord God will do nothing, until he revealeth his secret unto his servants the prophets." (Joseph Smith Translation, Amos 3:7, [in Amos 3:7, footnote *a*])

Wednesday 📖

"The word of the Lord came unto me [Jeremiah], saying, Before I formed thee in the belly I knew thee; and before thou camest forth out of the womb I sanctified thee, and I ordained thee a prophet unto the nations." (Jeremiah 1:4–5)

Thursday 📖

"Yea, behold, I will tell you in your mind and in your heart, by the Holy Ghost, which shall come upon you and which shall dwell in your heart. Now, behold, this is the spirit of revelation." (D&C 8:2–3)

Friday 📖

"If any of you lack wisdom, let him ask of God, that giveth to all men liberally, and upbraideth not; and it shall be given him. But let him ask in faith, nothing wavering. For he that wavereth is like a wave of the sea driven with the wind and tossed." (James 1:5–6)

Saturday 📖

"[Jesus] asked his disciples, saying, Whom do men say that I the Son of man am? And they said, Some say that thou art John the Baptist: some, Elias; and others, Jeremias, or one of the prophets. He saith unto them, But whom say ye that I am? And Simon Peter answered and said, Thou art the Christ, the Son of the living God. And Jesus answered and said unto him, Blessed art thou, Simon Bar-jona: for flesh and blood hath not revealed it unto thee, but my Father which is in heaven. And I say also unto thee, That thou art Peter, and upon this rock I will build my church; and the gates of hell shall not prevail against it. And I will give unto thee the keys of the kingdom of heaven: and whatsoever thou shalt bind on earth shall be bound in heaven: and whatsoever thou shalt loose on earth shall be loosed in heaven." (Matthew 16:13–19)

Article of Faith 10:
Zion

"We believe in the literal gathering of Israel and in the restoration of the Ten Tribes; that Zion (the New Jerusalem) will be built upon the American continent; that Christ will reign personally upon the earth; and, that the earth will be renewed and receive its paradisiacal glory." (Articles of Faith 1:10) 📖

LDS.org video "Teachings of Joseph Smith: Preparing for Zion" https://goo.gl/hY8kd8

Gospel Topics: Zion https://goo.gl/PZvaUG

Music from Children's Songbook & Hymns

* The Tenth Article of Faith (*CS*, 128)
* Kindness Begins with Me (*CS*, 145)
* Now Let Us Rejoice (*Hymns*, 3)
* Come, All Ye Saints of Zion (*Hymns*, 38)

Quote

"This gathering of Israel and this building of Zion in the last days occurs in stages. The early part of the work, which involved gathering to the United States and building stakes of Zion in North America, has already been accomplished. We are now engaged in gathering Israel within the various nations of the earth and in establishing stakes of Zion at the ends of the earth. . . . Each one of us can build up Zion in our own lives by being pure in heart" (Bruce R. McConkie, "Come: Let Israel Build Zion," *Ensign*, May 1977).

Scripture Stories

Oliver Cowdery receives a revelation through Joseph Smith shortly after becoming Joseph's scribe for the Book of Mormon. He is told that a marvelous work is happening, and he should keep the commandments and seek to bring forth and establish the cause of Zion (see D&C 6:1–6. See also Joseph Smith—History Note 1, which describes Oliver's feelings as Joseph's scribe).

Enoch is called to preach repentance, and he worries about his limitations. He says, "All the people hate me; for I am slow of speech" (Moses 6:31). Even though he feels inadequate, Enoch obeys, preaches righteousness, and establishes the city of Zion, which is taken up unto God (see Moses 6:26–34; Moses 7:1–19, 69).

Gospel Art Pictures

* *City of Zion Is Taken Up* (#6)
* *Joseph Smith Translating the Book of Mormon* (#92)

Church History

Establishing Zion, a geographical location where the Saints of God live, was a major focus of the early Saints. Joseph prophesied that if the Saints were faithful, Zion would be redeemed in Jackson County, Missouri, by September 1836. If they weren't, the Saints would be driven from city to city (see http://goo.gl/w6b2wx). Some people consider this one of several "false prophesies" from Joseph Smith. Faithful Saints realize that the conditions were not met to redeem Zion and the Saints were indeed driven from city to city, substantiating the prophecy. To see a list of other prophecies that have not been fulfilled, go to http://goo.gl/mqhLLS.

LDS.org video "Ministry of Howard W. Hunter: Love for the Holy Land" https://goo.gl/KahBfR

On April 3, 1836, Moses appeared to Joseph Smith and Oliver Cowdery and delivered the keys of the gathering of Israel (see D&C 110:11). Years later on Sunday, October 24, 1841, Elder Orson Hyde dedicated the Holy Land for the return of the children of Abraham (see David B. Galbraith, "Orson Hyde's 1841 Mission to the Holy Land," *Ensign*, October 1991; see also a picture at https://goo.gl/VvOs5m). From 1970–72, Howard W. Hunter, then the Church Historian, oversaw the building of the Orson Hyde Memorial Garden in Jerusalem, which was dedicated in 1979. From 1979–89, he oversaw the building of the BYU Jerusalem Center for Near Eastern Studies and then dedicated it on May 16, 1989 (see *Teachings of Presidents of the Church: Howard W. Hunter*, "Historical Summary," x–xi).

Howard W. Hunter: Documentary https://goo.gl/XWZPzD

Adaptations for Younger Children

Quote

"I will seek good friends and treat others kindly" ("My Gospel Standards").

Lessons from *Behold Your Little Ones*

"Jesus Christ Showed Us How to Love Others" (Lesson 5, pp. 24–27) and "I Will Love Others" (Lesson 18, pp. 76–79). Explain that Zion is where people love God and each other.

Faith in God

Memorize and pass off the tenth article of faith this week. Recite it or sing it every day during family scripture study (*Children's Songbook*, 128). For Article of Faith 10, the memory trick is the phrase "ten tribes." See page 230 in this book for the full list of memory helps. On a piece of paper, have your children write the tenth article of faith, draw a picture that represents it, and then tape it in a prominent place (*Faith in God*, pp. 16, 20).

Activity

Explain that Zion is a place where people love each other and God. They get along well and are friends. Have everyone share things they like about your home and family. Then take turns sharing something that would make home more "Zion-like." See if you can implement some of the things that would make home more like Zion for your family. Keep this activity light; don't feel responsible to do everything your family wants to do. Just get some insights into how your family members feel, and see what you could change for the better.

Adaptations for Older Children and Teens

Quote

"My dear brethren and sisters, we must prepare to redeem Zion. It was essentially the sin of pride that kept us from establishing Zion in the days of the Prophet Joseph Smith. It was the same sin of pride that brought consecration to an end among the Nephites (see 4 Ne. 1:24–25). Pride is the great stumbling block to Zion. I repeat: Pride *is* the great stumbling block to Zion. We must cleanse the inner vessel by conquering pride (see Alma 6:2–4; Matt. 23:25–26). We must yield 'to the enticings of the Holy Spirit,' put off the prideful 'natural man,' become 'a saint through the atonement of Christ the Lord,' and become 'as a child, submissive, meek, humble.' (Mosiah 3:19; see also Alma 13:28). That we may do so and go on to fulfill our divine destiny is my fervent prayer" (Ezra Taft Benson, "Beware of Pride," *Ensign*, May 1989; italics in original).

Preach My Gospel

Chapter 6: "How Do I Develop Christlike Attributes?," pp. 115–26. Zion is the pure in heart, the city of God. Developing Christlike attributes helps you build Zion.

Personal Progress

Divine Nature #3 and #7—Think about what you can do to make your home more like Zion (a place where the Spirit is and where people are cooperative and live in harmony). Work on becoming a peacemaker in your home (pp. 23–24).

Duty to God

"Make a list of ways you can help build a happy home. . . . Do those things, and record the difference it makes in your home" (p. 80).

Activity

Have everyone think about what could make your home more like Zion—a place where people love God and love each other. Have everyone take turns sharing their favorite things about home. Have everyone think about something that would make home more like Zion for them. What would they see, hear, smell, taste, and touch? What things would they like to do more or less of? Take turns sharing ideas. See if you can implement some of the things that would make home more like Zion for your family. Keep this activity light; don't feel responsible to do everything your family wants to do. Just get some insights into how your family members feel, what they like, and what could change for the better.

Daily Scriptures

Article of Faith 10: Zion

Sunday 📖

"We believe in the literal gathering of Israel and in the restoration of the Ten Tribes; that Zion (the New Jerusalem) will be built upon the American continent; that Christ will reign personally upon the earth; and, that the earth will be renewed and receive its paradisiacal glory." (Articles of Faith 1:10)

Monday

"Thus saith the Lord, let Zion rejoice, for this is Zion—the pure in heart; therefore, let Zion rejoice." (D&C 97:21)

Tuesday

"Keep my commandments, and seek to bring forth and establish the cause of Zion." (D&C 6:6)

Wednesday 📖

"And the Lord called his people Zion, because they were of one heart and one mind, and dwelt in righteousness; and there was no poor among them." (Moses 7:18)

Thursday

"And blessed are they who shall seek to bring forth my Zion at that day, for they shall have the gift and the power of the Holy Ghost; and if they endure unto the end they shall be lifted up at the last day, and shall be saved in the everlasting kingdom of the Lamb; and whoso shall publish peace, yea, tidings of great joy, how beautiful upon the mountains shall they be." (1 Nephi 13:37)

Friday

"Zion shall flourish, and the glory of the Lord shall be upon her; And she shall be an ensign unto the people." (D&C 64:41–42)

Saturday

"[After Christ visited the Nephites,] there was no contention in the land, because of the love of God which did dwell in the hearts of the people. And there were no envyings, nor strifes, nor tumults, nor whoredoms, nor lyings, nor murders, nor any manner of lasciviousness; and surely there could not be a happier people among all the people who had been created by the hand of God. There were no robbers, nor murderers, neither were there Lamanites, nor any manner of -ites; but they were in one, the children of Christ, and heirs to the kingdom of God. And how blessed were they! For the Lord did bless them in all their doings; yea, even they were blessed and prospered." (4 Nephi 1:15–18)

Article of Faith 11: The Privilege of Worshipping God

"We claim the privilege of worshiping Almighty God according to the dictates of our own conscience, and allow all men the same privilege, let them worship how, where, or what they may." (Articles of Faith 1:11) 📖

Gospel Topics: Worship.
https://goo.gl/jUvQYb

Music from *Children's Songbook* & *Hymns*

- The Eleventh Article of Faith (*CS*, 130)
- I Know My Father Lives (*CS*, 5; *Hymns*, 302)
- I Believe in Christ (*Hymns*, 134)
- Know This, That Every Soul Is Free (*Hymns*, 240)

Quote

"Each of us is an individual. Each of us is different. There must be respect for those differences. . . . We must work harder to build mutual respect, an attitude of forbearance, with tolerance one for another regardless of the doctrines and philosophies which we may espouse. Concerning these you and I may disagree. But we can do so with respect and civility" (Gordon B. Hinckley, *Teachings of Gordon B. Hinckley* (1997), 661, 665).

Scripture Stories

Shadrach, Meshach, and Abed-nego worship God instead of an idol (see Daniel 3).

Daniel worships God by praying, even though it is illegal in his country (see Daniel 6).

Jesus appears to Nephites at the temple. He invites each person to come to Him and see and feel the marks of His crucifixion, and they all worshiped Him (see 3 Nephi 11:1–17).

Jesus tells the Nephites to pray in their families, and to meet often to partake of the sacrament. He tells them to allow everyone to come and worship with them (see 3 Nephi 18: 21–23, 28–32).

Gospel Art Pictures

- *Three Men in the Fiery Furnace* (#25)
- *Daniel in the Lions' Den* (#26)
- *Jesus Teaching in the Western Hemisphere* (#82)
- *Family Prayer* (#112)

Church History

Joseph Smith and the early Church members were bitterly persecuted for their faith. In 1839, Joseph Smith said,

> "We ought always to be aware of those prejudices which sometimes so strangely present themselves, and are so congenial to human nature, against our friends, neighbors, and brethren of the world, who choose to differ from us in opinion and in matters of faith. Our religion is between us and our God. Their religion is between them and their God."
> (*Teachings of Presidents of the Church: Joseph Smith*, 345)

To read more quotes by Joseph Smith on the matter, see *Teaching of the Presidents of the Church: Joseph Smith*, pages 344–46, or go to https://goo.gl/JVSfWY. To watch a video of Elder Oaks explaining the importance of defending the freedom of religion, go to https://goo.gl/dMwUkW. For more resources, go to http://goo.gl/nHdt8g.

LDS.org video and article "People of Faith Should Defend Freedom of Religion, Elder Oaks Says." https://goo.gl/dMwUkW

MormonNewsroom.org article "Religious Freedom". This article includes videos and additional resources for study on this topic. http://goo.gl/nHdt8g

Adaptations for Younger Children

Quote

"I will live now to be worthy to go to the temple" ("My Gospel Standards").

Lesson from *Behold Your Little Ones*

"I Can Pray to Heavenly Father" (Lesson 3, pp. 16–19). We worship God as our Heavenly Father who knows us, loves us, and wants to talk with us.

Faith in God

Memorize and pass off the eleventh article of faith this week. Recite it or sing it every day during family scripture study (*Children's Songbook*, 130). For Article of Faith 11, the memory trick is the word "heaven." We claim the privilege of worshiping the God of heaven. See page 230 in this book for the full list of memory helps. On a piece of paper, have your children write the eleventh article of faith, draw a picture that represents it, and then tape it in a prominent place (*Faith in God*, pp. 16, 20).

Activity

Talk about the different ways we worship God. We go to church. We pray. We study His words in the scriptures. We treat others kindly. We think of Him. We thank Him and praise Him.

For fun, do the following hand play (https://goo.gl/BQP5D2):

"Here's the church. And here's the steeple." (Clasp your hands and interlace your fingers with your fingers pointing down against your palms. Point both index fingers up for the steeple.)
"Open the doors and see all the people." (Flip your palms up and wiggle your fingers to show all the "people.")
"Close the doors and hear them pray." (Bring your palms down and make the "church" again.)
"Open the doors and they all run away." (Flip your palms up and wiggle your fingers as you separate your hands and let your "people" fingers run away.)

Adaptations for Older Children and Teens

Quote

"Notwithstanding the significance of our doctrinal differences with other faiths, our attitude toward other churches has been to refrain from criticism. They do much good. They bless mankind. Many help their members learn of the Savior and His teachings. . . . Our leaders have consistently counseled us 'to live with respect and appreciation for those not of our faith. There is so great a need for civility and mutual respect among those of differing beliefs and philosophies.' It is equally important that we be loving and kind to members of our own faith, regardless of their level of commitment or activity. The Savior has made it clear that we are not to judge each other. This is especially true of members of our own families. Our obligation is to love and teach and never give up. The Lord has made salvation 'free for all men' but has 'commanded his people that they should persuade all men to repentance.'" (Quentin L. Cook, "Our Father's Plan—Big Enough for All His Children," *Ensign*, May 2009)

Preach My Gospel

"Keep the Sabbath Day Holy," p. 74.

Personal Progress

Virtue #3—Worshipping God in the temple is a special privilege. "Prepare to be worthy to enter the temple and to participate in temple ordinances. Read Alma chapter 5 [and] . . . answer the questions for yourself" (p. 71).

Duty to God

Study the doctrinal topic of "Agency," focusing on the War in Heaven over agency, as well as the Fall of Adam and Eve. Record what you learn and share what you learned with your parents or a priesthood leader (see pp. 18–21, 42–45, 66–69).

For a brief description of a variety of religions and how they compare to our Church's beliefs, see http://goo.gl/mNCyaN or http://eom.byu.edu/index.php/World_Religions_(Non-Christian)_and_Mormonism.

Activity

Talk about ways people worship God. Some ways of worshipping are common, though the specific ways they are done may differ. Things like prayer, reading sacred texts, loving others, and serving, are common among religions. Some things are different, like what names people call God, ceremonies, and sacred art. Talk about different world religions like Christian denominations, Islam, Hindu, Shinto, Native American religions, and so on. For a brief description of a variety of religions and how they compare to our Church's beliefs, see http://goo.gl/mNCyaN.

Daily Scriptures

Article of Faith 11: The Privilege of Worshipping God

Sunday 📖

"We claim the privilege of worshiping Almighty God according to the dictates of our own conscience, and allow all men the same privilege, let them worship how, where, or what they may." (Articles of Faith 1:11)

Monday

"We believe that religion is instituted of God; and that men are amenable to him, and to him only, for the exercise of it, unless their religious opinions prompt them to infringe upon the rights and liberties of others; but we do not believe that human law has a right to interfere in prescribing rules of worship to bind the consciences of men, nor dictate forms for public or private devotion." (D&C 134:4)

Tuesday

"Worship God, in whatsoever place ye may be in, in spirit and in truth; and . . . live in thanksgiving daily, for the many mercies and blessings which he doth bestow upon you." (Alma 34:38)

Wednesday

"We know that there is a God in heaven, who is infinite and eternal, from everlasting to everlasting the same unchangeable God, the framer of heaven and earth, and all things which are in them; And that he created man, male and female, after his own image and in his own likeness, created he them; And gave unto them commandments that they should love and serve him, the only living and true God, and that he should be the only being whom they should worship." (D&C 20:17–19)

Thursday

"Thus saith the scripture: Choose ye this day, whom ye will serve. Now if a man desired to serve God, it was his privilege; or rather, if he believed in God it was his privilege to serve him; but if he did not believe in him there was no law to punish him." (Alma 30:8–9)

Friday

"The people of Nephi . . . gave thanks unto the Lord their God; yea, and they did fast much and pray much, and they did worship God with exceedingly great joy." (Alma 45:1)

Saturday 📖

"Choose you this day whom ye will serve . . . but as for me and my house, we will serve the Lord." (Joshua 24:15)

Article of Faith 12: The Laws of the Land

"We believe in being subject to kings, presidents, rulers, and magistrates, in obeying, honoring, and sustaining the law." (Articles of Faith 1:12) 📖

Music from Children's Songbook & Hymns

Gospel Topics: Citizenship. https://goo.gl/psKsHL

- The Twelfth Article of Faith (*CS*, 131)
- My Country (*CS*, 224)
- My Flag, My Flag (*CS*, 225)
- Patriotic hymns (*Hymns*, 338–41)

Quote

"God intended men to be free. . . . No nation which has kept the commandments of God has ever perished" (Ezra Taft Benson, International Freedoms Conference, Philadelphia, Pennsylvania, October 26, 1979).

Scripture Stories

Moses receives the Ten Commandments, which become the "laws of the land" for the Israelites. (see Exodus 20).

In order to obey the law, Mary and Joseph travel to Bethlehem where they are taxed. Mary gives birth to the baby Jesus (see Luke 2:1–16).

Nephi is told to kill Laban. Under the biblical law, he had the right to do so because Laban had stolen his property and tried to kill him. Despite the fact that following the prompting to kill Laban was legal, Nephi did not want to do it and only did so when the Spirit explained that it would bless generations to have the plates (see 1 Nephi 4:5–18). (see also FairMormon's page, "Was Nephi's killing of Laban cold-blooded murder?" at http://goo.gl/DVGQbC and John Welch's publication "Legal Perspectives on the Slaying of Laban" in *Book of Mormon Studies* at http://goo.gl/ytgeVC).

Jacob speaks to his people and reviews both the civil laws and God's laws. One law he discusses refers to marriage. He teaches that monogamy is normally God's law, but at times God may command a polygamous state for His own reasons (see Jacob 2:27–30).

Gospel Art Pictures

The Ten Commandments (#14)

Joseph and Mary Travel to Bethlehem (#29)

King Benjamin Addresses His People (#74)

Church History

Polygamy was not against the law when the Lord told Joseph Smith to restore that ancient practice. When was the practice discontinued? *Wilford Woodruff received a revelation and announced the change on October 6, 1890* (see D&C Official Declaration 1). To see a documentary on his life, including issues surrounding the ending of polygamy in the Church, go to https://goo.gl/Kiwhwg.

What is the Church's position on polygamy now? Do Church members engage in polygamous relationships in countries where polygamy is legal? President Gordon B. Hinckley stated, "This Church has nothing whatever to do with those practicing polygamy. . . . If any of our members are found to be practicing plural marriage, they are excommunicated" ("What Are People Asking About Us?," *Ensign*, November 1998). To see a video clip of this talk go to https://goo .gl/XmJmnU). For more about plural marriage in Church history, see https://goo.gl/vHJ7pH.

Wilford Woodruff: Documentary
https://goo.gl/Kiwhwg

LDS.org video "Do Not Practice Polygamy": a talk by President Hinckley.
https://goo.gl/XmJmnU

Adaptations for Younger Children

Quote

"Keep the laws of God, and the laws of man, honor our membership in the kingdom of God, [and] our citizenship . . . in the nation of which we are a part" (Joseph F. Smith, *Teachings of Presidents of the Church: Joseph F. Smith*, 123).

Lesson from *Behold Your Little Ones*

"I Will Obey" (Lesson 14, pp. 60–63). We have rules in our homes, schools, and nations. Discuss anything you want to about government, laws, patriotic songs, or anything related.

Faith in God

Memorize and pass off the twelfth article of faith this week. Recite it or sing it every day during family scripture study (*Children's Songbook*, 131). For Article of Faith 12, the memory trick is "delve into the laws on the shelves." Imagine the country's laws written in books on shelves. See page 230 in this book for the full list of memory helps. On a piece of paper, have your children write the twelfth article of faith, draw a picture that represents it, and then tape it in a prominent place (*Faith in God*, pp. 16, 20).

Read and discuss the twelfth article of faith. Talk about what being a good citizen means and how our choices and actions affect other people. (p. 9)

Activity

Pretend you are Nephites preparing to protect yourselves from a Lamanite attack. You can draw a city or make one using toys and blocks, or furniture, blankets, and pillows. Make a city full of people standing guard, and surround the city with walls and huge piles of "dirt" (toys, pillows, or crumpled up paper) to make it harder for the Lamanite armies to get close to the city. Explain that God's commandments are like these walls. When we obey the commandments and the laws of our country, it's like we are staying inside the walls that protect us from Satan's attacks. Afterward, play together with whatever you made your city out of.

Adaptations for Older Children and Teens

Quote

"It is most important that all citizens be informed in matters of government; that they know and understand the laws of the land; and that they take an active part wherever possible in choosing and electing honest and wise men to administer the affairs of government. . . . There is no reason or justification for men to disregard or break the law or try to take it into their own hands. Christ gave us the great example of a law-abiding citizen. . . . It is the duty of citizens of any country to remember that they have individual responsibilities, and that they must operate within the law of the country in which they have chosen to live" (N. Eldon Tanner, "The Laws of God," *Ensign*, November 1975).

Preach My Gospel

"Obey and Honor the Law," p. 80–81.

Personal Progress

Knowledge or Integrity #8 or #9: Personalized Value Experience—Keeping the laws of the country you live in requires knowledge of those laws, as well as the personal integrity to keep them. Discuss the laws of your country and the importance of being a good citizen (pp. 41, 65).

Duty to God

Study the doctrinal topic of the "Apostasy and the Restoration of the Gospel." Record what you learn and share what you learned with your parents or a priesthood leader (see pp. 18–21, 42–45, 66–69). The gospel could not have been restored if the laws didn't allow freedom of worship.

Activity

Get a piece of wood (or a pencil) and hold it out. Ask what would happen if you let go of the piece of wood. Because of the law of gravity on Earth, the wood would drop. What would happen if you were on the moon and let go of the wood? It would not drop. It would stay where it was. What would happen if you were surrounded by water? The wood would float. Depending on circumstances, rules can change. God's law of marriage is usually monogamy unless He specifically says otherwise (see 2 Samuel 12:7–8; Jacob 2:27, 30).

If Nephi killed Laban in the United States today, it would be considered first-degree murder, but under the laws of his country, it was considered an act of self-defense (see http://goo.gl/DVGQbC for details). It would be against the law to destroy someone's printing press now, but it wasn't in Joseph Smith's day when he and others destroyed the *Nauvoo Expositor's* printing press (see Dallin H. Oaks, "Joseph, the Man and the Prophet," *Ensign*, May 1996; and a FairMormon.org page at http://goo.gl /zmwVfD). Discuss some common laws of your country, the consequences for breaking laws, and the importance of being a good citizen.

Daily Scriptures

Article of Faith 12: The Laws of the Land

Sunday 📖

"We believe in being subject to kings, presidents, rulers, and magistrates, in obeying, honoring, and sustaining the law." (Articles of Faith 1:12)

Monday

"We believe that governments were instituted of God for the benefit of man; and that he holds men accountable for their acts in relation to them, both in making laws and administering them, for the good and safety of society." (D&C 134:1)

Tuesday

"We believe that all men are bound to sustain and uphold the respective governments in which they reside, while protected in their inherent and inalienable rights by the laws . . . and that all governments have a right to enact such laws as in their own judgments are best calculated to secure the public interest." (D&C 134:5)

Wednesday

"Let no man break the laws of the land, for he that keepeth the laws of God hath no need to break the laws of the land." (D&C 58:21)

Thursday

"The laws and constitution of the people, which I have suffered to be established . . . should be maintained for the rights and protection of all flesh." (D&C 101:77)

Friday

"That law of the land which is constitutional, supporting that principle of freedom in maintaining rights and privileges, belongs to all mankind, and is justifiable before me. Therefore, I, the Lord, justify you, and your brethren of my church, in befriending that law which is the constitutional law of the land." (D&C 98:5–6)

Saturday

"I [the Lord] established the Constitution of this land, by the hands of wise men whom I raised up unto this very purpose." (D&C 101:80)

Article of Faith 13:
Focusing on Virtue

"We believe in being honest, true, chaste, benevolent, virtuous, and in doing good to all men; indeed, we may say that we follow the admonition of Paul—We believe all things, we hope all things, we have endured many things, and hope to be able to endure all things. If there is anything virtuous, lovely, or of good report or praiseworthy, we seek after these things." (Articles of Faith 1:13) 📖

LDS.org youth video 2011—"We Believe" about the thirteenth article of faith.
https://goo.gl/2b5QF7

In this LDS.org video, "Return to Virtue," Sister Elaine S. Dalton talks about the importance of virtuous living.
https://goo.gl/qAZ63f

Music from Children's Songbook & Hymns

- The Thirteenth Article of Faith (*CS*, 132)
- I Believe in Being Honest (*CS*, 149)
- More Holiness Give Me (*Hymns*, 131)
- True to the Faith (*Hymns*, 254)

Quotes

"Virtue is a prerequisite to entering the Lord's holy temples and to receiving the Spirit's guidance. Virtue 'is a pattern of thought and behavior based on high moral standards.' It encompasses chastity and moral purity. Virtue begins in the heart and in the mind. It is nurtured in the home. . . . *Virtue* is a word we don't hear often in today's society, but the Latin root word *virtus* means strength" (Elaine S. Dalton, "A Return to Virtue," *Ensign*, November 2008; italics in original).

"We as parents and leaders need to counsel with our children and youth on an ongoing basis, listening with love and understanding. They need to know the dangers of pornography and how it overtakes lives, causing loss of the Spirit, distorted feelings, deceit, damaged relationships, loss of self-control, and nearly total consumption of time, thought, and energy" (Linda S. Reeves, "Protection from Pornography—a Christ-Focused Home," *Ensign*, May 2014).

Scripture Stories

Ruth was a convert who was known for being virtuous (see Ruth 1:15-17; Ruth 3:11).

The two thousand stripling warriors were strong, virtuous, and faithful young men who "were true at all times" (Alma 53:20) (see also Alma 53:18–21; 56:45–48; 57:24–26).

Gospel Art Pictures

- *Ruth Gleaning in the Fields* (#17)
- *Two Thousand Young Warriors* (#80)

Church History

The Church has always emphasized and valued the arts. To see a history demonstrating this, see the *Ensign* article "'Virtuous, Lovely, or of Good Report': How the Church Has Fostered the Arts" (Ronald W. Walker and D. Michael Quinn, July 1977, https://goo.gl/2wrHb7).

The absolute antithesis of all things virtuous is the plague of pornography. As early as the 1970s, leaders of the Church were openly warning against the destructive power of pornography. One of these early talks is "Pornography— the Deadly Carrier" (Thomas S. Monson, *Ensign,* November 1979). A more recent talk was given in the April 2014 general conference by Linda S. Reeves, titled "Protection from Pornography—a Christ-Focused Home" (*Ensign*, May 2014). To see an article and several videos on LDS. org about pornography, go to https://goo.gl/7MRxmn. To watch a video that introduces pornography in a kid-friendly way, go to the LDS.org video "What Should I Do When I See Pornography?" at https://goo.gl/thu2EF.

Gospel Topic: Pornography
https://goo.gl/7MRxmn

LDS.org video "What Should I Do When I See Pornography?"
https://goo.gl/thu2EF

Adaptations for Younger Children

Quotes

"I will be honest with Heavenly Father, others, and myself" ("My Gospel Standards").

"I will not swear or use crude words" ("My Gospel Standards").

"I will only read and watch things that are pleasing to Heavenly Father. I will only listen to music that is pleasing to Heavenly Father" ("My Gospel Standards").

Lessons from *Behold Your Little Ones*

"I Will Be Thankful" (Lesson 15, pp. 64–67) and "I Can Be Happy" (Lesson 19, pp. 80–83). Gratitude is a great virtue; it brings us close to God very quickly. We are happier when we are honest, true, chaste, benevolent, and so on.

Faith in God

Memorize and pass off the thirteenth article of faith this week. Recite it or sing it every day during family scripture study (*Children's Songbook*, 132). For Article of Faith 13, the memory trick is the rhyme "thirteen fourteen," because there is a list of fourteen things in the thirteenth article of faith. Honest! It's true! See page 230 in this book for the full list of memory helps. On a piece of paper, have your children write the thirteenth article of faith, draw a picture that represents it, and then tape it in a prominent place (*Faith in God,* pp. 16, 20).

"After studying the thirteenth article of faith, make a list of things that are uplifting and virtuous. Discuss with a parent or leader how you can seek after these things" (*Faith in God for Girls*, p. 12).

Activity

Quickly think of everything you can that is "virtuous, lovely, of good report, or praiseworthy" (Articles of Faith 1:13). Discuss things that are wholesome and how they make you feel. Discuss things that are not wholesome and how they make you feel. You may wish to briefly introduce what pornography is during this family home evening.

Adaptations for Older Children and Teens

Quotes

"I will prepare to enter the temple and remain pure and worthy. My thoughts and actions will be based on high moral standards" (*Young Women Personal Progress*, p. 69).

"The thirteenth article of faith provides special insight into how we should conduct our lives and present ourselves. . . . All of us should aspire to embody these attributes and lead lives that exemplify them" (L. Tom Perry, "The Doctrines and Principles Contained in the Articles of Faith," *Ensign*, November 2013).

"Satan has become a master at using the addictive power of pornography to limit individual capacity to be led by the Spirit. The onslaught of pornography in all of its vicious, corroding, destructive forms has caused great grief, suffering, heartache, and destroyed marriages. It is one of the most damning influences on earth" (Richard G. Scott, "To Acquire Spiritual Guidance," *Ensign*, November 2009).

Preach My Gospel

"Virtue," pp. 118–19.

Personal Progress

Knowledge #3—Memorize and recite the thirteenth article of faith. Evaluate entertainment options using the thirteenth article of faith. Write about your thoughts in your journal (p. 38).

Review the section on Virtue. See what you've done and what you haven't done. Look over the value project of reading the Book of Mormon and writing what you learn in your journal (pp. 69–74).

Duty to God

Study Doctrine and Covenants 63:16, Doctrine and Covenants 121:45, and four sections from the *For the Strength of Youth* pamphlet that will help you develop the habit of having virtuous thoughts (p. 40).

Activity

Mosiah 4:30 encourages readers to watch their thoughts, words, and actions, and continue in the faith or they will perish. Try reading the verse but changing a few words to make the teaching tell us what *to* do. "But this much I can tell you, that if ye [do] watch yourselves, and your thoughts, and your words, and your deeds, and observe the commandments of God, and continue in the faith of what ye have heard concerning the coming of our Lord, even unto the end of your lives, ye must [live]. And now, O man, remember, and [live]." Try the same thing with 1 Nephi 7:11–12, 15:10–11; 2 Nephi 9:51, 26:32, 32:4.

Talk openly and appropriately about the dangers and destructiveness of pornography. The LDS.org video "What Should I Do When I See Pornography" (see QR code on page 69) can be a helpful introduction for you.

Daily Scriptures

Article of Faith 13: Focusing on Virtue

Sunday

We believe in being honest, true, chaste, benevolent, virtuous, and in doing good to all men; indeed, we may say that we follow the admonition of Paul—We believe all things, we hope all things, we have endured many things, and hope to be able to endure all things. If there is anything virtuous, lovely, or of good report or praiseworthy, we seek after these things." (Articles of Faith 1:13)

Monday

"Look unto me in every thought; doubt not, fear not." (D&C 6:36)

Tuesday

"Ye must give thanks unto God in the Spirit for whatsoever blessing ye are blessed with. And ye must practice virtue and holiness before me continually." (D&C 46:32–33)

Wednesday

"Who shall ascend into the hill of the Lord? or who shall stand in his holy place? He that hath clean hands, and a pure heart; who hath not lifted up his soul unto vanity, nor sworn deceitfully. He shall receive the blessing from the Lord." (Psalm 24:3–5)

Thursday

"Be full of charity towards all men, . . . and let virtue garnish thy thoughts unceasingly." (D&C 121:45)

Friday

"But this much I can tell you, that if ye do not watch yourselves, and your thoughts, and your words, and your deeds, and observe the commandments of God, and continue in the faith of what ye have heard concerning the coming of our Lord, even unto the end of your lives, ye must perish. And now, O man, remember, and perish not." (Mosiah 4:30)

Saturday

Jesus asked, "What manner of men ought ye to be? Verily I say unto you, even as I am." (3 Nephi 27:27)

For the Strength of Youth:
Introduction and Review

"Let no man despise thy youth; but be thou an example of the believers, in word, in conversation, in charity, in spirit, in faith, in purity. . . . Meditate upon these things; give thyself wholly to them; that thy profiting may appear to all." (1 Timothy 4:12, 15)

In the LDS.org video, "Message from President Thomas S. Monson," President Monson talks about the *For Strength of Youth* pamphlet.
https://goo.gl/sg20G2

Mormonads—Standards
https://goo.gl/PxFmUT

Music from Children's Songbook & Hymns

- Seek the Lord Early (*CS*, 108)
- I Will Be Valiant (*CS*, 162)
- True to the Faith (*Hymns*, 254)
- Who's on the Lord's Side? (*Hymns*, 260)

Quote

"Many scholars believe that Daniel was between 12 and 17 years old at the time [he was taken from Jerusalem] . . . to be educated in the language, laws, religion, and science of the worldly Babylon. . . . I don't know if it was easy for Daniel to be a believer in such an environment. . . . I imagine that Daniel was like many of us who have to work for our testimonies. I'm confident that Daniel spent many hours on his knees praying, laying his questions and fears on the altar of faith, and waiting upon the Lord for understanding and wisdom. And the Lord did bless Daniel. Though his faith was challenged and ridiculed, he stayed true to what he knew by his own experience to be right. Daniel believed. Daniel did not doubt. . . . Have courage to believe. . . . Stand with Daniel" (Dieter F. Uchtdorf, "Be Not Afraid, Only Believe," *Ensign*, November 2015).

Scripture Stories

Though living in enemy territory and being taught things contrary to his beliefs, Daniel held fast to his faith, developed a strong relationship with God, and saved himself and his friends from death by revealing and interpreting the dream of king Nebuchadnezzar (see Daniel 1–2).

As a twelve-year-old, Jesus astonished teachers in the temple with his knowledge. He grew mentally, physically, spiritually, and socially (see Luke 2:40–52).

Gospel Art Pictures

- *Daniel Interprets Nebuchadnezzar's Dream* (#24)
- *Boy Jesus in the Temple* (#34)

Church History

Using agency to follow the standards outlined in the *For the Strength of Youth* pamphlet prepares youth to be worthy to make covenants with God in sacred temples. To watch a short video of President Uchtdorf talking about the *For the Strength of Youth* pamphlet and the temple, see https://goo.gl/AxfNH8.

When and where were the first temple endowments performed? *May 4, 1842, in an upper room of Joseph Smith's red brick store.* (*Teachings of Presidents of the Church: Joseph Smith*, xxi)

When was the first edition of the *For the Strength of Youth* pamphlet printed, and who was the First Presidency of the Church at that point? *The first printing of the pamphlet was done in 1965 when the presidency consisted of David O. McKay, Hugh B. Brown, and N. Elson Tanner.* (The original 1965 *For the Strength of Youth* pamphlet is shown at http://www.barncow.com/mormon/youth-1965.html or at http://goo.gl/7AR8vR. The pamphlet published in 1990 is online at https://goo.gl/r8C94p. An article comparing the different versions is at UtahValley360.com "For the Strength of Youth: 1965 to today" at http://goo.gl/w76ubV).

Video "Counsel for Youth," from President Uchtdorf's Facebook page, is about the *For Strength of Youth* pamphlet and temple recommends. https://goo.gl/AxfNH8

In the LDS.org video "Temples are a Beacon," President Monson talks about the importance of temples. He shares a story of a family who sacrificed to travel participate in temple ordinances. https://goo.gl/8zD728

Adaptations for Younger Children

Quote

"I will follow Heavenly Father's plan for me" ("My Gospel Standards").

Lesson from *Behold Your Little Ones*

"I Will Follow the Prophet" (Lesson 24, pp. 100–103)

Faith in God

Look through the *Faith in God* booklet and get a good overview of the program, even if you have been working on it for a while. Read "My Gospel Standards" on the back cover of the booklet.

Activity ⏲

Get two cans of soda. Empty one and leave the other sealed. Holding the sealed can, squeeze it hard and show that it doesn't change. Then take the empty can and crush it. When we are full of the Spirit, outside pressures don't have the power to crush us. Using our agency to read, learn, and then personally embrace the standards in "My Gospel Standards" and the *For the Strength of Youth* pamphlet can help us be worthy of the Spirit in our lives. Make sure your family knows that you consider the standards in *For the Strength of Youth* to apply to every member of the Church, regardless of age (see Cheryl A. Esplin, "Filling Our Homes with Light and Truth," *Ensign*, May 2015).

Adaptations for Older Children and Teens

Quote

"The Lord has promised many wonderful blessings to those who are true to the standards He has set. Some are immediate: the companionship of the Holy Ghost, peace of conscience, and increased faith and confidence. Each time we obey a commandment, our ability to obey grows. . . . The world needs young people who understand the value of these blessings and how to qualify for them. There are many among your friends and your peers who are looking for an alternative to the world's ways, who want true principles to build their lives upon. All they need is your example and testimony" (David L. Beck, "Q&A on the new For the Strength of Youth," article can be found on youth.lds.org or at https://goo.gl/45SbYg).

Preach My Gospel

Chapter 4: "How Do I Recognize and Understand the Spirit?," pp. 89–102.

Personal Progress

Choice and Accountability #2—"Read the pamphlet *For the Strength of Youth*. . . . Practice living righteous standards by choosing three standards in which you need to improve. . . . After three weeks share your progress with your family, your class, or a leader" (p. 46).

Integrity #1—Living by the standards in *For the Strength of Youth* requires integrity (p. 62).

Duty to God

Read the following quotes from the *Duty to God* book. "This [*Duty to God*] book, along with the scriptures and *For the Strength of Youth*, will help you fulfill your responsibilities" (p. 5). "The Duty to God program is a tool to help Aaronic Priesthood holders: strengthen their testimony and their relationship with Heavenly Father[,] learn about and fulfill their priesthood duties[, and] apply the standards from *For the Strength of Youth*" (p. 94). Look over the *For the Strength of Youth* pamphlet.

Activity ⏲

Get a funnel and read this quote: "The world says, 'Try everything. Because you're young now, you can experiment.' What happens when you follow that message is like a funnel that starts out wide but gets pretty narrow at the bottom. Your agency becomes restricted by those decisions. Experimentation can lead to addiction. A moment of excitement can lead to pregnancy out of wedlock or a change in your life plan. But if you will walk a strict path—turn the funnel upside down—and obey the Lord's standards, the whole world opens up for you and grows wider as you keep the commandments. Instead of being bound to your mistakes, you have the freedom to live the kind of life that will make you happy" (Elaine S. Dalton, "Q&A on the new For the Strength of Youth," article can be found on youth.lds.org or at https://goo.gl/45SbYg).

Daily Scriptures

For the Strength of Youth: Introduction and Review

Sunday

"Let no man despise thy youth; but be thou an example of the believers, in word, in conversation, in charity, in spirit, in faith, in purity. Meditate upon these things; give thyself wholly to them; that thy profiting may appear to all." (1 Timothy 4:12, 15)

Monday

"O, remember, my son, and learn wisdom in thy youth; yea, learn in thy youth to keep the commandments of God." (Alma 37:35)

Tuesday 🔖

"Consider on the blessed and happy state of those that keep the commandments of God. For behold, they are blessed in all things, both temporal and spiritual." (Mosiah 2:41)

Wednesday

"Be strong in the Lord, and in the power of his might. Put on the whole armour of God, that ye may be able to stand against the wiles of the devil. For we wrestle not against flesh and blood, but against principalities, against powers, against the rulers of the darkness of this world, against spiritual wickedness in high places. Wherefore take unto you the whole armour of God, that ye may be able to withstand in the evil day, and having done all, to stand." (Ephesians 6:10–13)

Thursday 🔖

"If any man will do his will, he shall know of the doctrine, whether it be of God, or whether I speak of myself." (John 7:17)

Friday

"Ye are the salt of the earth: but if the salt have lost his savour, wherewith shall it be salted? it is thenceforth good for nothing, but to be cast out, and to be trodden under foot of men. Ye are the light of the world. A city that is set on an hill cannot be hid. Neither do men light a candle, and put it under a bushel, but on a candlestick; and it giveth light unto all that are in the house. Let your light so shine before men, that they may see your good works, and glorify your Father which is in heaven." (Matthew 5:13–16)

Saturday 🔖

"Arise and shine forth, that thy light may be a standard for the nations." (D&C 115:5)

Agency and Accountability

"Men should be anxiously engaged in a good cause, and do many things of their own free will, and bring to pass much righteousness; For the power is in them, wherein they are agents unto themselves."(D&C 58:27–28)

Music from Children's Songbook & Hymns

- The Second Article of Faith (*CS*, 122)
- Dare to Do Right (*CS*, 158)
- Choose the Right (*Hymns*, 239)
- Know This, That Every Soul Is Free (*Hymns*, 240)

Mormonads—Agency
and Accountability
https://goo.gl/qZVokt

Quotes

"Heavenly Father has given you agency, the ability to choose right from wrong and to act for yourself. . . . You are responsible for the choices you make. . . . While you are free to choose your course of action, you are not free to choose the consequences" (*For the Strength of Youth*, p. 2).

"It has been said that the door of history turns on small hinges, and so do people's lives. The choices we make determine our destiny" (Thomas S. Monson, "Choices," *Ensign*, May 2016).

Gospel Topics: Agency
https://goo.gl/ZxZvHb

Scripture Stories

God tells Adam and Eve they can eat any fruit except the fruit from the tree of knowledge of good and evil. If they do, they will become mortal and die, but He also tells them they can choose for themselves. The consequence of their choosing to eat the fruit is that they have to leave the Garden of Eden (see Moses 3:1–9, 15–25; 4:7–31), but they can also now have children (see 2 Nephi 2:22–23).

King Nebuchadnezzar commands everyone to worship a golden image, but Shadrach, Meshach, and Abed-nego choose to defy the king's command and worship God instead. The consequence for their obedience to God is that they are thrown into a fiery furnace. Amazingly, they are seen walking around in the fire unharmed. They come out of the fire and are just fine (see Daniel 3).

The Lord commands the Kirtland Temple to be built, and says no unclean thing should be allowed inside. Choices determine temple worthiness (see D&C 97:15–17).

Gospel Art Pictures

- *Adam and Eve Teaching Their Children* (#5)
- *Three Men in the Fiery Furnace* (#25)
- *Temple Pictures* (#117–21)

Church History

Using agency to follow the standards outlined in the *For the Strength of Youth* pamphlet prepares youth to be worthy to make covenants with God in sacred temples. What were the earliest temples built? *Kirtland Temple (1836), Nauvoo Illinois Temple (1846), St. George Utah Temple (1877), Logan Utah Temple (1884), Manti Utah Temple (1888), Salt Lake Temple (1893), Laie Hawaii Temple (1919).*

LDS.org video "Ministry of Gordon B. Hinckley: Temple Building" https://goo.gl/5PPMN3

When did President Hinckley announce the building of smaller temples? *October 4, 1997.* There were fifty operating temples at the time. To see a video about this, go to https://goo.gl/5PPMN3.

What was the first smaller temple? *The Monticello Utah Temple, the 53rd operating temple of the Church, was the first of the smaller temples to be built. It was dedicated on July 26–27, 1998.*

LDS.org video titled "Focus on the Temple." This page has other temple videos too. https://goo.gl/DfFfum

When did President Hinckley announce the goal of having 100 operating temples by the year 2000? *April 1998.* There were 51 operating temples at that time. By the end of the year 2000, 102 temples were in operation (see http://goo.gl/9bEacr for the LDS Temple Chronology webpage). To see a video titled "Focus on the Temple," go to https://goo.gl/DfFfum.

Adaptations for Younger Children

Quote

"I will choose the right. I know I can repent when I make a mistake" ("My Gospel Standards").

Lessons from *Behold Your Little Ones*

"Jesus Christ Created the World for Me" (Lesson 7, pp. 32–35) and "I Love the Scriptures" (Lesson 23, pp. 96–99). Tell the story of the Creation from lesson 7 and include Adam and Eve. Use the puppet activity from lesson 23.

Faith in God

"Learn to sing 'Choose the Right' (*Hymns*, 239). Explain what agency is and what it means to be responsible for your choices. Discuss how making good choices has helped you develop greater faith" (*Faith in God*, p. 7).

Activity

Talk about how a boomerang works. If you have one, show how it works. You can throw a boomerang and it will come back to you. Throwing the boomerang is like making a choice, and the boomerang coming back is like getting the consequence of that choice. Read what I call "the boomerang scripture," Alma 41:15: "That which ye do send out shall return unto you again."

Discuss some choices and consequences. For example, when we take care of our bodies by eating good foods, drinking lots of water, playing a lot, and sleeping when we are tired, the consequence is that our bodies feel good. When people choose to eat bad things, sit around too much, and go to bed too late, the consequence is that their bodies don't feel good and don't function as well.

Adaptations for Older Children and Teens

Quote

"I was surprised [that some people do] not understand what we mean by the word agency. I went to an online dictionary. Of the 10 definitions and usages of the word *agency*, none expressed the idea of making choices to act. We teach that agency is the ability and privilege God gives us to choose and 'to act for [ourselves] and not to be acted upon.' Agency is to act with accountability and responsibility for our actions. . . . The world teaches many falsehoods about agency. Many think we should 'eat, drink, and be merry; . . . and if it so be that we are guilty, God will beat us with a few stripes, and at last we shall be saved.' Others embrace secularism and deny God. . . . Contrary to the world's secular teaching, the scriptures teach us that we do have agency, and our righteous exercise of agency always makes a difference in the opportunities we have and our ability to act upon them and progress eternally" (Robert D. Hales, "Agency: Essential to the Plan of Life," *Ensign*, November 2010; italics in original).

Preach My Gospel

"Key Definitions: Agency," p. 44; "Obedience," p. 72; Chapter 8: "How Do I Use Time Wisely?," pp. 137–54; "Accountability," pp. 150–51.

Personal Progress

Review the "Choice and Accountability" section. See what you've done and what you haven't done. Look over the value project ideas (pp. 45–52).

Duty to God

Study the doctrinal topic of "Agency," focusing on personal agency and accountability. Record what you learn and share what you learned with your parents or a priesthood leader. (pp. 18–21, 42–45, 66–69)

Mormonad—What Goes Around Comes Around.
https://goo.gl/PCjt4a

Activity

Talk about how a boomerang works; if you have one, use it. You can throw a boomerang and it will come back to you. Throwing the boomerang is like making a choice, and the boomerang coming back is like getting the consequence of that choice. Read what I call the "boomerang scripture," Alma 41:15: "That which ye do send out shall return unto you again."

Discuss some choices and consequences. For example, when we take care of our bodies by eating good foods, drinking lots of water, playing a lot, and sleeping when we are tired, the consequence is that our bodies feel good. When people choose to eat or ingest bad things, sit around too much, go to bed too late, drink alcohol, or take drugs, the consequence is that their bodies don't feel good or function as well.

Daily Scriptures

Agency and Accountability

Sunday

"It is not meet that I should command in all things; for he that is compelled in all things, the same is a slothful and not a wise servant. . . . Verily I say, men should be anxiously engaged in a good cause, and do many things of their own free will, and bring to pass much righteousness; For the power is in them, wherein they are agents unto themselves." (D&C 58:26–28)

Monday

"Remember . . . that whosoever perisheth, perisheth unto himself; and whosoever doeth iniquity, doeth it unto himself; for behold, ye are free; ye are permitted to act for yourselves; for behold, God hath given unto you a knowledge and he hath made you free." (Helaman 14:30)

Tuesday

"Cheer up your hearts, and remember that ye are free to act for yourselves—to choose the way of everlasting death or the way of eternal life." (2 Nephi 10:23)

Wednesday 📖

"I give unto you directions how you may act before me, that it may turn to you for your salvation. I, the Lord, am bound when ye do what I say; but when ye do not what I say, ye have no promise." (D&C 82:9–10)

Thursday 📖

"The Messiah cometh in the fulness of time, that he may redeem the children of men from the fall. And because that they are redeemed from the fall they have become free forever, knowing good from evil; to act for themselves and not to be acted upon. . . . Wherefore, men . . . are free to choose liberty and eternal life, through the great Mediator of all men, or to choose captivity and death" (2 Nephi 2:26–27)

Friday

"Pray always, that you may come off conqueror; yea, that you may conquer Satan, and that you may escape the hands of the servants of Satan that do uphold his work." (D&C 10:5)

Saturday

"[Many] shall say: Eat, drink, and be merry, for tomorrow we die; and it shall be well with us. And . . . [many] say: Eat, drink, and be merry; nevertheless, fear God—he will justify in committing a little sin; yea, lie a little, take the advantage of one because of his words, dig a pit for thy neighbor; there is no harm in this; and do all these things, for tomorrow we die; and if it so be that we are guilty, God will beat us with a few stripes, and at last we shall be saved in the kingdom of God. Yea, and there shall be many which shall teach after this manner, false and vain and foolish doctrines, and shall be puffed up in their hearts, and shall seek deep to hide their counsels from the Lord." (2 Nephi 28:7–9)

Dating

"Who shall ascend into the hill of the Lord? or who shall stand in his holy place? He that hath clean hands, and a pure heart." (Psalm 24:3–4) 📖Ⓜ

LDS.org video "A Brand New Year: Dating." This video focuses on how dating can help you build lasting relationships. https://goo.gl/jbDzyT

Mormonads—Dating https://goo.gl/xLZEw8

Music from Children's Songbook & Hymns

- I Love to See the Temple (*CS*, 95)
- Let Us Oft Speak Kind Words (*Hymns*, 232)
- Choose the Right (*Hymns*, 239)
- As Zion's Youth in Latter Days (*Hymns*, 256 v. 2)

Quote

"[Years ago, my wife and I] concluded that the skill of developing worthwhile relationships is something a person indeed learns. . . . We began exploring ideas on how we could best teach our children to develop appropriate relationships. . . . We also wanted to teach realistic, proper, and practical behaviors that would empower self-confidence . . . and lay a foundation for healthy relationships. In all of this we felt that we needed to start early—long before our children began dating—and we wanted our experience to be filled with learning and teaching that were natural and hopefully fun. We fully understood, too, that we would be competing with the way the media portray relationships" (Matthew O. Richardson, "Dating Academy: Teaching Children about Relationships," *Ensign*, August 2014).

Scripture Stories

Abraham wants Isaac to marry a woman of faith. He prayerfully finds Rebekah. Later, Isaac wants Jacob to marry a woman of faith, and he is able to do so (see Genesis 24; Genesis 28:1–5; Genesis 29).

The Lord sends Nephi and his brothers to invite Ishmael's family to travel with them so they can marry and raise families (see 1 Nephi 7:1–5; 16:7).

Elijah appears to Joseph Smith and Oliver Cowdery to restore the sealing power. While dating can be a lot of fun, the ultimate purpose of dating is to find the person you want to marry (see D&C 110:13–16).

Gospel Art Pictures

- *Rebekah at the Well* (#10)
- *Lehi and His People Arrive in the Promised Land* (#71)
- *Elijah Appearing in the Kirtland Temple* (#95)
- *Young Couple Going to the Temple* (#120)

Church History

When was the idea of waiting to date until age sixteen first counseled? *In the 1965 (first edition) of* For the Strength of Youth *there was a section on dating.* It says, "To make dating wholesome, purposeful, protected, and really enjoyable experiences for young people, the Church recommends the following safeguards. There should be no dating before the age of sixteen. . . . Steady dating during the early dating years should not be practiced. . . . Love and affection are precious, and virtue must never be placed in jeopardy" (*For the Strength of Youth*, 1st ed., pp. 12–13, or go to http://www.barncow.com/mormon/youth-1965.html or http://goo.gl/bfv6Ts).

New Era article "Dating FAQs"
https://goo.gl/KLdKom

In February 1975, the *New Era* printed an article called "Questions and Answers." The first question addressed dating: what age range is appropriate for dating, and why? (https://goo.gl/kzm5M2). More recently, the *New Era* printed an article called "Dating FAQs" (see the April 2010 issue or go to https://goo.gl/KLdKom).

Adaptations for Younger Children

Quote

"Encourage your children to come to you for counsel with their problems and questions by listening to them every day. Discuss with them such important matters as dating, sex, and other matters affecting their growth and development, and do it early enough so they will not obtain information from questionable sources" (Ezra Taft Benson, "The Honored Place of Woman," *Ensign*, November 1981).

Lesson from *Behold Your Little Ones*

"I Love My Family" (Lesson 11, pp. 48–51).

Faith in God

"Plan and hold a parent-child activity, such as a dinner, picnic, hike, day trip, or service project." (p. 9).

Activity

Talk about what a date is. A date is a prearranged day and time when two people get together and do something specific. Young children can have dates with family members or "playdates" with friends. As they get older, they will have dates with special friends and will eventually date with the intention of getting married. Ask your children what they would like to do for a family date, a one-on-one parent-child date, and playdates. If possible, plan to do one or more dates.

Adaptations for Older Children and Teens

Quote

"Hanging out consists of numbers of young men and young women joining together in some group activity. It is very different from dating. . . . Unlike hanging out, dating is not a team sport. Dating is pairing off to experience the kind of one-on-one association and temporary commitment that can lead to marriage in some rare and treasured cases. . . . Simple and more frequent dates allow both men and women to 'shop around' in a way that allows extensive evaluation of the prospects. The old-fashioned date was a wonderful way to get acquainted with a member of the opposite sex. It encouraged conversation. It allowed you to see how you treat others and how you are treated in a one-on-one situation. It gave opportunities to learn how to initiate and sustain a mature relationship. None of that happens in hanging out. . . . A 'date' must pass the test of three *p*'s: (1) planned ahead, (2) paid for, and (3) paired off" (Dallin H. Oaks, "Dating versus Hanging Out," *Ensign,* June 2006).

Preach My Gospel

"Eternal Marriage," pp. 85–86.

Personal Progress

Divine Nature #6—Identify divine qualities and work on developing at least one of them (p. 24).

Choice and Accountability #6—Study YW theme and how it applies to dating choices (p. 48).

Duty to God

Study the doctrinal topic of "Temples" since dating ideally leads to a temple marriage. Record what you learn and share what you learned with your parents or a priesthood leader (see pp. 18–21, 42–45, 66–69)

Activity

Talk about dating. Remember that some youth aren't interested in dating and certainly shouldn't feel pressured to go on dates if they don't want to. See how your family members feel about dating. Are some people more interested in dating than others? What kinds of activities do people like to do on dates? Reminisce about fun dates, and talk about ideas you've heard of as a way to think up light, fun, and inexpensive dates. Plan special outings with parents and children, or between siblings as a way to try out ideas for dating. Have fun with this!

Daily Scriptures

Dating

Sunday

"Who shall ascend into the hill of the Lord? or who shall stand in his holy place? He that hath clean hands, and a pure heart." (Psalm 24:3–4)

Monday

"Watch yourselves, and your thoughts, and your words, and your deeds, and observe the commandments of God, and continue in the faith." (Mosiah 4:30)

Tuesday

"Look not on his countenance, or on the height of his stature; because I have refused him: for the Lord seeth not as man seeth; for man looketh on the outward appearance, but the Lord looketh on the heart." (1 Samuel 16:7)

Wednesday

"All things must be done in the name of Christ, whatsoever you do in the Spirit; And ye must give thanks unto God in the Spirit for whatsoever blessing ye are blessed with. And ye must practice virtue and holiness before me continually." (D&C 46:31–33)

Thursday

"Intelligence cleaveth unto intelligence; wisdom receiveth wisdom; truth embraceth truth; virtue loveth virtue; light cleaveth unto light." (D&C 88:40)

Friday

"Let no corrupt communication proceed out of your mouth, but that which is good to the use of edifying, that it may minister grace unto the hearers. And grieve not the holy Spirit of God . . . And be ye kind one to another." (Ephesians 4:29–30, 32)

Saturday

"Neither is the man without the woman, neither the woman without the man, in the Lord." (1 Corinthians 11:11)

Dress and Appearance

"God said, Let us make man in our image, after our likeness. . . . So God created man in his own image, in the image of God created he him; male and female created he them." (Genesis 1:26–27) 🄳🄼

Mormonads—Dress and Appearance
https://goo.gl/wkC34W

Music from Children's Songbook & Hymns

- The Lord Gave Me a Temple (*CS*, 153)
- Stand for the Right (*CS*, 159)
- The Things I Do (*CS*, 170)
- I Am a Child of God (*CS*, 2; *Hymns*, 301)

Quote

"By example we can . . . model that which is virtuous and lovely by our dress and appearance. As a covenant people we have the responsibility to care for, protect, and properly clothe our bodies. We must help our children and youth understand that we respect our bodies as temples and as gifts from God. We set the example by refusing to purchase or wear immodest clothing that is too tight, too sheer, or revealing in any other manner" (Mary N. Cook, "Be an Example of the Believers," *Ensign*, November 2010).

Scripture Stories

God creates mankind in His image, which means our bodies look like His (see Genesis 1:27–28).

The brother of Jared sees Jesus's spirit body, and is told our physical bodies look like His spirit body (see Ether 3:1–15).

Joseph Smith is concerned over which church to join. He decides to pray and ask God which church to join. When he does, he receives a physical visitation from Heavenly Father and Jesus Christ, known as the First Vision. He sees that God the Father and Jesus Christ have bodies like ours, and he speaks with Them (see Joseph Smith—History 1:5–20).

Gospel Art Pictures

- *Adam and Eve Kneeling at an Altar* (#4)
- *The Brother of Jared Sees the Finger of the Lord* (#85)
- *The First Vision* (#90)

Church History

When and where did the first full temple endowment take place? *On May 4, 1842, the first full temple endowment took place in the Nauvoo Illinois Temple.* During an endowment, a person is clothed in the holy temple garment. The temple garment is a sacred, personal reminder of covenants made between a person and God. The temple garment requires a standard for modest dress when worn correctly. To learn about the temple and the temple garment, read "Prepare for the Blessings of the Temple," (Russell M. Nelson, *Ensign*, November 2010); or watch an official church video showing, discussing, and honoring the sacred use of temple garments at http://goo.gl/jbb7xm.

Gospel Topics: Temples. https://goo.gl/XGm4rF

Before going to Carthage, Joseph Smith, Hyrum Smith, and John Taylor removed their temple garments. Accounts show that this was likely done to prevent the holy garments from being desecrated or ridiculed. Willard Richards kept his temple garments on and was the only one who came out unharmed— leading some to believe that his wearing of the garments provided him physical protection (see FairMormon's page "Did Joseph and other with him remove their garments in order to avoid being identified as polygamists?" at http://goo.gl/qvb65q). Leaders of the Church teach that the garment does not ensure physical protection but is "a protection against temptation and evil" and that protection is based on a person's faithfulness; the temple garment is not to be thought of as magical (First Presidency Letter, 10 October 1988; see Carlos E. Asay, "The Temple Garment: 'An Outward Expression of an Inward Commitment.'" *Ensign*, August 1997).

MormonNewsroom. org article and video "Temple Garments" http://goo.gl/jbb7xm

Adaptations for Younger Children

Quotes

"I will dress modestly to show respect for Heavenly Father and myself" ("My Gospel Standards").

"We [can] keep the outside of our bodily temples looking clean and beautiful to reflect the sacred and holy nature of what is inside, just as the Church does with its temples. We should dress and act in ways that reflect the sacred spirit inside us" (Susan W. Tanner, "The Sanctity of the Body," *Ensign*, November 2005).

Lesson from *Behold Your Little Ones*

"I Have a Body like Heavenly Father's" (Lesson 9, pp. 40–43).

Faith in God

"Learn about and practice . . . good grooming, including modest dress" (p. 11).

Activity

For tiny kids, play Name That Body Part. Just touch your nose and say, "Nose. My nose." Then touch their nose and say, "Your nose." Repeat for different parts of the body. Use your body to do different things like clap, crawl, and jump. With older kids, talk about guidelines for modest dress and appearance. Refer to *For the Strength of Youth* pages 6–8 for Church guidelines. Then just do some kind of physical play. You could dance, skip, hop, play outside, play with a ball, swing, and so on.

Adaptations for Older Children and Teens

Quotes

"Do not underestimate the important symbolic and actual effect of appearance. Persons who are well groomed and modestly dressed invite the companionship of the Spirit of our Father in Heaven and are able to exercise a wholesome influence upon those around them. Persons who are unkempt and careless about their appearance, or adopt the visual symbols of those who often oppose our ideals, expose themselves and persons around them to influences that are degrading and dissonant. Outward appearance is often a reflection of inward tendencies" (Harold B. Lee, *The Teachings of Harold B. Lee*, ed. Clyde J. Williams [1996], 220).

"Imagine the reaction you or I might have if we saw defacing graffiti on the exterior of one of our Church's temples. . . . Brothers and sisters, we must be particularly careful as the fads and fashions of the world entice us to mark or to pierce or to otherwise deface or disfigure our personal temples. . . . We now live in a world where people routinely do wear rings and other items in their noses, in their tongues, in their navels, and in their eyebrows because that is the current style. . . . Indeed, [our bodies] are temples, and the Spirit of the Lord should dwell therein and shine through. And, may I quickly add, it is harder for the Spirit to shine in and through our physical bodies when we are dozy and dull from foolishly going to bed at 1:30 A.M. or 2:30 A.M. or later night after night after night (see D&C 88:124)" (David A. Bednar, "Ye Are the Temple of God," *Ensign*, September 2001).

Preach My Gospel

"First Presidency Message," p. v; Chapter 1: "What Is My Purpose as a Missionary?," pp. 1–16 (see https://goo.gl/JzW8Xu for dress and grooming guidelines in the chapter titled "Missionary Conduct" of the missionary handbook).

Personal Progress

Individual Worth #8 or #9: Personalized Value Experience—Knowing your worth helps you respect yourself. The way you dress and present yourself to others reflects your level of respect for yourself and inspires others to respect you too. Look over your wardrobe and update it as necessary.

Duty to God

Study the doctrinal topic of "Temples," focusing on how your body is a temple. Record what you learn and share what you learned with your parents or a priesthood leader (see pp. 18–21, 42–45, 66–69).

Activity

Discuss Church standards of dress and appearance. Refer to *For the Strength of Youth* (pp. 6–8) and the missionary handbook for the dress and appearance guidelines (see https://goo.gl/JzW8Xu for the chapter titled "Missionary Conduct" in the missionary handbook). Think about current popular styles. Which reflect modesty and which don't? Talk about how to treat people whose dress and appearance is immodest, unkempt, or gaudy. What can you do if you find yourself in a group that is dressed inappropriately?

Daily Scriptures

Dress and Appearance

Sunday 📖

"And God said, Let us make man in our image, after our likeness: and let them have dominion over the fish of the sea, and over the fowl of the air, and over the cattle, and over all the earth, and over every creeping thing that creepeth upon the earth. So God created man in his own image, in the image of God created he him; male and female created he them." (Genesis 1:26–27)

Monday

"Look not on his countenance, or on the height of his stature; . . . for the Lord seeth not as man seeth; for man looketh on the outward appearance, but the Lord looketh on the heart." (1 Samuel 16:7)

Tuesday 📖

"Know ye not that your body is the temple of the Holy Ghost which is in you, which ye have of God, and ye are not your own? For ye are bought with a price: therefore glorify God in your body, and in your spirit, which are God's." (1 Corinthians 6:19–20)

Wednesday

"I also cast my eyes round about, and beheld, on the other side of the river of water, a great and spacious building; and it stood as it were in the air, high above the earth. And it was filled with people, both old and young, both male and female; and their manner of dress was exceedingly fine; and they were in the attitude of mocking and pointing their fingers towards those who had come at and were partaking of the fruit. And after they had tasted of the fruit they were ashamed, because of those that were scoffing at them; and they fell away into forbidden paths and were lost." (1 Nephi 8:26–28)

Thursday

"Thou shalt not be proud in thy heart; let all thy garments be plain, and . . . let all things be done in cleanliness before me." (D&C 42:40–41)

Friday

"The woman shall not wear that which pertaineth unto a man, neither shall a man put on a woman's garment: for all that do so are abomination unto the Lord thy God." (Deuteronomy 22:5)

Saturday

Church members "did impart of their substance, every man according to that which he had, to the poor, and the needy, and the sick, and the afflicted; and they did not wear costly apparel, yet they were neat and comely." (Alma 1:27)

Education

"Seek ye out of the best books words of wisdom; seek learning, even by study and also by faith." (D&C 88:118) 🔲

LDS.org video "Education." Elder and Sister Bednar discuss secular and spiritual learning. https://goo.gl/tGFjAS

Gospel Topics: Education https://goo.gl/jv6UUt

Music from Children's Songbook & Hymns

- Search, Ponder, and Pray (*CS*, 109)
- The Wise Man and the Foolish Man (*CS*, 281)
- Teach Me to Walk in the Light (*CS*, 177; *Hymns*, 304)
- True to the Faith (*Hymns*, 254)
- Oh Say, What Is Truth? (*Hymns*, 272)

Quote

"Work for an education. Get all the training that you can. The world will largely pay you what it thinks you are worth. . . . Education is the key to economic opportunity. The Lord has laid a mandate upon us as a people to acquire learning 'by study, and also by faith' (D&C 109:14)" (Gordon B. Hinckley, "Living Worthy of the Girl You Will Someday Marry," *Ensign*, May 1998).

Scripture Stories

Adam and Eve taught their children the things of God. They also taught them to read and write (see Moses 5:12, 58–59; Moses 6:6).

Jesus went to Jerusalem with His family for the Feast of the Passover when He was twelve years old. As was customary for boys of His age in that culture, He met with teachers on the temple grounds and was tested on His knowledge of His duties and privileges. Everyone was amazed at His knowledge and wisdom (see Luke 2:40–52; BD "Education.")

The Lord tells His disciples to learn a variety of subjects in order to be prepared for their future service (see D&C 88:76–80).

Gospel Art Pictures

- *Adam and Eve Teaching Their Children* (#5)
- *Jesus Praying with His Mother* (#33)
- *Boy Jesus in the Temple* (#34)

Church History

When was the Brigham Young Academy founded? *October 16, 1875.* When was the name changed to Brigham Young University? *1903.* What other Church educational establishments are there? *Brigham Young University–Idaho, Brigham Young University–Hawaii, and LDS Business College in Salt Lake City.* To see the BYU post "History of BYU," go to https://goo .gl/eB78tB. To view campus historical photographs, go to http://goo.gl /NC8xFe. To see a video documentary on the life of Brigham Young, go to https://goo.gl/MnSMGS.

Brigham Young: Documentary
https://goo.gl/MnSMGS

When was the Institute of Religion program started? *1926* (see *Teachings of Presidents of the Church: Heber J. Grant*, ix). Where was the first LDS Institute of Religion built? *The first building dedicated for that purpose was the Pocatello Institute in 1928, located in Moscow, Idaho* (see History. LDS.org's page "Pocatello Institute, dedicated 1929" at https://goo.gl /ZvrJW4).

LDS.org video "What is a
PEF Loan?"
https://goo.gl/R7x6wL

In the April 2001 general conference, President Gordon B. Hinckley announced the Perpetual Education Fund—a program by which worthy and qualified members of the Church can apply for a loan to get needed education, so they and their children may escape the cycle of poverty they have been born into ("The Perpetual Education Fund," *Ensign*, May 2001). To learn more about this incredible program, go to LDS.org's page "The Perpetual Education Fund" at https://goo.gl/P7Hwmh or watch the video "What is a PEF Loan?" at https://goo.gl/R7x6wL.

Adaptations for Younger Children

Quote

"Parents must diligently and effectively explain basic gospel doctrines, teach true principles, and share sacred experiences. But who truly does the teaching and certifies the truthfulness of what we come to know? The Holy Ghost, the third member of the Godhead" (David A. Bednar, "Understanding Is a Wellspring of Life," Ricks College Campus Education Week Devotional, June 3, 1999).

Lesson from *Behold Your Little Ones*

"The Holy Ghost Helps Me" (Lesson 6, pp. 28–31). The Holy Ghost helps us know whether or not the things we are learning are true and good for us.

Faith in God

"Read Doctrine and Covenants 88:77–80, 118 and Doctrine and Covenants 130:19. Discuss with a parent or Primary leader how important a good education is and how it can help you strengthen your home and family and the Church" (p. 12).

Activity

Talk about different ways we learn, such as going to a formal school, doing daily chores, talking with others, apprenticing, reading, watching television and movies, and praying and listening to the Spirit. After discussing various ways of learning, talk about what you like about each method and see if you prefer specific learning methods over others. Talk about how to determine if something is good to watch, read, listen to, or learn.

Adaptations for Older Children and Teens

Quote

"There can be no doubt, none whatever, that education pays. Do not short-circuit your lives. If you do so, you will pay for it over and over and over again. You have the potential to become anything to which you set your mind. You have a mind and a body and a spirit. With these three working together, you can walk the high road that leads to achievement and happiness. But this will require effort and sacrifice and faith. You must get all of the education that you possibly can. Life has become so complex and competitive. You cannot assume that you have entitlements due you. You will be expected to put forth great effort and to use your best talents to make your way to the most wonderful future of which you are capable. Sacrifice a car; sacrifice anything that is needed to be sacrificed to qualify yourselves to do the work of the world. That world will in large measure pay you what it thinks you are worth, and your worth will increase as you gain education and proficiency in your chosen field" (Gordon B. Hinckley, "Words of the Prophet: Seek Learning," *New Era*, September 2007).

Preach My Gospel

Chapter 2: "How Do I Study Effectively and Prepare to Teach?" pp. 17–28; "Knowledge," p. 119.

Personal Progress

Knowledge, #1—"Learn about the importance of gaining knowledge" (p. 38). Review the section on "Knowledge." See what you've done and what you haven't done. Look over the project ideas (pp. 38–44).

Duty to God

Look over the section "For the Strength of Youth: Education." Work on it, or review what you did if you have already done this section (pp. 55–59).

Activity

Discuss career ideas and options. Parents, talk to your children about your experience with your education. What subjects did you like to study when you were their age? How did you decide what you wanted to do for work? Have you changed your field of work?

List or discuss your favorite topics to study as well as your hobbies and talents. What kinds of careers do you think would be a good fit for your interests and current abilities (knowing you can always improve your skill sets)? Are there things you would like to learn more about? Do you have a career you are already interested in? Do you know anyone who does what you are interested in doing? See if you can shadow or apprentice with them.

In order to do as well as possible with your education, what habits do you think are important? Discuss positive study and education habits as well as positive time management and health habits that will help you get the most out of your education.

Daily Scriptures

Education

Sunday

"And as all have not faith, seek ye diligently and teach one another words of wisdom; yea, seek ye out of the best books words of wisdom; seek learning, even by study and also by faith." (D&C 88:118)

Monday

"Now these sons of Mosiah were with Alma at the time the angel first appeared unto him; therefore Alma did rejoice exceedingly to see his brethren; and what added more to his joy, they were still his brethren in the Lord; yea, and they had waxed strong in the knowledge of the truth; for they were men of a sound understanding and they had searched the scriptures diligently, that they might know the word of God." (Alma 17:2)

Tuesday

"O that cunning plan of the evil one! O the vainness, and the frailties, and the foolishness of men! When they are learned they think they are wise, and they hearken not unto the counsel of God, for they set it aside, supposing they know of themselves, wherefore, their wisdom is foolishness and it profiteth them not. And they shall perish. But to be learned is good if they hearken unto the counsels of God." (2 Nephi 9:28–29)

Wednesday

"And set in order the churches, and study and learn, and become acquainted with all good books, and with languages, tongues, and people." (D&C 90:15)

Thursday

"Be instructed . . . in all things that pertain unto the kingdom of God. . . . Of things both in heaven and in the earth, and under the earth; things which have been, things which are, things which must shortly come to pass; things which are at home, things which are abroad; the wars and the perplexities of the nations, and the judgments which are on the land; and a knowledge also of countries and of kingdoms—That ye may be prepared in all things . . . to magnify the calling whereunto I have called you, and the mission with which I have commissioned you." (D&C 88:78–80)

Friday

"And if a person gains more knowledge and intelligence in this life through his diligence and obedience than another, he will have so much the advantage in the world to come." (D&C 130:19)

Saturday

"Wisdom is the principal thing; therefore get wisdom: and with all thy getting get understanding." (Proverbs 4:7)

Entertainment and Media

"Woe unto them that call evil good, and good evil; that put darkness for light, and light for darkness; that put bitter for sweet, and sweet for bitter!" (Isaiah 5:20) 🅳🅼

Mormonads—Entertainment, Media, and Music
https://goo.gl/UTjdBs

Gospel Topics: Media
https://goo.gl/wkk5PM

Music from *Children's Songbook* & *Hymns*

- I'm Trying to Be like Jesus (*CS*, 78)
- Fun to Do (*CS*, 253)
- Choose the Right (*Hymns*, 239)
- Who's on the Lord's Side (*Hymns*, 260)

Quote

"Just as honest toil gives rest its sweetness, wholesome recreation is the friend and steadying companion of work. Music, literature, art, dance, drama, athletics—all can provide entertainment to enrich one's life and further consecrate it. At the same time, it hardly needs to be said that much of what passes for entertainment today is coarse, degrading, violent, mind-numbing, and time wasting. Ironically, it sometimes takes hard work to find wholesome leisure. When entertainment turns from virtue to vice, it becomes a destroyer of the consecrated life. 'Wherefore, take heed . . . that ye do not judge that which is evil to be of God' (Moroni 7:14)" (D. Todd Christofferson, "Reflections on a Consecrated Life," *Ensign*, November 2010).

Scripture Stories

In the parable of the prodigal son, a young man takes his inheritance early and wastes it on meaningless, unwholesome, and "riotous living" (Luke 15:13). When he returns, his father throws a wholesome, celebratory party for him (see Luke 15:11–32).

On the journey toward the promised land, Laman, Lemuel, and others entertain themselves in a way that results in them being very rude to others in their family (see 1 Nephi 18:9).

The Lord encourages the Saints to praise Him "with singing, with music, with dancing, and with a prayer of praise and thanksgiving" when they are happy (D&C 136:28).

Gospel Art Pictures

- *Lehi and His People Arrive in the Promised Land* (#71)
- *Mary Fielding Smith and Joseph F. Smith Crossing the Plains* (#101)

Church History

Brigham Young encouraged wholesome recreation as a way to relax. Between 1861 and 1862, he donated more than half the funds necessary to build the Salt Lake Theatre. (For details see http://goo.gl/eSd4fw). He said, "I built [the] theater to attract the young of our community and to provide amusement for the boys and girls, rather than have them running all over creation for recreation. [. . .] If you want to dance, run a foot-race, . . . or play at ball, do it, and exercise your bodies, and let your minds rest" (*Teaching of Presidents of the Church: Brigham Young*, pp. 188–89). "The blessings of food, sleep, and social enjoyment are ordained of God for his glory and our benefit; and it is for us to learn to use them and not abuse them, that his kingdom may advance on the earth, and we advance in it" (*Journal of Discourses*, 6:147–49).

LDS.org video "Things As They Really Are." Elder Bednar discusses technology, entertainment, and media. https://goo.gl/4wDp6V

Prior to technology, entertainment was found in lots of ways. President Benson recalls, "Our grandparents were very musical and always provided entertainment of various kinds. Grandma Dunkley, a convert to the Church from Scotland, would dance the Highland Fling for us, and we loved that" (*President Ezra Taft Benson Remembers the Joys of Christmas* (Deseret Book, 1988), 2–3). As an adult in 1954, President Benson shared a family home evening with United States President Eisenhower. They went to the home of J. Willard and Alice Marriott "for an evening of holiday fun and entertainment. Our sons performed comic skits and other readings, the girls sang, [my wife] Flora recited a reading, and I did my part by leading the whole group in singing. . . . It was plain, old-fashioned, homespun entertainment" (*President Ezra Taft Benson Remembers the Joys of Christmas*, 9).

In our day, entertainment and media can be wholesome and balancing, or spiritually destructive and out of balance. To watch a short video of Elder Bednar discussing technology, entertainment, and media, see https://goo.gl/4wDp6V.

Adaptations for Younger Children

Quotes

"I will keep my mind and body sacred and pure" ("My Gospel Standards").

"I will only read and watch things that are pleasing to Heavenly Father" ("My Gospel Standards").

Lesson from *Behold Your Little Ones*

"Heavenly Father and Jesus Christ Love Me" (Lesson 4, pp. 20–23).

Faith in God

"Visit an art museum or attend a concert, play, or other cultural event. Share your experience with your family or activity day group" (p. 10).

Activity

Talk about the work and entertainment your family engages in. Talk about what the children do to work, including helping around the house, learning, and playing. Talk about what the children do for fun and entertainment. Talk about some wholesome choices for entertainment they may not be aware of. Do some work together and then do something fun together.

Adaptations for Older Children and Teens

Quotes

"It is no coincidence that FamilySearch and other tools have come forth at a time when young people are so familiar with a wide range of information and communication technologies. Your fingers have been trained to text and tweet to accelerate and advance the work of the Lord—not just to communicate quickly with your friends. The skills and aptitude evident among many young people today are a preparation to contribute to the work of salvation" (David A. Bednar, "The Hearts of the Children Shall Turn," *Ensign*, November 2011).

"Don't do dumb things with your smartphone. You all know what I mean. . . . There are countless ways technology can distract you from what is most important. . . . The divine purpose of technology is to hasten the work of salvation. . . . The Lord expects you to use these great tools to take His work to the next level, to share the gospel in ways that are beyond my generation's wildest imagination. Where generations past influenced their neighbors and their town, you have the power through the Internet and social media to reach beyond borders and influence the whole world" (Randall L. Ridd, "The Choice Generation," *Ensign*, May 2014).

Preach My Gospel

"Media and Church Headquarters Referrals," p. 163.

Personal Progress

Knowledge #3—Use the thirteenth article of faith to evaluate entertainment options (p. 39).

Choice and Accountability #8 or #9: Personalized Value Experience—Evaluate your typical entertainment, media, and technology choices. Pay extra attention to your choices over the next couple of weeks. Write about how you are using these things to help you stay close to the Lord (p. 49).

Duty to God

Study, discuss, and personally apply the section on "Entertainment and Media" in the *For the Strength of Youth* pamphlet (pp. 11–13). This will help you do part of each section titled "Live Worthily" (see pp. 16–17, 40–41, 64–65).

Activity ⏲

Wrap some thread once or twice around someone's wrists. Have them break the thread. The thread represents bad habits. The first time someone does something not so great, like engaging in unwholesome entertainment or media, it is easy to choose whether *to do* it again or whether *not to do* it again. Now wrap the thread around the person's wrists many times and see if he or she can break the thread. Have the person ask for help from someone who can help unwrap the thread. If we let bad habits go on and on, we lose the power to easily return to something better.

Daily Scriptures

Entertainment and Media

Sunday 📖

"Woe unto them that call evil good, and good evil; that put darkness for light, and light for darkness; that put bitter for sweet, and sweet for bitter!" (Isaiah 5:20)

Monday 📖

"We believe in being honest, true, chaste, benevolent, virtuous, and in doing good to all men; indeed, we may say that we follow the admonition of Paul—We believe all things, we hope all things, we have endured many things, and hope to be able to endure all things. If there is anything virtuous, lovely, or of good report or praiseworthy, we seek after these things." (Articles of Faith 1:13)

Tuesday

"Wherefore, all things which are good cometh of God; and that which is evil cometh of the devil; for the devil is an enemy unto God, and fighteth against him continually, and inviteth and enticeth to sin, and to do that which is evil continually. But behold, that which is of God inviteth and enticeth to do good continually; wherefore, every thing which inviteth and enticeth to do good, and to love God, and to serve him, is inspired of God." (Moroni 7:12–13)

Wednesday

"The Spirit of Christ is given to every man, that he may know good from evil; wherefore, I show unto you the way to judge; for every thing which inviteth to do good, and to persuade to believe in Christ, is sent forth by the power and gift of Christ; wherefore ye may know with a perfect knowledge it is of God. But whatsoever thing persuadeth men to do evil, and believe not in Christ, and deny him, and serve not God, then ye may know with a perfect knowledge it is of the devil; for after this manner doth the devil work, for he persuadeth no man to do good, no, not one; neither do his angels; neither do they who subject themselves unto him." (Moroni 7:16–17)

Thursday 📖

"Do not suppose, because it has been spoken concerning restoration, that ye shall be restored from sin to happiness. Behold, I say unto you, wickedness never was happiness." (Alma 41:10)

Friday

"Beloved, believe not every spirit, but try the spirits whether they are of God: because many false prophets are gone out into the world." (1 John 4:1)

Saturday

"Come unto Christ, and lay hold upon every good gift, and touch not the evil gift, nor the unclean thing." (Moroni 10:30)

Family

"See that ye love one another; cease to be covetous; learn to impart one to another as the gospel requires. Cease to be idle; cease to be unclean; cease to find fault one with another. . . . And above all things, clothe yourselves with the bond of charity, as with a mantle, which is the bond of perfectness and peace." (D&C 88:123–25)

LDS.org video "Musical Presentation: The Family Is of God" https://goo.gl/qWB9Fj

Music from *Children's* Songbook & Hymns

- Family History—I Am Doing It (*CS*, 94)
- A Happy Family (*CS*, 198)
- *Children's Songbook* songs about family (188–211)
- Families Can Be Together Forever (*CS*, 188; *Hymns*, 300)
- Love at Home (*Hymns*, 294)

Quotes

"The ultimate end of all activity in the Church is that a man and his wife and their children can be happy at home" (Boyd K. Packer, "The Witness," *Ensign*, May 2014).

Mormonads—Family and Family History https://goo.gl/LDkH6S

"Parents should act to preserve time for family prayer, family scripture study, family home evening, and the other precious togetherness and individual one-on-one time that binds a family together and fixes children's values on things of eternal worth" (Dallin H. Oaks, "Good, Better, Best," *Ensign,* November 2007).

Scripture Stories

Sometimes Lehi's family works well together, and other times there is a lot of conflict. They travel in the wilderness together, get the brass plates, build a boat, cross the ocean, and build a new life in the promised land (see 1 Nephi 2–5, 7, 16–18).

Families come to the temple to offer sacrifices and listen to King Benjamin. He teaches them to serve and obey God, have faith, pray, and serve others. At one point he says, "Teach [your children] to love one another, and to serve one another" (Mosiah 4:15) (see also Mosiah 2–5).

Gospel Art Pictures

- *Jesus Praying with His Mother* (#33)
- *Lehi and His People Arrive in the Promised Land* (#71)
- *King Benjamin Addresses His People* (#74)

Church History

When did family home evening as a church program start? *1915.* Joseph F. Smith inaugurated family home evening in an official letter from the First Presidency. For the original letter, see the appendix, pages 236–37. For a short video on the inauguration of family home evening, see https://goo.gl/oXGvNF.

President David O. McKay reemphasized the family home evening program, and a family home evening manual was published to support families each year from 1970–85 (see a Church News article on LDS.org titled "2015 Marks Two Milestones for Family Home Evening" at https://goo.gl/EC8V3U).

On September 23, 1995, "The Family: A Proclamation to the World," a declaration from the First Presidency and Quorum of the Twelve Apostles, was published. President Gordon B. Hinckley read the proclamation in the women's session of general conference in October 1995 (see Gordon B. Hinckley, "Stand Strong against the Wiles of the World," *Ensign*, November 1995, or online at https://goo.gl/LzYTwL. President Hinckley introduces the proclamation at 19 minutes 32 seconds).

For the Church's views on same-sex attraction and marriage, see LDS.org's gospel topics "Same-Sex Attraction" at http://goo.gl/buPxcp and "Same-sex Marriage" at http://goo.gl/5HPZEQ.

LDS.org video "Ministry of Joseph F. Smith: Family Home Evening Inaugurated" https://goo.gl/oXGvNF

LDS.org video of President Hinckley's conference talk, "Stand Strong against the Wiles of the World," in which he introduced "The Family: A Proclamation to the World" https://goo.gl/LzYTwL

Adaptations for Younger Children

Quote

"I will honor my parents and do my part to strengthen my family" ("My Gospel Standards").

Lesson from *Behold Your Little Ones*

"I Love My Family" (Lesson 11, pp. 48–51) and "I Will Obey" (Lesson 14, pp. 60–63).

Faith in God

"Honor your parents and be kind to your family" (p. 4).

"Give an opening and a closing prayer in family home evening or at Primary. Share your feelings about how prayer protects us and helps us to stay close to Heavenly Father and the Savior" (p. 6).

"Read 'The Family: A Proclamation to the World.' Make a list of things you can do to help strengthen your family and make a happy home. Share the list with your parents or Primary leader" (p. 13).

Activity ⏰

Get a stack of wooden pencils (or thin, breakable sticks). Show your family the pencils. Pick one up and break it. Show how it isn't strong by itself. Then pick up as many pencils as you have people in your family and try to break the bunch. Show that together your family is stronger. Then look at fun family pictures together and reminisce. Talk about what you like about your family. Talk about what makes you strong and what could make you stronger.

Adaptations for Older Children and Teens

Quotes

"Understanding the eternal nature of the temple will draw you to your family; understanding the eternal nature of the family will draw you to the temple" (Gary E. Stevenson, "Sacred Homes, Sacred Temples," *Ensign*, May 2009).

"The devil is well organized. Never in our day has he had so many emissaries working for him. . . . Satan uses many tools to weaken and destroy the home and family and especially our young people. Today, as never before, it seems the devil's thrust is directed at our youth. . . . The family home evening is an important barrier to the works of Satan. The [Young Men and Young Women programs] must protect our youth against every evil influence and should fill a vacuum left by rejecting worldly enticements. And, of course, a great panacea for all problems and personal doubts: prayer—private and family prayer, night and morning" (Ezra Taft Benson, "Satan's Thrust—Youth," *Ensign*, December 1971).

Preach My Gospel

"The Gospel Blesses Families," pp. 3, 32; "Eternal Marriage," pp. 85–86; "Addressing the Importance of the Family," pp. 159–60.

Personal Progress

Knowledge #2—"Learn a new skill or talent that will help you care for your own future family" (p. 38).

Integrity #7—Make a list of things that strengthen families as well as things you are aware of that weaken families. Research the topic of how to create a strong family by reading conference talks and "The Family: A Proclamation to the World" (p. 64).

Duty to God

Study the doctrinal topic of "Eternal Families and Family History Work." Record what you learn and share what you learned with your parents or a priesthood leader (see pp. 18–21, 42–45, 66–69).

Look over the section "For the Strength of Youth: Family and Friends." Work on it, or review what you did if you have already done this section (*Duty to God*, pp. 79–83).

Activity

Have everyone write down their favorite things about each person in the family. Then have everyone share what they wrote. Talk about different things your family has done together that you've enjoyed. Make sure to talk about day-to-day things as well as occasional activities you've done. Tell your family that *what* the family does together isn't as important as the feeling of connectedness and closeness that everyone shares. Then talk about memories of big and little things that stand out— times when family members felt really close. It could be as small as a special moment during family prayer, or as big as a family trip. Look at family pictures together, either for family home evening or sometime during the week.

Daily Scriptures

Family

Sunday

"See that ye love one another; cease to be covetous; learn to impart one to another as the gospel requires. Cease to be idle; cease to be unclean; cease to find fault one with another. . . . And above all things, clothe yourselves with the bond of charity, as with a mantle, which is the bond of perfectness and peace." (D&C 88:123–25)

Monday

"A new commandment I give unto you, That ye love one another; as I have loved you. . . . By this shall all men know that ye are my disciples, if ye have love one to another." (John 13:34–35)

Tuesday

"Children are an heritage of the Lord: and the fruit of the womb is his reward. As arrows are in the hand of a mighty man; so are children of the youth. Happy is the man that hath his quiver full of them." (Psalm 127:3–5)

Wednesday

"Rejoice, and be filled with the love of God. . . . And ye will not have a mind to injure one another, but to live peaceably. . . . And ye will not suffer your children that they go hungry, or naked; neither will ye suffer that they transgress the laws of God, and fight and quarrel one with another, and serve the devil, who is the master of sin, or who is the evil spirit which hath been spoken of by our fathers, he being an enemy to all

righteousness. But ye will teach them to walk in the ways of truth and soberness; ye will teach them to love one another, and to serve one another." (Mosiah 4:12–15)

Thursday 🔖

"In the celestial glory there are three heavens or degrees; And in order to obtain the highest, a man must enter into this order of the priesthood [meaning the new and everlasting covenant of marriage]; And if he does not, he cannot obtain it. He may enter into the other, but that is the end of his kingdom; he cannot have an increase." (D&C 131:1–4)

Friday

"If ye keep my commandments, ye shall abide in my love; even as I have kept my Father's commandments, and abide in his love. These things have I spoken unto you, that my joy might remain in you, and that your joy might be full. This is my commandment, That ye love one another, as I have loved you." (John 15:10–12)

Saturday

"[The people of Nephi] did walk after the commandments which they had received from their Lord and their God, continuing in fasting and prayer, and in meeting together oft both to pray and to hear the word of the Lord. . . . There was no contention in the land, because of the love of God which did dwell in the hearts of the people." (4 Nephi 1:12, 15)

Friends

"A man that hath friends must shew himself friendly: and there is a friend that sticketh closer than a brother." (Proverbs 18:24)

Mormonads—Friendship
https://goo.gl/igzQ39

Music from *Children's Songbook* & *Hymns*

- I'm Trying to Be Like Jesus (*CS*, 78)
- Friends Are Fun (*CS*, 262)
- Love One Another (*CS*, 136; *Hymns*, 308)
- Should You Feel Inclined to Censure (*Hymns*, 235)

Quote

"Living the gospel and being true to gospel principles is the key to true, lasting, triumphant friendship. Weak bonds and less spiritual relationships will not hold up when confronted by a wicked person such as David and Jonathan faced, or an unbelieving background such as Ruth had known, or the youthful transgressions of the younger Alma and the sons of Mosiah. In each case it was gospel principles, commitments, associations, and covenants that led to the strong ties and triumphant friendship we celebrate in these examples. . . . *Real* friends share the gospel—the living of it and the loving of it. No stronger bond nor higher compliment can be given from one friend to another" (Jeffrey R. Holland, "Real Friendship," *New Era*, June 1998; italics in original).

LDS.org video "A True Friend: Tanya and Lada." Learn about the power of friendship from a member living in Kyiv, Uraine. https://goo.gl/8WyQMj

Scripture Stories

Daniel and his friends choose to follow Jehovah while living as captives in a country that believes in other gods. Together, they follow their code of health and are blessed for it (see Daniel 1).

Alma the Younger and his friends strive to destroy the Church and lead people into wickedness. An angel tells them to stop. They are converted and serve missions together (see Mosiah 27).

While in Liberty Jail, Joseph Smith pleads with God for help. He is told that the affliction will pass and that things could be worse because, unlike Job, Joseph's friends stand by him and support him. (see D&C 121:1–10).

Gospel Art Pictures

- *Daniel Refusing the King's Food and Wine* (#23)
- *Conversion of Alma the Younger* (#77)
- *Joseph Smith in Liberty Jail* (#97)

Church History

In 1832, Brigham Young was baptized into the Church. In 1833, Brigham Young traveled to Kirtland, Ohio, with Heber C. Kimball in order to meet Joseph Smith. He settled there and developed a very close friendship with Joseph. To see a short video representing Brigham Young meeting and becoming friends with Joseph Smith, go to https://goo.gl /K9caEP.

LDS.org video "Preparation of Brigham Young: A Friend of the Prophet Joseph Smith" https://goo.gl/K9caEP

In 1857, the United States had a serious banking problem. Joseph started a financial institution called the Kirtland Safety Society Anti-Banking Company, which he prophesied would never fail as long as the Saints followed his counsel, which they didn't. When it failed like nearly every other United States bank, many of Joseph's friends and followers, who had invested in the anti-banking society, blamed him for its failure and stopped following him. Of the original Twelve Apostles, only Brigham Young and Heber C. Kimball stood by Joseph through that time (Eugene England, "Brigham and Joseph," *New Era*, December 1977). To learn more about the Kirtland Safety Society, see a FairMormon article titled "The Kirtland Safety Society" at http://goo.gl/SVZkzc and a FairMormon page titled "What Is the Kirtland Safety Society and Why Did It Fail?" at http://goo .gl/XnYE26.

Adaptations for Younger Children

Quotes

"I will seek good friends and treat others kindly" ("My Gospel Standards").

"A true friend makes it easier for us to live the gospel by being around him" (Robert D. Hales, "The Aaronic Priesthood: Return with Honor," *Ensign*, May 1990).

Lesson from *Behold Your Little Ones*

"Jesus Christ Showed Us How to Love Others" (Lesson 5, pp. 24–27).

Faith in God

"Make a list of the qualities you like in a person. Choose one quality to develop in yourself. Discuss how showing respect and kindness strengthens you, your family, and others" (p. 9).

Activity

Think about your best friends. They could be members of your family. Talk about what you love about your best friends. Write a note, draw a picture, or make a gift for one or more of your best friends and decide on how to deliver it. Think about one thing you would like to do to be a better friend to others, including family members. It might be smiling, giving compliments, greeting them by name, hugging them, playing games they like, asking questions and listening more carefully, or praying for them specifically every day for a while. Tell your parents your plan.

Adaptations for Older Children and Teens

Quote

"Look closely at your friends. Cultivate good friends. They're so valuable. . . . Friendship is an extremely important part of your life. Someone has said a true friend is someone who makes it easier to live the gospel of Jesus Christ. . . . Some of the most trusted and loving friends you will ever have on this earth are your parents and family. . . . Cultivate our Savior and Redeemer Jesus Christ as your friend above all. Being his friend will without exception lift your vision and bring you comfort, guidance, peace, and, yes, even the companionship of other true friends. . . . Choose your friends wisely" (Malcolm S. Jeppsen, "Who Is a True Friend?," *Ensign*, May 1990).

Preach My Gospel

Chapter 6: "How Do I Develop Christlike Attributes," pp. 115–26; "Listen," pp. 185–86; Chapter 13: "How Do I Work with Stake and Ward Leaders?," pp. 213–24; "Friendship," p. 216. Choose friends who are striving to develop Christlike attributes and who support you in developing Christlike attributes. Good friends and good missionaries listen to and understand other people.

Personal Progress

Choice and Accountability #1—"A daughter of God can make wise decisions and solve problems. . . . Follow a pattern of regular scripture study and prayer to receive help in making personal decisions such as choosing good friends [and] being kind to others" (p. 46).

Good Works #3—Think about how you can be a better friend by applying Mosiah 18:7–10 (p. 54).

Duty to God

"Think about family members and friends whom you could invite to come unto Christ. Write down their names and what you will do to help them" (pp. 28, 52, 76).

Look over the section "For the Strength of Youth: Family and Friends." Work on it, or review what you did if you have already done this section (*Duty to God*, pp. 79–83).

Activity ⏲

Get three eggs, ideally with some differences such as color, size, or shape. If necessary, you can draw on the eggs to make them look different. Poke a small hole on each side of one egg and blow out the inside. Hard-boil another egg. Leave the third egg raw. Mark each egg in an inconspicuous spot so you know which is which. When it's time for the activity, tell your family that is important to be friendly to everyone, but it's also very important to be wise about who your closest friends are because you will become like them. Tell your family that the eggs represent different friends you can choose. Have everyone pick their favorite egg. Spin each egg to show that there's something different on the inside of each egg. Then crush the empty egg, crack the raw egg, and peel the third. Talk about how we want to have *solid* friends that won't be crushed by outside pressures and that won't crack at the smallest problem. We want to have, and be, friends that are solid and true on the inside.

Daily Scriptures

Friends

Sunday

"A man that hath friends must shew himself friendly: and there is a friend that sticketh closer than a brother." (Proverbs 18:24)

Monday

"Make no friendship with an angry man; and with a furious man thou shalt not go: Lest thou learn his ways, and get a snare to thy soul." (Proverbs 22:24–25)

Tuesday

"As the Father hath loved me, so have I loved you: continue ye in my love. If ye keep my commandments, ye shall abide in my love; even as I have kept my Father's commandments, and abide in his love. These things have I spoken unto you, that my joy might remain in you, and that your joy might be full. This is my commandment, That ye love one another, as I have loved you. Ye are my friends, if ye do whatsoever I command you." (John 15:9–12, 14)

Wednesday

"A new commandment I give unto you, That ye love one another; as I have loved you. . . . By this shall all men know that ye are my disciples, if ye have love one to another." (John 13:34–35)

Thursday

"And now it came to pass that as Alma was journeying from the land of Gideon southward, away to the land of Manti, behold, to his astonishment, he met with the sons of Mosiah journeying towards the land of Zarahemla. Now these sons of Mosiah were with Alma at the time the angel first appeared unto him; therefore Alma did rejoice exceedingly to see his brethren; and what added more to his joy, they were still his brethren in the Lord; yea, and they had waxed strong in the knowledge of the truth; for they were men of a sound understanding and they had searched the scriptures diligently, that they might know the word of God. (Alma 17:1–2)

Friday

"Know ye not that the friendship of the world is enmity with God? whosoever therefore will be a friend of the world is the enemy of God. But he giveth more grace. Wherefore he saith, God resisteth the proud, but giveth grace unto the humble. Submit yourselves therefore to God. Resist the devil, and he will flee from you. Draw nigh to God, and he will draw nigh to you. Cleanse your hands. . . . and purify your hearts." (James 4:4, 6–8)

Saturday

"Walk after the Lord your God, and fear him, and keep his commandments, and obey his voice, and ye shall serve him, and cleave unto him. If thy brother, the son of thy mother, or thy son, or thy daughter, or the wife of thy bosom, or thy friend, which is as thine own soul, entice thee secretly, saying, Let us go and serve other gods, which thou hast not known, thou, nor thy fathers; Thou shalt not consent unto him, nor hearken unto him." (Deuteronomy 13:4, 6, 8)

Gratitude

"He who receiveth all things with thankfulness shall be made glorious." (D&C 78:19)

LDS.org video "Tender Mercies of the Lord" with Elder Bednar https://goo.gl/4Qn9ut

LDS.org video "Highlight: Grateful in Any Circumstances— Dieter F. Uchtdorf" https://goo.gl/siuHB8

Music from *Children's Songbook* & *Hymns*

- Children All Over the World (*CS*, 16)
- I Am Glad for Many Things (*CS*, 151)
- I Think the World Is Glorious (*CS*, 230)
- Count Your Blessings (*Hymns*, 241)

Quote

"We can lift ourselves and others as well when we refuse to remain in the realm of negative thought and cultivate within our hearts an attitude of gratitude. If ingratitude be numbered among the serious sins, then gratitude takes its place among the noblest of virtues. Someone has said that 'gratitude is not only the greatest of virtues, but the parent of all others'" (Thomas S. Monson, "The Divine Gift of Gratitude," *Ensign*, November 2010).

Scripture Stories

Jesus heals ten lepers. One leper, when he sees he is healed, returns to Jesus and gives thanks (see Luke 17:11–19).

At the gates of the temple, Peter and John meet a lame man who asks for alms. Peter says he has no money, but that he will give the man what he has. In the name of Jesus Christ, Peter heals the man, "and he leaping up stood, and walked, and entered with them into the temple, walking, and leaping, and praising God" (Acts 3:8) (see also Acts 3:1–9).

Amulek teaches the Zoramites about Jesus Christ, His Atonement, faith, repentance, prayer, and redemption. Amulek tells them to worship God and live in gratitude every day, recognizing and giving thanks for all God's many blessings to them (see Alma 34).

Gospel Art Pictures

- *The Ten Lepers* (#46)
- *My Father's House* (#52)
- *Young Boy Praying* (#111)
- *Family Prayer* (#112)

Church History

In 1964, Joseph William Billy Johnson of Ghana was converted when he read the testimony of Joseph Smith in a pamphlet. For fourteen years, he shared the gospel, despite tremendous opposition. When Joseph Johnson heard the announcement that "all worthy male members of the Church may be ordained to the priesthood without regard for race or color" (Official Declaration 2), he said, "I jumped and started crying and rejoicing in the Lord with tears that now is the time that the Lord will send missionaries to Ghana and to other parts of Africa to receive the priesthood" ("A People Prepared," Elizabeth Maki, *Church History*, April 21, 2013, https://history.lds.org/article/ghana-pioneer-jwb -johnson?lang=eng). Missionaries were sent to Africa to organize branches. The Cape Coast Branch, with Joseph William Billy Johnson serving as branch president, was quickly organized. Johnson said, "It was a day of jubilation when they came. I was so happy that they came and so happy that the Church is not brand new; it's on its feet in Ghana" ("A People Prepared," Elizabeth Maki). To learn more, see History.LDS.org's article "A People Prepared" at https://goo.gl/KS8AyJ.

LDS.org video "Rare Footage of First Baptisms in West Africa" https://goo.gl/ZR5XVV

Adaptations for Younger Children

Quote

"Be grateful. There are two little words in the English language that perhaps mean more than all others. They are 'thank you.' . . . Be thankful to your parents, who care so very much about you. . . . Say thank you to your friends. Say thank you to your teachers. Express appreciation to everyone who does you a favor or assists you in any way" (Gordon B. Hinckley, "A Prophet's Counsel and Prayer for Youth," *Ensign*, January 2001).

Lesson from *Behold Your Little Ones*

"I Will Be Thankful" (Lesson 15, pp. 64–67).

Faith in God

"Plan and complete your own activity that will help you learn and live the gospel" (p. 7). Read the scriptures and quotes on gratitude included in this *FHEasy* lesson plan. Decide on a way to develop a habit of having a grateful heart. For example, every night, right before praying, think of ten things you are grateful for. Then write or draw them, and include them when you pray. Throughout the day, notice things you are grateful for and silently thank God for them. Daily go through the gratitude ABC game below.

Activity

Go on a gratitude walk. Walk around and talk about all the things you see that you are grateful for. Then, write or draw some of the things you saw and thought of that you are grateful for.

A fun way to make a gratitude list is to do it alphabetically. Start with the letter *A* and think of things your family is thankful for that start with the letter *A*. Then move to *B* and go through the alphabet. Brainstorm as a family for each letter or take turns. For more visual families, you can make a gratitude collage. Draw or cut and paste pictures of things you are grateful for.

Christina Shelley Albrecht

Adaptations for Older Children and Teens

Quote

"Why does God command us to be grateful? All of His commandments are given to make blessings available to us. Commandments are opportunities to exercise our agency and to receive blessings. Our loving Heavenly Father knows that choosing to develop a spirit of gratitude will bring us true joy and great happiness. But some might say, 'What do I have to be grateful *for* when my world is falling apart?' Perhaps focusing on what we are grateful *for* is the wrong approach. . . . I don't believe the Lord expects us to be less thankful in times of trial than in times of abundance and ease. In fact, most of the scriptural references do not speak of gratitude *for* things but rather suggest an overall spirit or attitude of gratitude. It is easy to be grateful *for* things when life seems to be going our way. But what then of those times when what we wish for seems to be far out of reach? Could I suggest that we see gratitude as a disposition, a way of life that stands independent of our current situation? In other words, I'm suggesting that instead of being thankful *for* things, we focus on being thankful *in* our circumstances—whatever they may be. . . . Being grateful in our circumstances is an act of faith in God. It requires that we trust God and hope for things we may not see but which are true. . . . Gratitude is a catalyst to all Christlike attributes! A thankful heart is the parent of all virtues" (Dieter . Uchtdorf, "Grateful in Any Circumstances," *Ensign*, May 2014; italics in original).

Preach My Gospel

"Pray with Faith," pp. 93–95.

Personal Progress

Good Works #1—Be grateful for the service others give to you. "For two weeks record in your journal the quiet acts of service your family members and other perform. Acknowledge their service in some meaningful way" (p. 54).

Duty to God

Study, discuss, and personally apply the section on "Gratitude" in the *For the Strength of Youth* pamphlet (*For the Strength of Youth*, 18). This will help you do part of each section titled "Live Worthily" (see *Duty to God*, pp. 16–17, 40–41, 64–65).

Activity

Have everyone look around the room and pay special attention to everything that is one color, for example, brown. Tell them that afterward, you will all close your eyes and see how many brown things everyone can remember. Let them look around for about thirty seconds and then have everyone close their eyes and report what they remember. Tell them to keep their eyes closed and report everything they remember that was a different color, for example, green. When everyone has shared what they recall, have them open their eyes and see what else is green, but didn't register in their minds because they were focused on the other color. Tell your family that what you focus on is what you notice, see, and remember the most, so focus on the things you are grateful for!

106

Daily Scriptures

Gratitude

Sunday

"Be of good cheer, for I will lead you along. The kingdom is yours and the blessings thereof are yours, and the riches of eternity are yours. And he who receiveth all things with thankfulness shall be made glorious; and the things of this earth shall be added unto him, even an hundred fold, yea, more." (D&C 78:18–19)

Monday

"Worship God, in whatsoever place ye may be in, in spirit and in truth; and that ye live in thanksgiving daily, for the many mercies and blessings which he doth bestow upon you." (Alma 34:38)

Tuesday

"It is a good thing to give thanks unto the Lord, and to sing praises unto thy name, O most High: To shew forth thy lovingkindness in the morning, and thy faithfulness every night. For thou, Lord, hast made me glad through thy work: I will triumph in the works of thy hands." (Psalm 92:1–2, 4)

Wednesday

"Let all thy thoughts be directed unto the Lord; yea, let the affections of thy heart be placed upon the Lord forever. Counsel with the Lord in all thy doings, and he will direct thee for good; yea, when thou liest down at night lie down unto the Lord, that he may watch over you in your sleep; and when thou risest in the morning let thy heart be full of thanks unto God; and if ye do these things, ye shall be lifted up at the last day." (Alma 37:36–37)

Thursday

"He that asketh in the Spirit asketh according to the will of God; wherefore it is done even as he asketh. And again, I say unto you, all things must be done in the name of Christ, whatsoever you do in the Spirit; And ye must give thanks unto God in the Spirit for whatsoever blessing ye are blessed with. And ye must practice virtue and holiness before me continually." (D&C 46:30–33)

Friday

"Rejoice evermore. Pray without ceasing. In every thing give thanks: for this is the will of God in Christ Jesus concerning you." (1 Thessalonians 5:16–18)

Saturday

"Thou shalt thank the Lord thy God in all things." (D&C 59:7)

Honesty and Integrity

"All the while my breath is in me, and the spirit of God is in my nostrils; My lips shall not speak wickedness, nor my tongue utter deceit. . . . Till I die I will not remove mine integrity from me. My righteousness I hold fast, and will not let it go: my heart shall not reproach me so long as I live." (Job 27:3–6)

Gospel Topics: Honesty
https://goo.gl/4fk2cm

LDS.org video "Honesty: You Better Believe It!" President Faust tells a story about honesty.
https://goo.gl/6aDRgw

Music from Children's Songbook & Hymns

- The Thirteenth Article of Faith (*CS*, 132)
- I Believe in Being Honest (*CS*, 149)
- Do What Is Right (*Hymns*, 237)
- Choose the Right (*Hymns*, 239)

Quotes

"We all need to know what it means to be honest. Honesty is more than not lying. It is truth telling, truth speaking, truth living, and truth loving" (James E. Faust, "Honesty—A Moral Compass," *Ensign*, November 1996).

"We cannot be less than honest. . . . Once it was said among our people that a man's word was as good as his bond. Shall any of us be less reliable, less honest than our forebears?" (Gordon B. Hinckley, "An Honest Man—God's Noblest Work," *Ensign*, May 1976).

Scripture Stories

God gives Moses the Ten Commandments. The ninth one is "Thou shalt not bear false witness against thy neighbor" (Exodus 20:16). In other words, be honest (see Exodus 20:1–17).

Job is a wealthy man who loves God. Satan believes that if Job were not so wealthy, he wouldn't love God anymore. All of Job's possessions, his family, and his health are taken from him to see if he will turn away from God. His friends encourage him to curse God and die. He replies, "I will not remove mine integrity from me" (Job 27:5). He recovers in every way and prospers even more than before (see the book of Job).

As a teenager, Joseph Smith tells people about his vision and is severely persecuted. Even so, he does not deny it. He chooses to be honest, even at the cost of his personal comfort (see Joseph Smith—History 1:21–25).

Gospel Art Pictures

- *The Ten Commandments* (#14)
- *The First Vision* (#90)

Church History

Though all the of the three witnesses to the Book of Mormon—David Whitmer, Oliver Cowdery, and Martin Harris—left the Church, they consistently bore strong testimony of their experience when the angel Moroni appeared to the them and showed them the gold plates. To read more about the Three Witnesses, see History.LDS.org's article "The Experience of the Three Witnesses" at https://goo.gl/KNhgk2 and FairMormon's page "Witnesses who left the Church continued to maintain their witness of the Book of Mormon" at http://goo.gl/DzvSc8.

LDS.org video "The Testimony of the Three Witnesses" with Elder Oaks https://goo.gl/NVR7EC

In 1857, when Joseph F. Smith was nineteen years old, he was returning from a five-year mission to Hawaii. As he went through San Fransisco, California, a group of anti-Mormons stopped him on the road, pointed a gun at him, and asked if he was a Mormon—clearly threatening his life if he answered affirmatively. He responded, "Yes, sirre; dyed in the wool; true blue, through and through." The man shook Joseph's hand and said, "Well, you are the——pleasantest man I ever met! Shake, young fellow, I am glad to see a man that stands up for his convictions" (*Teachings of Presidents of the Church: Joseph F. Smith*, 104). To see a video representation of this event go to https://goo.gl/vYy2Gh.

LDS.org video "Preparation of Joseph F. Smith: True Blue, Through and Through" https://goo.gl/vYy2Gh

Some people accuse members and leaders of "lying for the Lord." They say the Church is not honest about things like First Vision accounts, the history of the Church, artistic portrayal of Church history, polygamy, the witnesses of the Book of Mormon, and so on. To learn more about these accusations and faithful responses to them, see FairMormon's page "Lying for the Lord" at http://goo.gl/iTqF9j.

Adaptations for Younger Children

Quote

"I will be honest with Heavenly Father, others, and myself" ("My Gospel Standards").

Lesson from *Behold Your Little Ones*

"I Can Be Happy" (Lesson 19, pp. 80–83). Honesty and integrity support individual happiness.

Faith in God

Review the *Faith in God* Award Requirements on pages 4–5. One of the requirements is to live "My Gospel Standards," which are listed on the back cover of the booklet. Review the standards. The fourth standard on the list is "I will be honest with Heavenly Father, others, and myself." Talk about the importance of honesty with your family, leaders, or friends.

Activity

Tell Aesop's fable of the boy who cried wolf, or read the version in the appendix on page 234. You may want to have your children act it out. Ask the children why no one came to help the boy when there was a real wolf. Talk about how important it is to be honest and trustworthy.

Adaptations for Older Children and Teens

Quote

"The words *integrity* and *honesty* are closely associated and often used interchangeably. We must remember, however, that these terms are related but are not exactly the same. . . . As Elder Joseph B. Wirthlin . . . has explained: 'Integrity means always doing what is right and good, . . . not only in our actions but, more important, in our thoughts and in our hearts.' . . . Honesty is the quality or condition of being truthful, sincere, candid, and worthy of honor . . . being genuine, trustworthy, upright, respectable, and decent. . . . Cheating in academic work is unprincipled, dishonest, and a form of self-deception and betrayal. No student can hope to ultimately succeed in a career or profession if he or she builds upon a foundation of fraud. . . . The very fountain and foundation of our daily discipleship are integrity and honesty. People of integrity and honesty not only practice what they preach, they are what they preach" (David A. Bednar, "Be Honest," *New Era*, October 2005; italics in original).

Preach My Gospel

Chapter 11: "How Do I Help People Make and Keep Commitments?," pp. 195–202.

Personal Progress

Integrity #4—Define *integrity* and discuss its meaning and application (p. 63). Review the section on "Integrity." See what you've done and what you haven't. Look over the project ideas (pp. 61–68).

Duty to God

Study, discuss, and personally apply the section on "Honesty and Integrity" in the *For the Strength of Youth* pamphlet (*For the Strength of Youth*, p. 19). This will help you do part of each section titled "Live Worthily" (see *Duty to God*, pp. 16–17, 40–41, 64–65).

Activity ☺

Get an orange and fill a container with water. Ask your family to shout out different standards, like modesty, honesty, and language. Write the standards, in permanent marker, on the orange peel. Hold up the orange and ask your family if they think it will sink or float. Put the orange in the water and see that it floats. Now peel off the skin, taking the standards with it. Ask your family if the orange will sink or float now. Put the peeled orange in water and watch it sink. Discuss how our standards keep us afloat. They don't pull us down; they lift us up! Sometimes people think that living by a good set of moral standards robs them of freedom and drags them down, but it's really the opposite. Like a life jacket, standards can save us when we find ourselves in compromising situations, but if we shed our standards, we'll sink like the orange. (Adapted from a lesson idea on LDS.org/youth. Go to https://goo.gl/UepBkh for the online version of this lesson.)

Daily Scriptures

Honesty and Integrity

Sunday

"All the while my breath is in me, and the spirit of God is in my nostrils; My lips shall not speak wickedness, nor my tongue utter deceit. . . . Till I die I will not remove mine integrity from me. My righteousness I hold fast, and will not let it go: my heart shall not reproach me so long as I live." (Job 27:3–6)

Monday 📖

"Thou shalt not kill. Thou shalt not commit adultery. Thou shalt not steal. Thou shalt not bear false witness against thy neighbour." (Exodus 20:13–16)

Tuesday

"Judge me, O Lord; for I have walked in mine integrity: I have trusted also in the Lord; therefore I shall not slide. Examine me, O Lord, and prove me. . . . For thy lovingkindness is before mine eyes: and I have walked in thy truth. I have not sat with vain persons, neither will I go in with dissemblers. . . . [I] will not sit with the wicked. . . . But as for me, I will walk in mine integrity." (Psalm 26:1–5, 11)

Wednesday

Helaman's stripling warriors "were all young men, and they were exceedingly valiant for courage, and also for strength and activity; but behold, this was not all—they were men who were true at all times in whatsoever thing they were entrusted. Yea, they were men of truth and soberness, for they had been taught to keep the commandments of God and to walk uprightly before him." (Alma 53:20–21)

Thursday

"Blessed is my servant Hyrum Smith; for I, the Lord, love him because of the integrity of his heart, and because he loveth that which is right before me, saith the Lord. . . . My servant George Miller is without guile; he may be trusted because of the integrity of his heart; and for the love which he has to my testimony I, the Lord, love him." (D&C 124:15, 20)

Friday

The people of Ammon "were among the people of Nephi, and also numbered among the people who were of the church of God. And they were also distinguished for their zeal towards God, and also towards men; for they were perfectly honest and upright in all things; and they were firm in the faith of Christ, even unto the end." (Alma 27:27)

Saturday

"We have a good conscience, [because] in all things [we are] willing to live honestly." (Hebrews 13:18)

Language

"Watch yourselves, and your thoughts, and your words, and your deeds, and observe the commandments of God, and continue in the faith of what ye have heard concerning the coming of our Lord, even unto the end of your lives." (Mosiah 4:30)

Mormonads—Language
https://goo.gl/XxEK96

Music from Children's Songbook & Hymns

- I'll Walk with You (*CS*, 140)
- Kindness Begins with Me (*CS*, 145)
- Let Us Oft Speak Kind Words (*Hymns*, 232)
- Nay, Speak No Ill (*Hymns*, 233)
- I'll Go Where You Want Me to Go (*Hymns*, 270 v. 2)

Quote

"I wish to caution us, if caution is needed, regarding how we speak to each other and how we speak of ourselves. . . . There is a line from the Apocrypha which puts the seriousness of this issue better than I can. It reads, 'The stroke of the whip maketh marks in the flesh: but the stroke of the tongue breaketh the bones.' . . . Speak hopefully. Speak encouragingly, including about yourself. . . . Please accept one of Elder Holland's maxims for living—no misfortune is so bad that whining about it won't make it worse" (Jeffrey R. Holland, "The Tongue of Angels," *Ensign*, May 2007).

Mormonad—Cutting Remarks
Are Really Hurting
https://goo.gl/VrGnnB

Scripture Stories

James describes the power of words to either hurt or perfect people (see James 3).

Moroni's writes a condemning epistle to Pahoran, lashing out at him for not sending more help during a war. Pahoran's writes back and explains his need for help and that he is not offended by Moroni's anger (see Alma 60–61).

Jesus visits the Nephites and teaches them many things, including that "contention is . . . of the devil" (3 Nephi 11:29). All the people in the area are converted and there is no contention in the land because of the love of God they feel. (see 3 Nephi 11–18; 4 Nephi 1:1–15).

Gospel Topics—Profanity
https://goo.gl/aM2dJc

Gospel Art Pictures

- *Captain Moroni Raises the Title of Liberty* (#79)
- *Jesus Teaching in the Western Hemisphere* (#82)

Church History

In 1978, Elder Nelson performed an open-heart surgery on President Spencer W. Kimball that saved his life (see Russell M. Nelson, "A Plea to My Sisters," *Ensign*, November 2015). President Kimball had severe health problems and was in the hospital on and off. During one of his visits to the hospital, an employee was pushing him in a wheelchair when he stumbled, and cursed, taking the Lord's name in vain. President Kimball, though unwell and only partially conscious, begged the employee not to disrespect his Lord in that way. Clean language, and especially respecting the name of the Lord, was something President Kimball talked about a number of times (see "President Kimball Speaks Out on Profanity," *Ensign*, February 1981). To watch a video about choosing to use clean language, go to https://goo.gl/YyB8Px.

LDS.org video "Swearing." This video shows how a young man decided to commit to using clean language. https://goo.gl/YyB8Px

Adaptations for Younger Children

Quote

"I will use the names of Heavenly Father and Jesus Christ reverently. I will not swear or use crude words" ("My Gospel Standards").

Lesson from *Behold Your Little Ones*

"I Will Be Reverent" (Lesson 20, pp. 84–87). Reverence conveys respect. We can always use our words to show respect no matter where we are. Even when we are joking and playing and our voices are louder than normal, we can still make sure our words are uplifting and respectful.

Faith in God

"Learn about and practice good manners and courtesy" (p. 9). Talk about the importance of kindness and courtesy. Saying *please* and *thank you*, giving sincere compliments, sending thank-you notes or gifts, and other things convey respect and appreciation. Think of some way you'd like to practice being more well-mannered and courteous. Share your plan with a parent or leader and follow up with them in a week or two to share your progress.

Activity ⏲

Get a paper doll or a toy doll and several necklaces or pieces of thread. The doll represents someone who has some bad habits. Brainstorm some bad habits like lying, saying mean words, hitting, or taking things without asking. For each thing you come up with, tie up the doll with the necklaces or thread, binding it up. The best thing to do is to develop good habits like telling the truth, saying nice things, and always using God's name reverently. These habits make you feel free and good. If you do something that weighs you down or ties you up, you can get help to repent and feel better. Take the necklaces or thread off the doll and give it a big hug. (Adapted from *Young Women Manual 2*, "Lesson 40: Self-Mastery," p. 154–56. See https://goo.gl/mGDD6L for the online version of this lesson.)

Adaptations for Older Children and Teens

Quotes

"Many movies and television shows portray behavior which is in direct opposition to the laws of God. Do not subject yourself to the innuendo and outright filth which are so often found there. The lyrics in much of today's music fall in the same category. The profanity so prevalent around us today would never have been tolerated in the not-too-distant past. Sadly, the Lord's name is taken in vain over and over again. . . . I am sorry that any of us is subjected to profane language, and I plead with you not to use it. I implore you not to say or to do anything of which you cannot be proud" (Thomas S. Monson, "Priesthood Power," *Ensign*, May 2011).

"The people of God have always been commanded to abstain from language that is profane or vulgar. . . . Members of the Church, young or old, should never allow profane or vulgar words to pass their lips. The language we use projects the images of our hearts, and our hearts should be pure. . . . The language of Latter-day Saints should be reverent and clean. . . . I testify of God the Father and his Son, Jesus Christ, and pray that we may be more faithful in honoring their holy names" (Dallin H. Oaks, "Reverent and Clean," *Ensign*, May 1986).

Preach My Gospel

"Charity and Love," p. 118; "The Gift of Tongues," p. 133; "Listen." pp. 185–86.

Personal Progress

Individual Worth #3—Practice using language that builds people up and helps them feel their worth (p. 30).

Integrity #2—"Ask yourself . . . Do I avoid gossip, inappropriate jokes, swearing and profanity, and being light-minded about sacred subjects? Am I completely truthful . . . [and] honest?" (p. 62)

Duty to God

Study, discuss, and personally apply the section on "Language" in the *For the Strength of Youth* pamphlet (*For the Strength of Youth*, pp. 20–21). This will help you do part of each section titled "Live Worthily" (see *Duty to God*, pp. 16–17, 40–41, 64–65).

Activity ☺

Get five or six small rocks, marbles, balls, or anything you can throw and someone can catch. Tell everyone that these things represent bad habits. Talk about common bad habits like lying, using bad language, and saying unkind things. Have someone stand a few feet away from you and ask them to catch the items you throw at them. Throw all of them at once so that the person will not be able to catch them all. Share that trying to address and change everything you might like to change at once is generally impractical and can be very frustrating. Instead, it's important to work on making small, practical changes over a long period of time rather than trying to make numerous, large changes all at once. When it comes to language, what are your strengths? What would you like to improve?

Daily Scriptures
Language

Sunday

"Watch yourselves, and your thoughts, and your words, and your deeds, and observe the commandments of God, and continue in the faith of what ye have heard concerning the coming of our Lord, even unto the end of your lives." (Mosiah 4:30)

Monday 📖

"Who shall ascend into the hill of the Lord? or who shall stand in his holy place? He that hath clean hands, and a pure heart; who hath not lifted up his soul unto vanity, nor sworn deceitfully." (Psalm 24:3–4)

Tuesday

"Be not deceived: evil communications corrupt good manners. (1 Corinthians 15:33)

Wednesday 📖

"I am the Lord thy God, which have brought thee out of the land of Egypt, out of the house of bondage. Thou shalt have no other gods before me. [I show] mercy unto thousands of them that love me, and keep my commandments. Thou shalt not take the name of the Lord thy God in vain; for the Lord will not hold him guiltless that taketh his name in vain." (Exodus 20:2–3, 6–7)

Thursday

"I am from above, and my power lieth beneath. I am over all, and in all, and through all, and search all things, and the day cometh that all things shall be subject unto me. Behold, I am Alpha and Omega, even Jesus Christ. Wherefore, let all men beware how they take my name in their lips—For behold, verily I say, that many there be who are under this condemnation, who use the name of the Lord, and use it in vain, having not authority. Remember that that which cometh from above is sacred, and must be spoken with care, and by constraint of the Spirit; and in this there is no condemnation." (D&C 63:59–62, 64)

Friday

"The Lord God hath commanded that men . . . should not lie; that they should not steal; that they should not take the name of the Lord their God in vain; that they should not envy; that they should not have malice; that they should not contend one with another." (2 Nephi 26:32)

Saturday 📖

"Do ye not remember that I said unto you that after ye had received the Holy Ghost ye could speak with the tongue of angels? And now, how could ye speak with the tongue of angels save it were by the Holy Ghost? Angels speak by the power of the Holy Ghost; wherefore, they speak the words of Christ. Wherefore, I said unto you, feast upon the words of Christ; for behold, the words of Christ will tell you all things what ye should do." (2 Nephi 32:2–3)

Music and Dancing

"If thou art merry, praise the Lord with singing, with music, with dancing, and with a prayer of praise and thanksgiving." (D&C 136:28)

Gospel Topics: Music
goo.gl/4xqx5A

Music from *Children's Songbook* & *Hymns*

- Hum Your Favorite Hymns (*CS*, 152)
- Sing Your Way Home (*CS*, 193)
- With Songs of Praise (*Hymns*, 71)
- There Is Sunshine in My Soul Today (*Hymns*, 227)

Quote

LDS.org video "The Song of the Heart." This video is about a young Hawaiian girl and how her love of music has helped her come closer to God. goo.gl/k4JMVg

"'Hymns . . . invite the Spirit of the Lord.' They often do this quicker than anything else we may do. President J. Reuben Clark Jr. said, 'We get nearer to the Lord through music than perhaps through any other thing except prayer.' . . . Singing hymns and listening to appropriate music begin at home. The First Presidency has reminded us: 'Latter-day Saints should fill their homes with the sound of worthy music. . . . The hymns can bring families a spirit of beauty and peace and can inspire love and unity among family members. Teach your children to love the hymns. Sing them on the Sabbath, in [family] home evening, during scripture study, at prayer time. Sing as you work, as you play, and as you travel together. Sing hymns as lullabies to build faith and testimony in your young ones.' . . . I pray that we may eliminate any inappropriate music from our lives and follow the counsel of the First Presidency" (Jay E. Jensen, "The Nourishing Power of Hymns," *Ensign*, May 2007; brackets in original).

Scripture Stories

On the journey toward the promised land, Laman, Lemuel, and others sing, dance, and make merry in a way that results in them being very rude to others in their family (see 1 Nephi 18:9).

David is chosen to be king and receives the spirit of God. King Saul has an evil spirit and requests someone who can play beautiful music. David brings his harp and plays for him. The music makes Saul feel better and the evil spirit leaves him. The Israelites go to war with the Philistines, and David slays Goliath (see 1 Samuel 16–17).

Gospel Art Pictures

- *David Slays Goliath* (#19)
- *Lehi and His People Arrive in the Promised Land* (#71)

Church History

When did the first Mormon choir sing together in a Church conference in Salt Lake City? *August 22, 1847.* To learn about the choir, go to its website: MormonTabernacleChoir.org or goo.gl/LjSyVf.

President Heber J. Grant (1856–1945) was a great example of persistence in personal improvement and achieving high goals. He always loved to sing, though he had no natural talent for it. When he was forty-three years old, he began taking voice classes and after much persistence, he learned to sing. He often encouraged members to sing but cautioned, "The more beautiful the music by which false doctrine is sung, the more dangerous it becomes. I appeal to all Latter-day Saints . . . never to sing the words of a song, no matter how beautiful and inspiring the music may be, where the teachings are not in perfect accord with the truths of the gospel" (*Teachings of Presidents of the Church: Heber J. Grant*, 167). To learn more about President Grant's experiences learning to sing, see the article "'I Have Learned to Sing': President Heber J. Grant's Struggle to Sing the Hymns of Zion'" (Joan Oviatt, *Ensign*, September 1984, or see goo.gl/hvsjWz). To read a collection of quotes by Church leaders on music, including two from Heber J. Grant, go to https://goo.gl/YbrGCi.

The Mormon Tabernacle Choir's official website: MormonTabernacleChoir.org or goo.gl/LjSyVf

Heber J. Grant: Documentary https://goo.gl/xLi24W

Adaptations for Younger Children

Quotes

"I will only listen to music that is pleasing to Heavenly Father" ("My Gospel Standards").

"Encourage our young people to learn to sing. . . . The singing of our sacred hymns . . . has a powerful effect in converting people to the principles of the gospel and in promoting peace and spiritual growth" (*Teachings of Presidents of the Church: Heber J. Grant*, 166).

Lesson from *Behold Your Little Ones*

"I Can Be Happy" (Lesson 19, pp. 80–83). The music you listen to affects the way you think, feel, and act. Listen to music that has melodies and lyrics that make you feel good.

Faith in God

"Learn to sing, play, or lead a song from the *Children's Songbook*. Teach or share the song in a family home evening or at Primary. Discuss how developing talents helps prepare us for service to Heavenly Father and others" (p. 10).

Activity

Ask your family members what their favorite songs are and why. Share some of your favorite songs. Ask if they have ever heard music that makes them feel bad. Talk about what they can do if they hear music that makes them feel bad. *They can change or turn off the song, leave the room, or ask whoever is in charge of the music to change it.* Share your feelings about music and its importance in life. Listen to several uplifting songs with different beats, melody lines, and lyrics, and discuss what makes them feel uplifting. Dance together to fun, upbeat songs.

Adaptations for Older Children and Teens

Quotes

"Young people, you cannot afford to fill your minds with the unworthy music of our day. *It is not harmless.* . . . You degrade yourself when you identify with those things that at times surround extremes in music—the shabbiness, the irreverence, the immorality, the addictions. Such music is not worthy of you. Be selective in what you listen to and produce. It becomes part of you. It controls your thoughts and influences the lives of others as well. I would recommend that you go through your music and throw away that which promotes degrading thoughts. Such music ought not to belong to young people concerned with spiritual development. . . . I would counsel you to develop your talents, and if you have musical talent, think of this: There is much music yet to be created, much to be performed. Yours can be the worthy music that will be uplifting, that will spread the gospel, touch hearts, give comfort and strength to troubled minds" (Boyd K. Packer, "Worthy Music, Worthy Thoughts," *New Era*, April 2008, italics added).

"You don't need to know the 1, 2, 3s of *every* dance step to make dances enjoyable, but knowing the basics and having a desire to learn can be valuable. 'I love to go to school dances and actually dance,' Brock [a BYU ballroom dancer] says. 'I just can't do the slow dance thing where you shuffle around in a circle. Dance is great for the youth of the Church: physically, socially, emotionally, and spiritually'" (Shanna Butler, "Why Dance?," *New Era*, August 2004; italics in original).

Preach My Gospel

"Virtue," pp. 118–19.

Personal Progress

Individual Worth #5—Participate in a dance, speech, music, or theater performance, and record how your participation increased your confidence and feelings of worth (p. 31).

Knowledge #6—Learn to lead music for a church meeting (p. 39).

Duty to God

Study, discuss, and personally apply the section on "Music and Dancing" in the *For the Strength of Youth* pamphlet (*For the Strength of Youth*, pp. 22–23). This will help you do part of each section titled "Live Worthily" (see *Duty to God*, pp. 16–17, 40–41, 64–65).

Activity

Dance together! If you know any kinds of dances like ballroom, ballet, folk, or international dances, teach some dance moves to your family and practice them. Learning to dance at home gives you the confidence to have more fun at public social dances. Ask your family members if they would like to learn to dance well, and see what you can do to support them if that is something they are interested in.

Daily Scriptures

Music and Dancing

Sunday

"If thou art merry, praise the Lord with singing, with music, with dancing, and with a prayer of praise and thanksgiving." (D&C 136:28)

Monday 📖

"Woe unto them that call evil good, and good evil; that put darkness for light, and light for darkness; that put bitter for sweet, and sweet for bitter!" (Isaiah 5:20)

Tuesday

"Whatsoever is good cometh from God, and whatsoever is evil cometh from the devil." (Alma 5:40)

Wednesday

"For behold, my brethren, it is given unto you to judge, that ye may know good from evil; and the way to judge is as plain, that ye may know with a perfect knowledge, as the daylight is from the dark night. For behold, the Spirit of Christ is given to every man, that he may know good from evil; wherefore, I show unto you the way to judge; for every thing which inviteth to do good, and to persuade to believe in Christ, is sent forth by the power and gift of Christ; wherefore ye may know with a perfect knowledge it is of God." (Moroni 7:15–16)

Thursday

"But whatsoever thing persuadeth men to do evil, and believe not in Christ, and deny him, and serve not God, then ye may know with a perfect knowledge it is of the devil; for after this manner doth the devil work, for he persuadeth no man to do good, no, not one; neither do his angels; neither do they who subject themselves unto him. Wherefore, I beseech of you, brethren, that ye should search diligently in the light of Christ that ye may know good from evil; and if ye will lay hold upon every good thing, and condemn it not, ye certainly will be a child of Christ." (Moroni 7:17, 19)

Friday

"For my soul delighteth in the song of the heart; yea, the song of the righteous is a prayer unto me, and it shall be answered with a blessing upon their heads. Wherefore, lift up thy heart and rejoice." (D&C 25:12–13)

Saturday

"Let thy bowels also be full of charity towards all men, and to the household of faith, and let virtue garnish thy thoughts unceasingly; then shall thy confidence wax strong in the presence of God." (D&C 121:45)

Physical and Emotional Health
Part 1: Physical Health

"Know ye not that ye are the temple of God, and that the Spirit of God dwelleth in you? For the temple of God is holy, which temple ye are." (1 Corinthians 3:16–17)

Mormonads—Physical Health
and Emotional Health
https://goo.gl/Zcm2NZ

Music from Children's Songbook & Hymns

- The Lord Gave Me a Temple (*CS*, 153)
- The Word of Wisdom (*CS*, 154)
- Head, Shoulders, Knees, and Toes (*CS*, 275)
- Hinges (*CS*, 277)
- Healthy, Wealthy, and Wise (*CS*, 280)
- Choose the Right (*Hymns*, 239)
- In Our Lovely Deseret (*Hymns*, 307 v.2)

Quote

Gospel Topic: Word of Wisdom
https://goo.gl/pbkYsy

"You should always take care of your body. Take nothing into your body that will harm it, such as we are counseled in the Word of Wisdom: tea, coffee, liquor, tobacco, or anything else that is habit-forming, addictive, or harmful. Read section 89 in the Doctrine and Covenants. You will find great promises" (Body K. Packer, "Counsel to Young Men," *Ensign*, May 2009).

Scripture Stories

Daniel and his friends eat healthy foods and are found to be the healthiest of the young men in the king's court (see Daniel 1:3–20).

Ammon's physical strength and service lead to a significant missionary opportunity (see Alma 17:21–Alma 19).

In 1833, Joseph Smith receives the revelation introducing the Word of Wisdom as "a principle with promise" and "not by commandment or constraint" (D&C 89:2–3). Later, in 1921, it is adopted as a general health code and a requirement for Church members (see D&C 89).

Gospel Art Pictures

- *Daniel Refusing the King's Food and Wine* (#23)
- *Ammon Defends the Flocks of King Lamoni* (#78)
- *Brother Joseph* (#87)

Church History

Did Joseph Smith and early Church leaders use tobacco or drink alcoholic beverages contrary to the Word of Wisdom? *No.* The Word of Wisdom was given to Joseph Smith in 1833 when Joseph was thinking about his brethren chewing tobacco during their meetings. The Lord specified that the guidelines at that time were not a commandment. Almost one hundred years later, after the Saints had time to adjust their habits, the First Presidency felt inspired to require compliance to the Word of Wisdom for all who wished to serve in the temple. For more information about the how Word of Wisdom was implemented early on, as well as how it is being implemented in our modern day, go to FairMormon's page "The Word of Wisdom" at http://goo.gl/hNjeq7.

Why did Brigham Young create and run a distillery in Utah? *For medicinal reasons.* At the time, the Word of Wisdom was not a requirement for church members. For more information about Brigham Young's distillery, go to FairMormon's page "Brigham Young built a whiskey distillery in Utah: Did this violate the Word of Wisdom?" at http://goo.gl/6u7z4U. To see videos about people following the Word of Wisdom, go to https://goo.gl/t2KCNe and http://goo.gl/JTM42J.

LDS.org video "A Brand New Year: Physical Health" https://goo.gl/t2KCNe

LDS.org video "Word of Wisdom." A man shares his experience with, and testimony of, the Word of Wisdom. http://goo.gl/JTM42J

Adaptations for Younger Children

Quote

"I will keep my mind and body sacred and pure, and I will not partake of things that are harmful to me" ("My Gospel Standards").

Lesson from *Behold Your Little Ones*

"I Will Take Care of My Body" (Lesson 10, pp. 44–47).

Faith in God

"Read Doctrine and Covenants 89. Discuss how Heavenly Father blesses us when we faithfully live the Word of Wisdom. Help plan and conduct an activity to teach the Word of Wisdom to others" (p. 6 for boys; p. 7 for girls). Lead the family in the activity below.

"Plan, prepare, and serve a nutritious meal" (p. 9).

"Learn about and practice good nutrition, good health, and good grooming, including modest dress" (p. 11).

Activity

Play a game called How I Take Care of My Temple. Each person says something we can do with or to our bodies. If it is good, everyone acts it out; if it is not good, everyone crosses their arms in front of them in an "X" to show they will not do that to their bodies. For example, if someone says, "Eat fruits and vegetables," everyone pretends to eat. If someone says, "Never ever take a shower," everyone makes an "X". You can talk about eating healthy food, practicing good hygiene and grooming, having good sleep habits, exercising, listening to good music, watching wholesome movies, and so on.

Adaptations for Older Children and Teens

Quote

"President Boyd K. Packer [counseled]: 'Our physical body is the instrument of our spirit. In that marvelous revelation the Word of Wisdom we are told how to keep our bodies free from impurities which might dull, even destroy, those delicate physical senses which have to do with spiritual communication. The Word of Wisdom is a key to individual revelation. . . . If we abuse our body with habit-forming substances, or misuse prescription drugs, we draw curtains which close off the light of spiritual communication.' The primary blessing that comes from obedience to the Word of Wisdom is spiritual in nature, not necessarily physical. Certainly, we all recognize the physical benefits of adhering to the lifestyle and dietary guidelines contained in the Word of Wisdom. But please notice [that] . . . the Word of Wisdom is about readiness and receptiveness to receive revelation. And secondarily the Word of Wisdom also produces physical benefits" (David A. Bednar, "Ye Are the Temple of God," *Ensign*, September 2001).

Preach My Gospel

"Obey the Word of Wisdom," p. 78.

Personal Progress

Knowledge #7—Learn first aid, safety, sanitation, and survival skills (p. 40).

Knowledge Value Project #3—Read Doctrine and Covenants 89 and work on physical health and fitness (p. 42).

Good Works #2—Help with all phases of meal preparation, service, and clean up. Collect recipes you want to have for use in your future home (p. 54) (see also the related value project on page 58).

Duty to God

Study the doctrinal topic of "The Word of Wisdom." Record what you learn and share what you learned with your parents or a priesthood leader (see pp. 18–21, 42–45, 66–69).

Look over the section "For the Strength of Youth: Physical Health." Work on it, or review what you did if you have already done this section (*Duty to God,* pp. 31–35).

Activity

Consider your physical health habits as individuals and as a family. Share what is going well and what improvements could be made to create better health.

Discuss situations where you would choose to refuse something because of your commitment to keeping the Word of Wisdom. How do you think it would feel? How do you think other people would react? Role-play a variety of situations, like deciding what foods and beverages to eat and drink, what time to go to bed, what activities to participate in, and what kinds of exercise to do.

Play together doing something physical that strengthens and invigorates the body—play a sport, go on a walk, jog, hike, or bike ride.

Daily Scriptures

Physical and Emotional Health Part 1: Physical Health

Sunday

"Know ye not that ye are the temple of God, and that the Spirit of God dwelleth in you? . . . For the temple of God is holy, which temple ye are." (1 Corinthians 3:16–17)

Monday

"Yea, all things which come of the earth, in the season thereof, are made for the benefit and the use of man, both to please the eye and to gladden the heart; Yea, for food and for raiment, for taste and for smell, to strengthen the body and to enliven the soul." (D&C 59:18–19)

Tuesday

"Cease to be idle; cease to be unclean; cease to find fault one with another; cease to sleep longer than is needful; retire to thy bed early, that ye may not be weary; arise early, that your bodies and your minds may be invigorated." (D&C 88:124)

Wednesday

"Inasmuch as any man drinketh wine or strong drink among you, behold it is not good, neither meet in the sight of your Father. . . . Tobacco is not for the body, neither for the belly, and is not good for man. . . . And again, hot drinks are not for the body or belly." (D&C 89:5, 8–9)

Thursday

"All wholesome herbs God hath ordained for the constitution, nature, and use of man—Every herb in the season thereof, and every fruit in the season thereof; all these to be used with prudence and thanksgiving. Yea, flesh also of beasts and of the fowls of the air, I, the Lord, have ordained for the use of man with thanksgiving; nevertheless they are to be used sparingly." (D&C 89:10–12)

Friday

"All grain is good for the food of man; as also the fruit of the vine; that which yieldeth fruit, whether in the ground or above the ground." (D&C 89:16)

Saturday 📖

"And all saints who remember to keep and do these sayings, walking in obedience to the commandments, shall receive health in their navel and marrow to their bones; And shall find wisdom and great treasures of knowledge, even hidden treasures; And shall run and not be weary, and shall walk and not faint. And I, the Lord, give unto them a promise, that the destroying angel shall pass by them, as the children of Israel, and not slay them." (D&C 89:18–21)

Physical and Emotional Health
Part 2: Emotional Health

"Look unto me in every thought; doubt not, fear not." (D&C 6:36)

Mormonads—Attitude
http://goo.gl/ZyD3aA

LDS.org article "Preparing
Emotionally for Missionary
Service" (Robert K. Wagstaff,
Ensign, March 2011)
https://goo.gl/wcYQgw

Music from Children's Songbook & Hymns

- Jesus Wants Me for a Sunbeam (*CS*, 60)
- If You're Happy (*CS*, 266)
- Master, the Tempest Is Raging (*Hymns*, 105)
- Scatter Sunshine (*Hymns*, 230)

Quotes

"So many people today are waiting for their own golden ticket—the ticket that they believe holds the key to the happiness they have always dreamed about. . . . The happiest people I know are not those who find their golden ticket; they are those who, while in pursuit of worthy goals, discover and treasure the beauty and sweetness of the everyday moments. . . . These are they who are truly happy" (Dieter F. Uchtdorf, "Forget Me Not," *Ensign*, November 2011).

"How do you best respond when mental or emotional challenges confront you or those you love? Above all, never lose faith in your Father in Heaven, who loves you more than you can comprehend. . . . If things [get] debilitating, seek the advice of reputable people with certified training, professional skills, and good values. . . . Our Father in Heaven expects us to use *all* of the marvelous gifts He has provided in this glorious dispensation" (Jeffrey R. Holland, "Like a Broken Vessel," *Ensign*, November 2013; italics in original).

Scripture Stories

Jesus is sleeping on a boat when a terrible storm comes up. His friends awaken Him and He commands the sea to be still. The Lord has the power to calm our emotional "storms" as well (see Matthew 8:23–27; Mark 4:36–41; Luke 8:22–25).

While living in Liberty Jail, Joseph Smith's family and other Saints are driven from their homes in the winter. During this difficult time, Joseph receives some incredible revelations (see D&C 121–22).

Gospel Art Pictures

- *Jesus Calms the Storm* (#40)
- *Emma Crossing the Ice* (#96)
- *Joseph Smith in Liberty Jail* (#97)

Church History

In early Church history, Saints experienced both rapturous joy and deep depression. Emma Smith enjoyed being the scribe for the Book of Mormon. She led the Relief Society. She wrote the first LDS Hymnbook. On the other hand, she was tormented by the law of plural marriage. She saw her husband return home after being beaten, tarred, feathered, and imprisoned, and finally the day came when he did not return home at all. Lucy Mack Smith, Joseph Smith's mother and Emma's mother-in-law, wrote,

> "I have never seen a woman in my life, who would endure every species of fatigue and hardship, from month to month, and from year to year, with that unflinching courage, zeal, and patience, which [Emma] has ever done." (Gracia N. Jones, "My Great-Great-Grandmother, Emma Hale Smith," *Ensign*, August 1992)

During the winter of 1838–1839, Joseph Smith and a few others were imprisoned in the Liberty Jail in Missouri. Jeffrey R. Holland said, "There was no more burdensome time in Joseph's life than this cruel, illegal, and unjustified incarceration" ("Lessons from Liberty Jail," *Ensign*, September 2009). To learn more about Joseph and Emma's joys and sorrows, see "Joseph and Emma: Moments in Their Lives," *Ensign*, July 2012 or go to https://goo.gl/NFvQEe. To see some pictures of Church history sites, including Liberty Jail, go to http://goo.gl/A8uaQd.

LDS.org Images: Missouri— Church History Sites http://goo.gl/A8uaQd

Adaptations for Younger Children

Quote

"In all of living have much of fun and laughter. Life is to be enjoyed, not just endured" (Gordon B. Hinckley, "Stand True and Faithful," *Ensign*, May 1996).

Lesson from *Behold Your Little Ones*

"I Can Be Happy" (Lesson 19, pp. 80–83).

Faith in God

Working on earning your *Faith in God* award can be a very emotionally healthy thing to do. It can be enjoyable and rewarding, and it can help you feel peace. Review your progress in the *Faith in God* program. Look over the entire book, including the introductory pages and "My Gospel Standards" on the back cover. Share with your family, leaders, or a friend what you most enjoy about the *Faith in God* program as well as anything you haven't enjoyed. Decide what to do next to continue working on earning your *Faith in God* award.

Activity

Ask each person what makes them particularly happy. Write, draw, or act out each thing. Invite anyone who would like to share something that makes them feel sad to do so privately and set up a time to do this. Think of something you can do that night as a family that makes everyone feel happy, then do it. You could read books, dance to fun music, play inside or outside, tell jokes, make popcorn, do puzzles, make ice cream, draw, or color.

Adaptations for Older Children and Teens

Quotes

"In times of darkness, remember there is a difference between passing local cloud cover and general darkness" (Neal A. Maxwell, "Jesus, the Perfect Mentor," *Ensign*, February 2001).

President Uchtdorf shared a story about a girl named Eva who went to live with her odd, old great-aunt Rose for a summer. After a while, she discovered that Aunt Rose was likely the happiest person she had ever met. When she asked her Aunt Rose why she was so happy, she answered: "There is enough that doesn't go right in life, so anyone can work themselves into a puddle of pessimism and a mess of melancholy. But I know people who, even when things don't work out, focus on the wonders and miracles of life. These folks are the happiest people I know. . . . God didn't design us to be sad. He created us to have joy! So if we trust Him, He will help us to notice the good, bright, hopeful things of life. And sure enough, the world will become brighter. No, it doesn't happen instantly, but honestly, how many good things do? . . . Faith and hope will open your eyes to the happiness that is placed before you. . . . Busy, unhappy people have forgotten the one thing that matters most in all the world—the thing Jesus said is the heart of His gospel. . . . It is love—the pure love of Christ. . . . *That* is what makes us happy" ("A Summer with Great-Aunt Rose," *Ensign*, November 2015, italics in original).

Preach My Gospel

"Hope," p. 117.

Personal Progress

Look over the section on "Faith" (p. 13–20). Review what you have done and what you have left to do. Decide what to work on next.

Duty to God

Study the doctrinal topic of "Faith." Record what you learn and share what you learned with your parents or a priesthood leader (see pp. 18–21, 42–45, 66–69).

Activity ⏲ 📖

Get the largest bill you have in your wallet, ideally one that's crisp and clean and $20 or more. Ask who would like it, and acknowledge everyone who responds. Then crumple it up in a wad, and ask who would like to have it. Then grind it on the floor under your shoe, and ask who would like it. Dip it in dirty water, and ask who would like it. Explain that no matter what you do yourself, or what happens to you, just like the money, you never decrease in your worth. Your circumstances will affect you, helping you feel generally happy or generally sad. Your choices will increase or decrease your personal freedom, helping you feel good or bad. Regardless, your worth in the eyes of God and those who truly love you will never decrease. "Remember the worth of souls is great in the sight of God" (D&C 18:10).

Daily Scriptures

Physical and Emotional Health Part 2: Emotional Health

Sunday

"Look unto me in every thought; doubt not, fear not. Behold the wounds which pierced my side, and also the prints of the nails in my hands and feet; be faithful, keep my commandments, and ye shall inherit the kingdom of heaven." (D&C 6:36–37)

Monday

"The fruit of the Spirit is love, joy, peace, longsuffering, gentleness, goodness, faith, meekness. . . . Let us also walk in the Spirit." (Galatians 5:22–23, 25)

Tuesday

"Adam fell that men might be; and men are, that they might have joy." (2 Nephi 2:25)

Wednesday

"If thou art merry, praise the Lord with singing, with music, with dancing, and with a prayer of praise and thanksgiving. If thou art sorrowful, call on the Lord thy God with supplication, that your souls may be joyful." (D&C 136:28–29)

Thursday

"Remember, remember that it is upon the rock of our Redeemer, who is Christ, the Son of God, that ye must build your foundation; that when the devil shall send forth his mighty winds, yea, his shafts in the whirlwind, yea, when all his hail and his mighty storm shall beat upon you, it shall have no power over you to drag you down to the gulf of misery and endless wo, because of the rock upon which ye are built, which is a sure foundation, a foundation whereon if men build they cannot fall." (Helaman 5:12)

Friday

"Learn of me, and listen to my words; walk in the meekness of my Spirit, and you shall have peace in me. I am Jesus Christ; I came by the will of the Father, and I do his will." (D&C 19:23–24)

Saturday

"Wherefore, I say unto you, that ye ought to forgive one another; for he that forgiveth not his brother his trespasses standeth condemned before the Lord; for there remaineth in him the greater sin. I, the Lord, will forgive whom I will forgive, but of you it is required to forgive all men. And ye ought to say in your hearts—let God judge between me and thee, and reward thee according to thy deeds." (D&C 64:9–11)

Repentance

"Come now, and let us reason together, saith the Lord: though your sins be as scarlet, they shall be as white as snow; though they be red like crimson, they shall be as wool." (Isaiah 1:18) 🔖

Mormonads—Repentance
http://goo.gl/d7zCb8

Music from *Children's Songbook* & *Hymns*

- Help Me, Dear Father (*CS*, 99)
- The Fourth Article of Faith (*CS*, 124)
- Lead, Kindly Light (*Hymns*, 97 v. 2)
- How Gentle God's Commands (*Hymns*, 125)

Quote

"My invitation to all of us is to evaluate our lives, repent, and keep on trying. If we don't try, we're just latter-day sinners; if we don't persevere, we're latter-day quitters; and if we don't allow others to try, we're just latter-day hypocrites. As we try, persevere, and help others to do the same, we are true Latter-day Saints. As we change, we will find that God indeed cares a lot more about who we are and about who we are becoming than about who we once were" (Dale G. Renlund, "Latter-day Saints Keep On Trying," *Ensign*, May 2015).

Scripture Stories

The Lord tells Jonah to call the people of Nineveh to repentance, but Jonah boards a ship headed for Tarshish instead. A great storm arises. Jonah admits that he is the cause of it and he is thrown overboard. The Lord sends a great fish to swallow Jonah. After three days and three nights, the fish spits him out. Jonah cries repentance to the people in Nineveh, and they repent (see the book of Jonah).

Enos prays for forgiveness and is forgiven. He teaches and testifies to the Nephites and the Lamanites. The Nephites continue to have faith in God, but the Lamanites do not repent (see Enos 1).

Alma the Younger and the four sons of Mosiah fight against the Church. They are stopped by an angel who tells them to repent. Alma is unconscious for several days. He has faith in Jesus Christ, repents, and becomes a missionary (see Mosiah 27:8–37; Alma 36:3–24).

Aaron teaches the gospel King Lamoni's father. King Lamoni's father prays and asks God if He exists. He promises to "give away all my sins to know thee" (Alma 22:18). He and others convert (see also Alma 22:2–23).

Gospel Art Pictures

- *Jonah* (#27)
- *Enos Praying* (#72)
- *Conversion of Alma the Younger* (#77)

Church History

While the Saints were in Kirtland, Martin Harris decided Joseph Smith was a fallen prophet. He was excommunicated in 1837. He even did missionary work for a splinter church. However, he repented and was rebaptized in 1842. In 1870, at age 87, he was invited by Brigham Young to join the Saints in Utah. Brigham Young even sent him a train ticket and an escort.

Despite Martin Harris's misdeeds, Elder Oaks says we should always honor him for his great financial contribution to the printing of the Book of Mormon. To learn more about Martin Harris see MormonWiki. com/Martin_Harris or http://goo.gl/fsnJiw (see Dallin H. Oaks, "The Witness: Martin Harris," *Ensign*, May 1999 and the LDS.org page "Martin Harris, the Great Benefactor" at http://goo.gl/3gWTTF).

In September 1832, Joseph Smith received the revelation recorded in Doctrine and Covenants 84 in which the Lord told the people to "repent and remember . . . the Book of Mormon and the former commandments which I have given" (D&C 84:57). During Ezra Taft Benson's service as a leader of the Church, he repeatedly focused on the Book of Mormon (see *Teachings of Presidents of the Church: Ezra Taft Benson*, 125–35). He also warned the Saints against pride, which he called "the stumbling block of Zion" (see "Beware of Pride," *Ensign*, May 1989).

LDS.org page "Martin Harris, the Great Benefactor" http://goo.gl/3gWTTF

LDS.org video of President Benson's conference talk "Beware of Pride," read by his counselor Elder Hinckley. https://goo.gl/6MFLvY

Adaptations for Younger Children

Quote

"I will choose the right. I know I can repent when I make a mistake" ("My Gospel Standards").

Lesson from *Behold Your Little Ones*

"I Will Say, 'I'm Sorry'" (Lesson 16, pp. 68–71).

Faith in God

Read "My Baptismal Covenant," which says, "Through the Atonement of Jesus Christ, I can be forgiven of my sins when I repent" (p. 2).

Activity

Repentance means changing one's mind or actions. Have everyone face a picture of Christ (*Gospel Art Book* #64). Alternate saying things people do to stay close to God and things that pull them away from God. When you say something that brings people close to God, have everyone turn to face the picture of Christ. When you say something that pulls people away from God, have everyone turn around so their backs are to the picture of Christ. Have kids say what they could do differently to remain close to God. For example, "Someone invites you to watch an inappropriate movie." The kids can say, "I would tell them I don't want to watch that movie and help choose an appropriate movie." Ideas for positive things include praying, walking in nature, serving others, and learning about Jesus and Heavenly Father. Ideas for negative things could include taking candy without asking, hitting someone, and saying mean words to someone.

Adaptations for Older Children and Teens

Quotes

"The message I would give to the youth is that repentance is not a bad thing; it's a blessing. The Savior provided for us the ability to repent. Don't wait. We can change, and that will help us live the standards. One virtuous young man or young woman led by the Spirit can change the world. You can be that one" (Elaine S. Dalton, "Q&A on the new For the Strength of Youth," LDS.org, http://goo.gl/w2XXNc).

"The message of repentance is often not welcomed. . . . But in reality the prophetic call should be received with joy. Without repentance, there is no real progress or improvement in life. . . . Repentance is a divine gift, and there should be a smile on our faces when we speak of it. It points us to freedom, confidence, and peace. Rather than interrupting the celebration, the gift of repentance is the cause for true celebration" (D. Todd Christofferson, "The Divine Gift of Repentance," *Ensign*, November 2011).

Preach My Gospel

"Repentance," pp. 62–63; "Repentance and Addiction Recovery," pp. 187–88.

Personal Progress

Choice and Accountability #4 and Virtue #4—Study scriptures about repentance, write about what repentance means to you in your journal, and prepare a family home evening lesson on it. (pp. 47, 71)

Duty to God

Study the doctrinal topic of "Repentance." Record what you learn and share what you learned with your parents or a priesthood leader (see pp. 18–21, 42–45, 66–69).

Study, discuss, and personally apply the section on "Repentance" in the *For the Strength of Youth* pamphlet (*For the Strength of Youth*, pp. 28–29). This will help you do part of each section titled "Live Worthily" (see *Duty to God*, pp. 16–17, 40–41, 64–65).

Activity ⏲

Boil a clean white egg ahead of time. Tell everyone that when we come to earth, we are pure and clean like the egg. During our lives, we make mistakes. Ask what types of mistakes are common, and write the mistakes on the egg in pencil or crayon. When we are baptized and then weekly renew our covenants by taking the sacrament, we get a chance to shed our sins and return to our pure state. Peel the egg and show the pure, white egg under the shell.

Daily Scriptures

Repentance

Sunday

"Come now, and let us reason together, saith the Lord: though your sins be as scarlet, they shall be as white as snow; though they be red like crimson, they shall be as wool." (Isaiah 1:18)

Monday

"Remember the worth of souls is great in the sight of God; For, behold, the Lord your Redeemer suffered death in the flesh; wherefore he suffered the pain of all men, that all men might repent and come unto him. And he hath risen again from the dead, that he might bring all men unto him, on conditions of repentance. And how great is his joy in the soul that repenteth!" (D&C 18:10–13)

Tuesday

"Behold, he who has repented of his sins, the same is forgiven, and I, the Lord, remember them no more. By this ye may know if a man repenteth of his sins—behold, he will confess them and forsake them." (D&C 58:42–43)

Wednesday

"Believe in God; believe that he is, and that he created all things, both in heaven and in earth; believe that he has all wisdom, and all power, both in heaven and in earth;

believe that man doth not comprehend all the things which the Lord can comprehend. And again, believe that ye must repent of your sins and forsake them, and humble yourselves before God; and ask in sincerity of heart that he would forgive you; and now, if you believe all these things see that ye do them." (Mosiah 4:9–10)

Thursday

"O that I were an angel, and could have the wish of mine heart, that I might go forth and speak with the trump of God, with a voice to shake the earth, and cry repentance unto every people! Yea, I would declare . . . the plan of redemption, that they should repent and come unto our God, that there might not be more sorrow upon all the face of the earth." (Alma 29:1–2)

Friday

"I beseech of you in words of soberness that ye would repent, and come with full purpose of heart, and cleave unto God as he cleaveth unto you." (Jacob 6:5)

Saturday

"Those things, which God before had shewed by the mouth of all his prophets, that Christ should suffer, he hath so fulfilled. Repent ye therefore, and be converted, that your sins may be blotted out." (Acts 3:18–19)

Sabbath Day Observance

"Call the sabbath a delight, the holy of the Lord, . . . not doing thine own ways, nor finding thine own pleasure, nor speaking thine own words: Then shalt thou delight thyself in the Lord; and I will cause thee to ride upon the high places of the earth." (Isaiah 58:13–14) 📖

Music from Children's Songbook & Hymns

- When I Go to Church (*CS*, 157)
- Saturday (*CS*, 196)
- Thanks for the Sabbath School (*Hymns*, 278)
- Welcome, Welcome Sabbath Morning (*Hymns*, 280)

Mormonads—Sabbath Day and Sacrament
https://goo.gl/pTfZUy

Quotes

"A family council, when conducted with love and with Christlike attributes, will counter the impact of modern technology that often distracts us from spending quality time with each other and also tends to bring evil right into our homes. . . . You may want to consider holding the general family council on Sunday, which is the first day of the week; families can review the past week and plan for the coming week. This may be exactly what your family needs to help make the Sabbath a delightful experience" (M. Russell Ballard, "Family Councils," *Ensign*, May 2016).

"How can you ensure that your behavior on the Sabbath will lead to joy and rejoicing? In addition to your going to church, partaking of the sacrament, and being diligent in your specific call to serve, what other activities would help to make the Sabbath a delight for you?" (Russell M. Nelson, "The Sabbath Is a Delight," *Ensign*, May 2015).

Gospel Topics: Sabbath Day
https://goo.gl/JEjJ96

Scripture Stories

Moses tells the Israelites God's Ten Commandments. The fourth commandment is "Remember the Sabbath day, to keep it holy" (Exodus 20:8) (see also Exodus 20:1–17).

Jesus goes to a synagogue on the Sabbath and heals a man with a withered hand. The Pharisees ask Jesus if it is lawful to heal (which was considered a form of work) on the Sabbath. He replies, "It is lawful to do well on the sabbath days" (Matthew 12:12) (see also Matthew 12:1–13).

Jesus talks about what to do on the Sabbath day, including going to church, worshipping God, and resting from the regular work of the week (see D&C 59:9–13).

Gospel Art Pictures

- *The Ten Commandments* (#14)
- *Christ Healing the Sick at Bethesda* (#42)
- *Blessing the Sacrament* (#107)
- *Passing the Sacrament* (#108)

Church History

On July 25, 1847, the day after arriving in the Salt Lake Valley, President Brigham Young talked to Church members about keeping the Sabbath day holy. Even though there was a tremendous amount of work to do in order to establish a new home in the mountains, President Young said they would hold Church meetings every Sunday. He also told them "they must not work on Sunday, that [if they did] they would lose five times as much as they would gain by it, and they must not hunt or fish on that day" (*Teachings of Presidents of the Church: Brigham Young*, 145; brackets in original). In our day, prophets continue to remind us to keep the Sabbath day holy. To watch a video of Elder Holland talking about the Sabbath holy, go to https://goo.gl/D55gMi.

LDS.org video "'Upon My Holy Day.'" Elder Holland talks to the youth about keeping the Sabbath day holy. https://goo.gl/D55gMi

In September 1972, President Spencer W. Kimball visited Jerusalem, where the Jews observe the Sabbath on Saturday. Branch president David Galbraith presented the idea that Church members living in Israel could start observing the Sabbath on Saturday as well, for a variety of practical reasons. Two months afterward, on November 20, 1972, the First Presidency authorized the observance of the Sabbath day on Saturday for Saints who live in Israel. Later, it was authorized that members in Islamic countries, like Egypt and Jordan, observe the Sabbath on Friday along with their neighbors. For more information, see FairMormon's page "Sabbath changed to Sunday" at http://goo.gl/BD969q.

Adaptations for Younger Children

Quote

I will do those things on the Sabbath that will help me feel close to Heavenly Father and Jesus Christ" ("My Gospel Standards").

Lesson from *Behold Your Little Ones*

"Sunday Is a Day to Remember Heavenly Father and Jesus Christ" (Lesson 8, pp. 36–39).

Faith in God

"Attend sacrament meetings and Primary regularly" (p. 4).

"Explain how taking the sacrament helps you renew your baptismal covenant. In a family home evening, teach others about things we can do to remain faithful" (p. 6).

Activity

Ask everybody to share their favorite things to do on Sunday. Find out what people like and dislike about going to church, and about Sundays in general. If someone shares something they do not like, don't make a big deal of it or try to "make" them feel differently. Be understanding of what people don't like, but try to focus on what they do like and how to make Sundays and Church experiences positive. Brainstorm ways for your family to get more out of Sundays. You could prepare for Church on Saturday night, plan special family activities, go out in nature or watch nature programs, or visit with people.

Adaptations for Older Children and Teens

Quote

"Parents, now is the time to teach our children to be examples of the believers by attending sacrament meeting. When Sunday morning arrives, help them to be well rested, properly dressed, and spiritually prepared to partake of the emblems of the sacrament and receive the enlightening, edifying, ennobling power of the Holy Ghost. Let your family be filled with love as you honor the Sabbath all day long and experience its spiritual blessings throughout the week. . . . I bear my special witness that the greatest joy we receive in this life is in following the Savior. May we keep His commandments by keeping His sacred day holy" (L. Tom Perry, "The Sabbath and the Sacrament," *Ensign*, May 2011).

Preach My Gospel

Lesson 4: "The Commandments," pp. 71–81; "Keep the Sabbath Day Holy," p. 74.

Personal Progress

Faith #3—Learn about how Jesus instituted the sacrament. Make partaking of the sacrament more meaningful to you by paying attention to the sacrament hymn and sacrament prayers and thinking of the purpose of taking the sacrament (p. 15).

Duty to God

Look over the sections titled "Administer Priesthood Ordinances" (pp. 24, 48, 72). Work on the one for your age group. Also read page 103 titled, "Blessing the Sacrament."

Study, discuss, and personally apply the section on "Sabbath Day Observance" in the *For the Strength of Youth* pamphlet (pp. 30–31). This will help you do part of each section titled "Live Worthily" (see pp. 16–17, 40–41, 64–65).

Activity ⏲

Get some ice cream and toppings to make an ice cream sundae. Gather ketchup, mayonnaise, and mustard as well. Alternatively, you can use a piece of bread and get butter, honey, ketchup, mayo, and mustard. Put a scoop of ice cream in a bowl and ask what toppings the family would like on a sundae. Put the toppings on and ask if anyone would like it. Tell everyone that you just *love* ketchup on your sundaes and squirt a bunch of ketchup, mayo, and mustard on the ice cream. Ask who would like a taste now. If someone is interested, let them have a bite and report on the taste. Tell everyone that nothing's wrong with ketchup, mayo, and mustard, they just don't taste the best on a sundae, just like some activities are really great to do on Sundays and others, while fine on other days, aren't best to do on Sundays. Talk about how to have a great Sunday, focusing on the underlying purpose of the Sabbath day, which is to draw closer to the Lord and your family and to serve others. (Adapted from Richard R. Eubank, *Is There an Object to Your Lesson?*, 66.)

Daily Scriptures

Sabbath Day Observance

Sunday 📖

"If thou turn away thy foot . . . from doing thy pleasure on my holy day; and call the sabbath a delight, the holy of the Lord, honourable; and shalt honour him, not doing thine own ways, nor finding thine own pleasure, nor speaking thine own words: Then shalt thou delight thyself in the Lord; and I will cause thee to ride upon the high places of the earth, and feed thee with the heritage of Jacob thy father: for the mouth of the Lord hath spoken it." (Isaiah 58:13–14)

Monday 📖

"Remember the sabbath day, to keep it holy. Six days shalt thou labour, and do all thy work: But the seventh day is the sabbath of the Lord thy God: in it thou shalt not do any work. . . . For In six days the Lord made heaven and earth, the sea, and all that in them is, and rested the seventh day: wherefore the Lord blessed the sabbath day, and hallowed it." (Exodus 20:8–11)

Tuesday

Jesus "went into their synagogue: And, behold, there was a man which had his hand withered. And they asked him, saying, Is it lawful to heal on the sabbath days? that they might accuse him. And he said unto them, . . . it is lawful to do well on the sabbath days. Then saith he to the man, Stretch forth thine hand. And he stretched it forth; and it was restored whole, like as the other." (Matthew 12:9–13)

Wednesday

"And that thou mayest more fully keep thyself unspotted from the world, thou shalt go to the house of prayer and offer up thy sacraments upon my holy day; For verily this is a day appointed unto you to rest from your labors, and to pay thy devotions unto the Most High; Nevertheless thy vows shall be offered up in righteousness on all days and at all times; But remember that on this, the Lord's day, thou shalt offer thine oblations and thy sacraments unto the Most High." (D&C 59:9–12)

Thursday

"Inasmuch as parents have children in Zion, . . . their children shall be baptized for the remission of their sins when eight years old, and receive the laying on of the hands. And they shall also teach their children to pray, and to walk uprightly before the Lord. And the inhabitants of Zion shall also observe the Sabbath day to keep it holy." (D&C 68:25, 27–29)

Friday

"Wherefore the Sabbath was given unto man for a day of rest; and also that man should glorify God." (Joseph Smith Translation, Mark 2:28, [in the Bible appendix])

Saturday

"Verily my sabbaths ye shall keep: for it is a sign between me and you throughout your generations; that ye may know that I am the Lord that doth sanctify you." (Exodus 31:13)

Service

"When ye are in the service of your fellow beings ye are only in the service of your God." (Mosiah 2:17) 🔲

Music from *Children's Songbook* & *Hymns*

Mormonads—Service
https://goo.gl/P6tfVY

- Go the Second Mile (*CS*, 167)
- When We're Helping (*CS*, 198)
- A Poor Wayfaring Man of Grief (*Hymns*, 29)
- Have I Done Any Good? (*Hymns*, 223)
- You Can Make the Pathway Bright (*Hymns*, 228 v. 3)

Quote

"President Monson [said]: 'We are surrounded by those in need of our attention, our encouragement, our support, our comfort, our kindness. . . . We are the Lord's hands here upon the earth, with the mandate to serve and to lift His children. He is dependent upon each of us.' . . . I would like to suggest four words to remember: 'First observe, then serve.' . . . May we all seek to first observe, then serve. As we do so, we are keeping covenants, and our service . . . will be evidence of our discipleship" (Linda K. Burton, "First Observe, Then Serve," *Ensign*, November 2012).

LDS.org video "The Good Samaritan"
https://goo.gl/WvvZLE

Scripture Stories

Jesus tells the story of a Samaritan who serves a man he does not know. Jesus finishes the story by saying, "Go, and do thou likewise" (Luke 10:37) (see also Luke 10:25–37).

Jesus washes His disciples' feet. Peter objects to his Master serving him this way, but Jesus insists. Jesus tells the Apostles to serve each other as He has served them (see John 13:1–17).

LDS.org video "Humanitarian Visitor Center Film"
https://goo.gl/J7vvk5

Ammon goes to be a missionary among the Lamanites, but before he says anything about the gospel, he focuses on serving the king in every way that he can. King Lamoni is amazed by his power and is then open to the gospel message. Ammon teaches Lamoni about God and the plan of salvation. Lamoni is converted and teaches his people the gospel (see Alma 17:20–Alma 19).

Gospel Art Pictures

- *The Good Samaritan* (#44)
- *Jesus Washing the Apostles' Feet* (#55)
- *Ammon Defends the Flocks of King Lamoni* (#78)

Church History

Service can be performed on a large scale, on a small scale, formally, or informally. On June 24, 1844, John Taylor served the little group in Carthage Jail by singing "A Poor Wayfaring Man of Grief," a hymn about how serving people is the same as serving God. Shortly afterward, a mob attacked and murdered Joseph and Hyrum (see *Teachings of Presidents of the Church: John Taylor*, xvi). To see a video documentary of John Taylor, including this eventful night in his life, go to http://goo.gl/PYqG6s.

John Taylor: Documentary
http://goo.gl/PYqG6s

Throughout the Doctrine and Covenants, the Lord calls early Church members to serve in the Church in various ways. Outside of Church callings, we can serve in our community. The Church now provides a website to connect volunteers with community service opportunities. Go to JustServe. org and enter your zip code to view a list of service opportunities in your area.

LDS.org video "Testimony of the Book of Mormon." Elder Holland reviews the martyrdom of Joseph and Hyrum Smith and bears his testimony of the Book of Mormon.
https://goo.gl/XTYxMb.

Adaptations for Younger Children

Quote

"Many years ago I heard a poem which has stayed with me, by which I have tried to guide my life. It's one of my favorites:

> *I have wept in the night*
> *For the shortness of sight*
> *That to somebody's need made me blind;*
> *But I never have yet*
> *Felt a tinge of regret*
> *For being a little too kind.*"

(Thomas S. Monson, "What Have I Done for Someone Today?," *Ensign*, November 2009)

Lesson from *Behold Your Little Ones*

"I Will Love Others" (Lesson 18, pp. 76–79).

Faith in God

"Read and discuss the parable of the Good Samaritan (Luke 10:30–37). Plan and complete a service project that helps a family member or neighbor. After completing the project, discuss how it helped your faith grow stronger" (p. 8). For example, you could help around the house, pull a neighbor's weeds, volunteer at a school or a library, or "help your Primary leaders plan and carry out an upcoming quarterly activity" (p. 9).

Activity ⏲

Have everyone take turns sharing what they notice other members of the family do to love and serve each other. Get a jar and some candies and call them "kindness candies." Encourage the family to be kind to each other and notice when others are kind to them. At the end of each day for the next week, have each person share what kind things they did and what kind things others did. Thank everyone for being kind and share some of the candies, because life is sweet when we are kind to each other.

Adaptations for Older Children and Teens

Quote

"Unless we lose ourselves in service to others, there is little purpose to our own lives. Those who live only for themselves eventually shrivel up and figuratively lose their lives, while those who lose themselves in service to others grow and flourish—and in effect save their lives. . . . Many years ago I heard a poem which has stayed with me, by which I have tried to guide my life. It's one of my favorites:

> *I have wept in the night*
> *For the shortness of sight*
> *That to somebody's need made me blind;*
> *But I never have yet*
> *Felt a tinge of regret*
> *For being a little too kind.*

My brothers and sisters, we are surrounded by those in need of our attention, our encouragement, our support, our comfort, our kindness—be they family members, friends, acquaintances, or strangers. We are the Lord's hands here upon the earth, with the mandate to serve and to lift His children. He is dependent upon each of us" (Thomas S. Monson, "What Have I Done for Someone Today?," *Ensign*, November 2009).

Preach My Gospel

"Service," p. 87; Chapter 9: "How Do I Find People to Teach?," pp. 155–74; "Go About Doing Good," pp. 168–70.

Personal Progress

Individual Worth #7—Identify some of your natural gifts and think about how you can use them to serve God and other people (p. 32).

Good Works #4—"Teach a lesson about service in family home evening" (p. 55). Look over the "Good Works" section. See what you have and haven't done, and what you'd like to do next (pp. 53–60).

Duty to God

Study the doctrinal topic of "Service." Record what you learn and share what you learned with your parents or a priesthood leader (see pp. 18–21, 42–45, 66–69).

Look over each section titled "Serve Others" (pp. 26, 50, 74). Work on the one for your age group, or review what you have already done.

Activity

Have everyone write down the names of a few people who have influenced their lives. Invite everyone to share the name of someone they wrote down. Point out that the person's service is what makes him or her memorable. Talk about how each person in the family serves others, and discuss different ways people serve in families, Church, and the community. (Adapted from *Young Women Manual 2*, Lesson 30: "Strengthening Testimony through Service," pp. 112–15.)

Daily Scriptures

Service

Sunday 📖

"I [King Benjamin] say unto you that because I said unto you that I had spent my days in your service, I do not desire to boast, for I have only been in the service of God. And behold, I tell you these things that ye may learn wisdom; that ye may learn that when ye are in the service of your fellow beings ye are only in the service of your God." (Mosiah 2:16–17)

Monday 📖

"Ye are the salt of the earth: but if the salt have lost his savour, wherewith shall it be salted? it is thenceforth good for nothing, but to be cast out, and to be trodden under foot of men. Ye are the light of the world. A city that is set on an hill cannot be hid. Neither do men light a candle, and put it under a bushel, but on a candlestick; and it giveth light unto all that are in the house. Let your light so shine before men, that they may see your good works, and glorify your Father which is in heaven." (Matthew 5:13–16)

Tuesday

"But ye will teach them to walk in the ways of truth and soberness; ye will teach them to love one another, and to serve one another. And also, ye yourselves will succor those that stand in need of your succor; ye will administer of your substance unto him that standeth in need; and ye will not suffer that the beggar putteth up his petition to you in vain, and turn him out to perish." (Mosiah 4:15–16)

Wednesday

"I [Jesus] was an hungred, and ye gave me meat: I was thirsty, and ye gave me drink: I was a stranger, and ye took me in: Naked, and ye clothed me: I was sick, and ye visited me: I was in prison, and ye came unto me. Then shall the righteous answer him, saying, Lord, when saw we thee an hungred, and fed thee? or thirsty, and gave thee drink? When saw we thee a stranger, and took thee in? or naked, and clothed thee? Or when saw we thee sick, or in prison, and came unto thee? And the King shall answer and say unto them, Verily I say unto you, Inasmuch as ye have done it unto one of the least of these my brethren, ye have done it unto me." (Matthew 25:35–40)

Thursday

"Whosoever will be great among you, shall be your minister: And whosoever of you will be the chiefest, shall be servant of all. For even the Son of man came not to be ministered unto, but to minister, and to give his life a ransom for many." (Mark 10:43–45)

Friday

"No man can serve two masters: for either he will hate the one, and love the other; or else he will hold to the one, and despise the other. Ye cannot serve God and mammon." (Matthew 6:24)

Saturday

"By love serve one another." (Galatians 5:13)

Sexual Purity

"Therefore shall a man leave his father and his mother, and shall cleave unto his wife: and they shall be one flesh." (Genesis 2:24) 🄳🄼

Gospel Topic: Chastity
https://goo.gl/Bng4Cj

Music from Children's Songbook & Hymns

- The Lord Gave Me a Temple (*CS*, 153)
- Keep the Commandments (*CS*, 146; *Hymns*, 303)
- Families Can Be Together Forever (*CS*, 188; *Hymns*, 300)
- As Zion's Youth in Latter Days (*Hymns*, 256)

Quote

"We believe in chastity before marriage and total fidelity after marriage. That sums it up. That is the way to happiness in living. That is the way to satisfaction. It brings peace to the heart and peace to the home" (Gordon B. Hinckley, "This Thing Was Not Done in a Corner," *Ensign*, November 1996).

Gospel Topic: Same-Sex Attraction
https://goo.gl/iJDgt3

Scripture Stories

Alma confronts Corianton about the fact that he chose to pursue a harlot and that his example led others to choose unrighteousness. He counsels him to repent, counsel with his faithful brothers, and return to God wholeheartedly (see Alma 39:1–13).

Joseph serves Potiphar as head of the servants. Potiphar's wife pursues him relentlessly trying to get him to "lie with her," or more plainly, to have illicit sex with her (see Genesis 39:7, 12, 14). He consistently refuses and literally runs from her. She falsely accuses him of pursuing her, and Joseph gets thrown in jail (see Genesis 39:1–20).

LDS.org video "Standards: Sexual Purity and Modesty—True Confidence"
https://goo.gl/BUZ7ph

During His Sermon on the Mount, Jesus compares the lower law of sexual purity to the higher law. The law of Moses says to commit no adultery, but in the higher law He teaches not to even think lustful thoughts or allow lust into one's heart (see Matthew 5:27–28; 3 Nephi 12:27–30; D&C 42:22–26).

Gospel Art Pictures

- *Joseph Resists Potiphar's Wife* (#11)
- *The Sermon on the Mount* (#39)
- *Young Couple Going to the Temple* (#120)

Church History

John C. Bennett was the cofounder of Nauvoo, and, at one time, he was a confidant of Joseph Smith. He deceived Joseph and others by presenting himself as a solid and reliable person of character. After Joseph taught him and other close associates about the law of plural marriage, Bennett began seducing married and unmarried women, claiming that illicit sexual relations were approved of if kept secret, and that Joseph and others were engaged in such relationships. He constructed a brothel next to the Nauvoo temple with a large sign that named the place and its purpose. Members were so offended that they put the building on rollers and dumped it in a ditch. Bennett was excommunicated for his blatant lies and lascivious actions. He became furious, left Nauvoo, and vowed for revenge. He had lies about Joseph and the Mormons published. To learn more, see FairMormon's page "John C. Bennett" at http://goo.gl/EgxknX and FairMormon's page "Did Joseph have 'lustful motives' for practicing polygamy?" at http://goo.gl/bQzPD2.

LDS.org video "Law of Chastity"
https://goo.gl/vrjP9x

LDS.org Church News article "Elder Christofferson Says Handbook Changes Regarding Same-Sex Marriages Help Protect Children" Video interview link included as well.
https://goo.gl/X7Nstg

Adaptations for Younger Children

Quote

"We live in a time when the world considers virtue lightly. You young men and women of the Church cannot consider it lightly. . . . I am not asking you to be prudish. I am asking you to be virtuous, and I think there is a vast difference between the two" (Gordon B. Hinckley, "The Body Is Sacred," *New Era*, November 2006).

Lesson from *Behold Your Little Ones*

"I Have a Body like Heavenly Father's" (Lesson 9, pp. 40–43).

Faith in God

Write in your journal how you can serve the Lord as you stand for truth and righteousness and participate in Young Women classes or the deacons quorum. (p. 12). As young men and women in the Church, you will be an example of purity. This will be a great blessing to you and to others.

Activity

Get a treat or some money and tell everyone that it will go to the person who can pick it up off of the floor without bending their legs or falling over. Tell them there are a couple more conditions. They have to have their backs to the wall with their feet touching at the ankles and their heels touching the wall. Have everyone try it. (It's unlikely that anyone can do it.) Tell them that some things are easy to do in certain situations and much harder to do in others. In order to protect your body, wear clothes and make sure to be modest. If anyone asks or tries to touch your body in any way that makes you feel uncomfortable, make sure to tell one of your parents about it even if the person tells you not to. (Adapted from Richard R. Eubank, *Is There An Object to Your Lesson*, p. 81.)

Adaptations for Older Children and Teens

LDS.org video "Should parents just talk about the physical aspect of healthy sexuality?" This video addresses the emotional side of sexuality and its importance. https://goo.gl/GMk7Qk

Quote

"Question: How do we keep bad thoughts from entering our minds, and what do we do when they come?

Answer: Some bad thoughts come by themselves. Others come because we invite them by what we look at and listen to. . . . The mind can think of only one thing at a time. Use that fact to crowd out ugly thoughts. Above all, don't feed thoughts by reading or watching things that are wrong. . . . When you are mature enough to plan seriously for marriage, keep your expressions of feelings to those that are comfortable in the presence of your parents. . . . You know how to be clean. We trust you to do it" (Richard G. Scott, "Making the Right Choices," *Ensign*, November 1994).

Preach My Gospel

"Live the Law of Chastity," p. 77; "Eternal Marriage," pp. 85–86.

Personal Progress

Integrity #1—"Read the pamphlet *For the Strength of Youth*. . . . Write your plan to stay morally clean and worthy to attend the temple" (p. 62).

Virtue #1—"Study the meaning and importance of chastity and virtue" (p. 70).

Duty to God

Study the doctrinal topic of "The Law of Chastity." Record what you learn and share what you learned with your parents or a priesthood leader (see pp. 18–21, 42–45, 66–69).

"Interview a mother, grandmother, sister, or other woman to learn about how to show proper respect to women. Make a plan to apply what you learn" (p. 81). Focus on how to respect young women you are dating or may date in the future.

Activity

Get a treat or some money and tell everyone that it will go to the person who can pick it up off of the floor without bending their legs. Have everyone see if they can bend over and touch the floor without bending their legs or falling over. Tell them there are a couple more conditions. They have to have their backs to the wall with their feet touching at the ankles and their heels touching the wall. Have everyone try it. (It's unlikely that anyone can do it.) Tell them that some things are easy to do in certain situations and much harder to do in others. Guarding your virtue is much easier to do if you put up your own "walls" or boundaries based on the "Sexual Purity" section in the *For the Strength of Youth* pamphlet. Having these "walls" in place will keep dating cleaner, lighter, and more fun. (Adapted from Richard R. Eubank, *Is There An Object to Your Lesson*, p. 81.)

Daily Scriptures

Sexual Purity

Sunday 📖

"Therefore shall a man leave his father and his mother, and shall cleave unto his wife: and they shall be one flesh." (Genesis 2:24)

Monday 📖

"Joseph was a goodly person, and well favoured. And it came to pass after these things, that his master's wife cast her eyes upon Joseph; and she said, Lie with me. But he refused, and said unto his master's wife, Behold, my master wotteth not what is with me in the house, and he hath committed all that he hath to my hand; There is none greater in this house than I; neither hath he kept back any thing from me but thee, because thou art his wife: how then can I do this great wickedness, and sin against God? And it came to pass, as she spake to Joseph day by day, that he hearkened not unto her, to lie by her, or to be with her." (Genesis 39:6–10)

Tuesday 📖

"Repent and forsake your sins, and go no more after the lusts of your eyes, but cross yourself in all these things." (Alma 39:9)

Wednesday 📖

"Flee fornication. Every sin that a man doeth is without the body; but he that committeth fornication sinneth against his own body. What? know ye not that your body is the temple of the Holy Ghost which is in you, which ye have of God, and ye are not your own? For ye are bought with a price: therefore glorify God in your body, and in your spirit, which are God's." (1 Corinthians 6:18–20)

Thursday

"See that ye bridle all your passions, that ye may be filled with love." (Alma 38:12)

Friday 📖

"Whoso forbiddeth to marry is not ordained of God, for marriage is ordained of God unto man. Wherefore, it is lawful that he should have one wife, and they twain shall be one flesh, and all this that the earth might answer the end of its creation; And that it might be filled with the measure of man, according to his creation before the world was made." (D&C 49:15–17)

Saturday

"Hear me, and hearken to the word of the Lord: For there shall not any man among you have save it be one wife; and concubines he shall have none; For I, the Lord God, delight in the chastity of women. And whoredoms are an abomination before me; thus saith the Lord of Hosts. Wherefore, this people shall keep my commandments, saith the Lord of Hosts, or cursed be the land for their sakes." (Jacob 2:27–29)

Tithes and Offerings

"Bring ye all the tithes into the storehouse, that there may be meat in mine house, and prove me now herewith, saith the Lord of hosts, if I will not open you the windows of heaven, and pour you out a blessing, that there shall not be room enough to receive it." (Malachi 3:10) 🔖Ⓜ

Mormonads—Tithes and Offerings
https://goo.gl/HRbAiX

Music from Children's Songbook & Hymns

- I Love to See the Temple (*CS*, 95)
- I'm Glad to Pay a Tithing (*CS*, 150)
- I Want to Give the Lord My Tenth (*CS*, 150)
- "Give," Said the Little Stream (*CS*, 236)
- Because I Have Been Given Much (*Hymns*, 219)

Quote

"Often as we teach and testify about the law of tithing, we emphasize the immediate, dramatic, and readily recognizable temporal blessings that we receive. And surely such blessings do occur. . . . I testify that by your obedience to this law of the Lord, the windows of heaven will be opened to you. . . . I testify spiritual and temporal blessings come into our lives as we live the law of tithing. I bear witness that such blessings often are significant but subtle" (David A. Bednar, "The Windows of Heaven," *Ensign*, November 2013).

Scripture Stories

While in Kirtland, Ohio, the Lord commands the early Saints to build a temple by the use of tithing, which was understood as all free will offerings (see D&C 97:10–16). Later the Lord sets the standard of tithing at 10 percent of one's profit (see D&C 119).

A rich man asks Jesus what he must do to be saved. Jesus tells him to sell all his possessions, give them to the poor, and follow Him. The man grieves. Jesus says it is hard for men *who trust in riches* to enter the kingdom of God, but it is possible with those "who trust in God and leave all for [Christ's] sake" (Joseph Smith Translation, Mark 10:27 [in Mark 10:27, footnote *a*]) (see also Mark 10:17–26).

Gospel Art Pictures

- *Christ and the Rich Young Ruler* (#48)
- *Payment of Tithing* (#113)
- *A Tithe is a Tenth Part* (#114)
- *Kirtland Temple* (#117)

Church History

The Kirtland Temple, "built . . . by the tithing [or free-will offerings] of my people" (D&C 97:11), was dedicated on March 27, 1836. Doctrine and Covenants 109 is the revealed dedicatory prayer for the Kirtland Temple.

When did the Lord command members to start paying tithing, and when did He define it as ten percent of one's annual profit? *On July 8, 1838, Joseph Smith received the revelation recorded in Doctrine and Covenants 119.* In Doctrine and Covenants 119, the Lord stops the requirement to live the law of consecration (which many Saints did not keep). He replaces the law of consecration with the law of tithing and defines "tithing" as "one-tenth of all [Church members'] interest annually" (D&C 119:4). Before this definition, tithing was referred to as any free-will offering (D&C 119, section heading).

On May 17, 1899, in St. George, Utah, President Lorenzo Snow was inspired to emphasize the importance of paying a full tithe and the promised blessings from the Lord if the people would do so (see Malachi 3:8–10; Church History timeline http://goo.gl/KZNJVF). To see a short video clip on this subject, see https://goo.gl/UR9SSA.

LDS.org video "Ministry of Lorenzo Snow: Leading the Church Out of Financial Bondage" https://goo.gl/UR9SSA

Adaptations for Younger Children

Quote

Read this quote that President Hinckley recited as a boy: "What is tithing? I will tell you every time. Ten cents from a dollar, and a penny from a dime" (Gordon B. Hinckley, "Tithing: An Opportunity to Prove Our Faithfulness," *Ensign*, May 1982).

Lesson from *Behold Your Little Ones*

"I Will Share" (Lesson 17, pp. 72–75).

Faith in God

"Pay your tithing and attend tithing settlement" (p. 4).

"Plan and complete your own activity that will help you learn and live the gospel" (p. 7). Practice filling out a tithing slip. Plan a way to earn some money this week, fill out a tithing slip, and turn in your own tithing. Talk about what a tithing settlement is and how paying a full tithe is required for people to gain a temple recommend and attend the temple.

Activity 🕐

Make or buy a pizza for dinner. A pie (or anything else that is round) would work equally well. Alternatively, you can draw a pizza. The pizza represents all your money. Cut the pizza into ten pieces and take one piece out. That piece represents your tithing. Show how much there is left. There is a lot! Giving your tithing before you spend all your money allows you to give tithing and still have lots of money to use. Some people wait to pay tithing and it looks like there will not be much left when they finally pay their tithing. Ask which method the family prefers.

Adaptations for Older Children and Teens

Quotes

"The leaders of the Lord's restored Church feel a tremendous responsibility to care appropriately for the consecrated offerings of Church members. We are keenly aware of the sacred nature of the widow's mite. . . . I know from firsthand experience that the Council on the Disposition of the Tithes is vigilant in caring for the widow's mite. . . . The honest payment of tithing is much more than a duty; it is an important step in the process of personal sanctification. To those of you who pay your tithing, I commend you. To those of you who presently are not obeying the law of tithing, I invite you to consider your ways and repent. I testify that by your obedience to this law of the Lord, the windows of heaven will be opened to you. Please do not procrastinate the day of your repentance" (David A. Bednar, "The Windows of Heaven," *Ensign*, November 2013).

"Pay your tithing as a declaration that possession of material goods and the accumulation of worldly wealth are *not* the uppermost goals of your existence. . . . We should pay [our tithes and offerings] as a personal expression of love to a generous and merciful Father in Heaven" (Jeffrey R. Holland, "Like a Watered Garden," *Ensign*, November 2001, italics in original).

Preach My Gospel

"Keep the Law of Tithing," pp. 78–79; "How to Donate Tithes and Offerings," p. 80.

Personal Progress

Faith #7 or Choice and Accountability #7—Pay a full tithing, which demonstrates faith. Make a budget and include payment of tithes. Ask the Lord to help you notice the blessings you receive by paying your tithing, and write about those blessings in your journal (see pp. 16, 48).

Duty to God

Study the doctrinal topic of "Tithing." Record what you learn and share what you learned with your parents or a priesthood leader (see pp. 18–21, 42–45, 66–69).

"Sample Monthly Budget for Kids" worksheet from MoneyAndStuff.info http://goo.gl/3wGR9t

Activity ☺

Make or buy a pizza for dinner, or you can draw a pizza. The pizza represents all your money. Cut the pizza into ten pieces and take one piece out. That piece represents your tithing. The remaining nine pieces represent the rest of your money. Giving your tithing first allows you to still have lots of money to use. It also shows Heavenly Father that it is a priority for you to keep the commandment of tithing; it demonstrates faith that He will provide for your needs. Some people wait to pay tithing and it looks like there will not be much left when they finally pay their tithing. Ask which method the family prefers. Talk about budgeting in general.

Daily Scriptures

Tithes and Offerings

Sunday 📖

"Will a man rob God? Yet ye have robbed me. But ye say, Wherein have we robbed thee? In tithes and offerings. . . . Bring ye all the tithes into the storehouse, that there may be meat in mine house, and prove me now herewith, saith the Lord of hosts, if I will not open you the windows of heaven, and pour you out a blessing, that there shall not be room enough to receive it." (Malachi 3:8–10)

Monday

"Think of your brethren like unto yourselves, and be familiar with all and free with your substance, that they may be rich like unto you." (Jacob 2:17)

Tuesday

"God loveth a cheerful giver." (2 Corinthians 9:7)

Wednesday

The members of the Church "were liberal to all, both old and young, both bond and free, both male and female, whether out of the church or in the church, having no respect to persons as to those who stood in need." (Alma 1:30)

Thursday

"If God, who has created you, on whom you are dependent for your lives and for all that ye have and are, doth grant unto you whatsoever ye ask that is right, in faith, believing that ye shall receive, O then, how ye ought to impart of the substance that ye have one to another." (Mosiah 4:21)

Friday

Jesus said, "I was an hungred, and ye gave me meat: I was thirsty, and ye gave me drink: I was a stranger, and ye took me in: Naked, and ye clothed me: I was sick, and ye visited me: I was in prison, and ye came unto me. Then shall the righteous answer him, saying, Lord, when saw we thee an hungred, and fed thee? or thirsty, and gave thee drink? When saw we thee a stranger, and took thee in? or naked, and clothed thee? Or when saw we thee sick, or in prison, and came unto thee? And the King shall answer and say unto them, Verily I say unto you, Inasmuch as ye have done it unto one of the least of these my brethren, ye have done it unto me." (Matthew 25:34–40)

Saturday

"Impart of your substance to the poor, every man according to that which he hath, such as feeding the hungry, clothing the naked, visiting the sick and administering to their relief, both spiritually and temporally." (Mosiah 4:26)

Work and Self-Reliance

"Thou shalt not be idle; for he that is idle shall not eat the bread nor wear the garments of the laborer." (D&C 42:42)

Music from Children's Songbook & Hymns

- Go the Second Mile (*CS*, 167)
- When We're Helping (*CS*, 198)
- The Prophet Said to Plant a Garden (*CS*, 237)
- Today, While the Sun Shines (*Hymns*, 229)
- Put Your Shoulder to the Wheel (*Hymns*, 252)

Mormonads—Goals, Work, and Self-Reliance
https://goo.gl/938N7K

Quote

"The Lord's way is not to sit at the side of the stream and wait for the water to pass before we cross. It is to come together, roll up our sleeves, go to work, and build a bridge or a boat to cross the waters of our challenges. . . . We must not turn aside our hearts or our heads from becoming more self-reliant, caring better for the needy, and rendering compassionate service. The temporal is intertwined with the spiritual" (Dieter F. Uchtdorf, "Providing in the Lord's Way," *Ensign*, November 2011).

Scripture Stories

After Joseph of Egypt is put in jail for resisting the advances of Potiphar's wife's, Joseph interprets the Pharaoh's dream that warns about an upcoming famine. Joseph proposes a food storage program. Pharaoh puts Joseph in charge of the program and makes him a ruler in Egypt (see Genesis 39–40, 41:1–49).

Nehemiah goes to Jerusalem to rebuild the city. Enemies try to draw him away and stop the work. Nehemiah responds, "I am doing a great work, so that I cannot come down: why should the work cease, whilst I leave it, and come down to you?" (Nehemiah 6:3) (see also Nehemiah 1–6).

The Lord commands Nephi to build a ship. Nephi asks where he can find materials to make tools. He convinces his rebellious brothers to help. When the ship is finished, they pack their things, including food, provisions, and seeds, and sail to the promised land (see 1 Nephi 17–18).

Gospel Art Pictures

- *Joseph Resists Potiphar's Wife* (#11)
- *Nephi Subdues His Rebellious Brothers* (#70)
- *Lehi and His People Arrive in the Promised Land* (#71)

Church History

When was the Church's welfare program started? *April 1936.* In 1935, Harold B. Lee, then a stake president in his thirties during the Great Depression, was called by the First Presidency to create a welfare system, called the Church Security Plan, to assist the poor and needy in the Church. That day he humbly prayed and received guidance as to how to organize the Church's welfare program. To see a video documentary of the life of Harold B. Lee, go to https://goo.gl/RxFizX.

Harold B. Lee: Documentary
https://goo.gl/RxFizX

The Church's welfare program assists members in difficult circumstances while emphasizing self-reliance. It educates members on how to become self-reliant or connects them with resources that can help them become self-reliant. To see a chronological history of the Church's welfare program, go to the Church News article called "Timeline: A Look Back at the Church Welfare Plan" at http://goo.gl/pMngS4. To read a talk on the Welfare Program, see Dieter F. Uchtdorf's article, "Providing in the Lord's Way," found in the November 2011 *Ensign*.

In 2016, the Church announced a program called "I Was A Stranger" (Linda K. Burton, "I Was a Stranger," *Ensign*, May 2016. See also Patrick Kearon, "Refuge from the Storm," *Ensign*, May 2016). This program assists members in helping refugees from war-torn areas. Learn more about this at IWasAStranger.LDS.org.

I Was A Stranger is a relief effort that assists members in helping refugees from war-torn area.
IWasAStranger.LDS.org

Adaptations for Younger Children

Quote

"Children, please listen to me because there are some simple things you can do to help. . . . You can pick up your toys when you are finished playing with them, and when you get a little older, you can make your bed, help with the dishes, and do other chores—without being asked. . . . [I] add my testimony, along with all of the others, that Jesus is the Christ and this is His Church. We are doing His work" (M. Russell Ballard, "Daughters of God," *Ensign*, May 2008).

Lesson from *Behold Your Little Ones*

"I Will Follow the Prophet" (Lesson 24, pp. 100–103).

Faith in God

"Sample Monthly Budget for Kids" worksheet from MoneyAndStuff.info
http://goo.gl/3wGR9t

"Learn how to budget and save money. Discuss why it is important to faithfully pay our tithing and how Heavenly Father blesses us when we do (see 3 Nephi 24:10–11). Pay your tithing and begin saving for a mission" (p. 10). For a simple budgeting sheet, go to http://goo.gl/3wGR9t.

"List five things you can do to help around your home. Discuss the importance of obeying and honoring your parents and learning how to work" (p. 11).

Activity

Parents, talk about what you do for work and what your parents do for work. Talk about your family's food storage and self-reliance plans. Ask your kids what kind of work interests them.

Adaptations for Older Children and Teens

Quotes

"The Lord's way is not to sit at the side of the stream and wait for the water to pass before we cross. It is to come together, roll up our sleeves, go to work, and build a bridge or a boat to cross the waters of our challenges" (Dieter F. Uchtdorf, "Providing in the Lord's Way," *Ensign*, November 2011).

"How I admire men, women, and children who know how to work! How the Lord loves the laborer! . . . Those who are unafraid to roll up their sleeves and lose themselves in the pursuit of worthwhile goals are a blessing to their families, communities, nations, and to the Church. . . . Work is an antidote for anxiety, an ointment for sorrow, and a doorway to possibility. Whatever our circumstances in life, my dear brethren, let us do the best we can and cultivate a reputation for excellence in all that we do. Let us set our minds and bodies to the glorious opportunity for work that each new day presents. . . . I pray that during the coming months and years we can fill our hours and days with righteous work" (Dieter F. Uchtdorf, "Two Principles for any Economy," *Ensign*, November 2009).

Preach My Gospel

"Diligence," pp. 121–22; Chapter 10: "How Can I Improve My Teaching Skills?," pp. 175–94.

Personal Progress

Knowledge #5—"Learn about an area of work . . . that interests you" (p. 39).

Good Works #5—Read and apply Doctrine and Covenants 58:26–28. An idea for the service required for this experience is to help your parents inventory your food and home storage (p. 55).

Duty to God

"Learn about occupations or careers that interest you. . . . If you have income, develop and follow a personal savings and spending plan" (p. 57).

Activity

Gather and display several portable tools and talk about the use of each one. Would it work well to use a screwdriver to pound a nail into wood? Would it work well use a hammer to kill a fly? Would it work well to use a saw to cut paper? Of course not! We are each made by our Heavenly Father for our specific mission; it's important to know what we were made to do in order to be the best instrument in His hands that we can be. It's also important not to try to make ourselves into something else. Think about your gifts and talents and how you can use them in your life's work to best serve God and His children.

Daily Scriptures

Work and Self-Reliance

Sunday

"Thou shalt not be idle; for he that is idle shall not eat the bread nor wear the garments of the laborer." (D&C 42:42)

Monday

"Cease to be idle; cease to be unclean; cease to find fault one with another; cease to sleep longer than is needful; retire to thy bed early, that ye may not be weary; arise early, that your bodies and your minds may be invigorated." (D&C 88:124)

Tuesday

"Go to the ant, thou sluggard; consider her ways, and be wise: Which having no guide, overseer, or ruler, Provideth her meat in the summer, and gathereth her food in the harvest." (Proverbs 6:6–8)

Wednesday

"In all labour there is profit: but the talk of the lips tendeth only to penury." (Proverbs 14:23)

Thursday

"It came to pass that [the Nephites] began to prosper exceedingly, and to multiply in the land. And I did teach my people to build buildings, and to work in all manner of wood, and of iron, and of copper, and of brass, and of steel, and of gold, and of silver, and of precious ores, which were in great abundance. And I, Nephi, did build a temple . . . and the workmanship thereof was exceedingly fine. And it came to pass that I, Nephi, did cause my people to be industrious, and to labor with their hands." (2 Nephi 5:13, 15–17)

Friday

The people of Alma "fled [from King Noah's army for] eight days' journey into the wilderness. And they came to a land, yea, even a very beautiful and pleasant land, a land of pure water. And they pitched their tents, and began to till the ground, and began to build buildings; yea, they were industrious, and did labor exceedingly." (Mosiah 23:3–5)

Saturday

"For behold, it is not meet that I should command in all things; for he that is compelled in all things, the same is a slothful and not a wise servant; wherefore he receiveth no reward. Verily I say, men should be anxiously engaged in a good cause, and do many things of their own free will, and bring to pass much righteousness; For the power is in them, wherein they are agents unto themselves. And inasmuch as men do good they shall in nowise lose their reward." (D&C 58:26–28)

Go Forward with Faith

"I can do all things through Christ which strengtheneth me." (Philippians 4:13)

Mormonads—Faith,
Testimony, and Spirituality
https://goo.gl/U7yXhY

Music from Children's Songbook & Hymns

- Nephi's Courage (*CS*, 120)
- Dare to Do Right (*CS*, 158)
- Choose the Right (*Hymns*, 239)
- I'll Go Where You Want Me to Go (*Hymns*, 270)

Quote

"Men and women who turn their lives over to God will discover that He can make a lot more out of their lives than they can. He will deepen their joys, expand their vision, quicken their minds, strengthen their muscles, lift their spirits, multiply their blessings, increase their opportunities, comfort their souls, raise up friends, and pour out peace. Whoever will lose his life in the service of God will find eternal life" (Ezra Taft Benson, *Teachings of Presidents of the Church: Ezra Taft Benson*, 42–43).

Scripture Stories

Jacob gives his sons patriarchal blessings (see Genesis 48:14–Genesis 49).

Nephi demonstrates great faith. He gets the brass plates, sees his father's dream, makes a new bow when his breaks and is able to get food, and leads the construction of a ship (see 1 Nephi 3–4; 1 Nephi 10:17–1 Nephi 14; 1 Nephi 16:18–32; 1 Nephi 17–18:4).

Mormon abridges and compiles records through the promptings of the Spirit (see Words of Mormon 1:1–11; 3 Nephi 5:9–18).

In a variety of ways, Joseph Smith exercises faith and acts. He ponders which church to join, prays and speaks with God the Father and Jesus Christ, speaks with Moroni, receives the gold plates, translates the Book of Mormon, and receives the priesthood (see Joseph Smith—History).

Gospel Art Pictures

- *Jacob Blessing His Sons* (#12)
- *Lehi and His People Arrive in the Promised Land* (#71)
- *Mormon Abridging the Plates* (#73)
- *Brother Joseph* (#87)

Church History

Who was the first Patriarch to the Church? *Joseph Smith, Sr., father of the Prophet Joseph Smith.* He was ordained as the first Patriarch to the Church in the latter days on December 18, 1833. (*Teachings of Presidents of the Church: Joseph Smith*, xviii)

On June 27, 1839, exactly five years before his death, Joseph Smith taught about patriarchs.

> "An evangelist is a Patriarch. . . . Wherever the Church of Christ is established in the earth, there should be a Patriarch for the benefit of the posterity of the Saints, as it was with Jacob in giving his patriarchal blessing unto his sons." (*Teachings of Presidents of the Church: Joseph Smith*, 140)

To learn more about patriarchal blessings, go to https://goo.gl /FHyWGN. To watch James E. Faust talking about the declaration of lineage in patriarchal blessings, go to https://goo.gl/xzqECe.

LDS.org video "Declaration of Lineage in Patriarchal Blessings" https://goo.gl/xzqECe

Gospel Topic: Patriarchal Blessings https://goo.gl/FHyWGN

Adaptations for Younger Children

Quote

"I am a child of God. I know Heavenly Father loves me, and I love Him. I can pray to Heavenly Father anytime, anywhere. I am trying to remember and follow Jesus Christ" ("My Gospel Standards").

Lesson from *Behold Your Little Ones*

"I Will Obey" (Lesson 14, pp. 60–63).

Faith in God

"Pray daily to Heavenly Father" (p. 4).

"Give a family home evening lesson on Joseph Smith's First Vision (see Joseph Smith—History 1:1–20). Discuss how Heavenly Father answers our sincere prayers" (p. 6).

"Mark these verses about the Holy Ghost in your scriptures: John 14:16–17, 2 Nephi 32:5, and Moroni 10:5. Discuss ways the Holy Ghost helps you" (p. 6).

Activity

Tell or act out the story of Lehi's family leaving Jerusalem and going to the promised land (1 Nephi–2 Nephi 4:12). The family's journey, and many things they do on their journey, shows how they go forward with faith. You can do an overview of the whole journey or you can focus in on one of these stories: Nephi and his brothers going to get the plates (see 1 Nephi 3–4), traveling through the wilderness with the Liahona (see 1 Nephi 16:10–16, 28), dealing with the loss of hunting bows (see 1 Nephi 16:14–31), building the boat (see 1 Nephi 17:7–1 Nephi 18:5), or starting out in the promised land (see 1 Nephi 18:23–25).

Briefly introduce patriarchal blessings as special blessings people receive to help guide their lives.

Adaptations for Older Children and Teens

President Uchtdorf has a handwritten note to the youth on his Facebook page. To see "A note from me to you about faith," go to https://goo.gl/nyWt7x

Quotes

"Firmly determine the direction in which you will face—toward the Lord—and then let the secular spinmeisters do their thing. Your hearts and your heads will not be turned by their ceaseless and clever spinning, however they may try. And try they will! You must determine the direction in which you face" (Neal A. Maxwell, "Jesus, the Perfect Mentor," *Ensign*, February 2001).

"Do not become sidetracked by the wiles of Satan that seem so rampant in our era. Then as now we have critics. We even have those inside the Church who seem to delight in looking for every element of weakness in the past or the present. Rather, let us go forward with faith and with the vision of the great and marvelous future that lies ahead as this work grows in strength and gains in momentum. Build faith in the hearts of all those around you" (Gordon B. Hinckley, "Go Forward With Faith," *Ensign*, August 1986).

Preach My Gospel

"Endure to the End," p. 66; "Key Definitions: Endure to the End," p. 70; Chapter 9: "How Do I Find People to Teach?," pp. 155–74.

Personal Progress

Faith #1—Study the topic of "Faith," read conference talks about it, and pray morning and night (p. 14).

Individual Worth #2—Getting and reading your patriarchal blessing can be a great source of strength as you "go forward with faith" in your life (p. 30).

Individual Worth #4—Write down hopes and dreams for the future as well as a plan to work toward those goals with faith (p. 31).

Duty to God

"The Duty to God program is a tool to help Aaronic Priesthood holders strengthen their testimony and their relationship with Heavenly Father" (p. 94). It is designed to help you go forward with faith. Review what you have done in the program and what you plan to do next.

Activity ☺

Take a quick look at the paper cutting instructions on page 235 of the appendix and make sure you know how to cut the paper properly. When you're ready for the activity, set a pile of paper and some scissors on a table and ask how someone could cut one piece of paper and make a hole large enough for a person to climb through. Try any suggestions offered, then ask if they believe it can actually be done or not. Cut the paper and let everyone take a turn climbing through. Tell your family that the Lord never tells us to do things that are impossible; we can trust that He knows how to accomplish all things. (Adapted from Richard R. Eubank, *Is There an Object to Your Lesson?*, 54.)

Discuss what patriarchal blessings are and how they can help people go forward with faith.

Daily Scriptures

Go Forward with Faith

Sunday

"I can do all things through Christ which strengtheneth me." (Philippians 4:13)

Monday 📖M

"Now we beseech you, brethren, by the coming of our Lord Jesus Christ, and by our gathering together unto him, That ye be not soon shaken in mind, or be troubled, neither by spirit, nor by word, nor by letter as from us, as that the day of Christ is at hand. Let no man deceive you by any means: for that day shall not come, except there come a falling away first, and that man of sin be revealed, the son of perdition." (2 Thessalonians 2:1–3)

Tuesday 📖M

"Your faith should not stand in the wisdom of men, but in the power of God. But God hath revealed them unto us by his Spirit: for the Spirit searcheth all things, yea, the deep things of God. For what man knoweth the things of a man, save the spirit of man which is in him? even so the things of God knoweth no man, but the Spirit of God." (1 Corinthians 2:5, 10–11)

Wednesday 📖M

"Faith, if it hath not works, is dead, being alone. Yea, a man may say, Thou hast faith, and I have works: shew me thy faith without thy works, and I will shew thee my faith by my works." (James 2:17–18)

Thursday

"Faith is the substance of things hoped for, the evidence of things not seen. By faith Noah, being warned of God of things not seen as yet, . . . prepared an ark to the saving of his house. . . . Through faith also Sara herself received strength to conceive seed, and was delivered of a child when she was past age. . . . By faith Moses, when he was born, was hid three months of his parents . . . and they were not afraid of the king's commandment. By faith [Moses] forsook Egypt, not fearing the wrath of the king. . . . He kept the passover, . . . [and the Israelites] passed through the Red sea as by dry land. . . . By faith the walls of Jericho fell down. . . . These all, [have] obtained a good report through faith." (Hebrews 11:1, 7, 11, 23, 27–29, 30, 39)

Friday 📖M

"I will go and do the things which the Lord hath commanded, for I know that the Lord giveth no commandments unto the children of men, save he shall prepare a way for them that they may accomplish the thing which he commandeth them." (1 Nephi 3:7)

Saturday 📖M

"Trust in the Lord with all thine heart; and lean not unto thine own understanding. In all thy ways acknowledge him, and he shall direct thy paths." (Proverbs 3:5–6)

The First Great Commandment: Love God

*"The love of God . . . is the most desirable of all things. . . .
Yea, and the most joyous to the soul." (1 Nephi 11:22–23)*

LDS.org video "The First Great Commandment" with Elder Holland
https://goo.gl/7aRoUp

LDS.org video and transcript of President Uchtdorf's conference talk, "The Love of God."
https://goo.gl/ZTpb69

Music from *Children's Songbook* & *Hymns*

- I Feel My Savior's Love (*CS*, 74)
- My Heavenly Father Loves Me (*CS*, 228)
- I Am a Child of God (*CS*, 2; *Hymns* 301)
- God Is Love (*Hymns*, 87)
- Our Savior's Love (*Hymns*, 113)

Quote

"When asked to name the greatest commandment, [Jesus] did not hesitate. 'Thou shalt love the Lord thy God with all thy heart, and with all thy soul, and with all thy mind,' He said. 'This is the first and great commandment.' . . . What we love determines what we seek. What we seek determines what we think and do. What we think and do determines who we are—and who we will become. . . . Let us be known as a people who love God with all our heart, soul, and mind and who love our neighbor as ourselves" (Dieter F. Uchtdorf, "The Love of God," *Ensign*, November 2009).

Scripture Stories

In an attempt to trick Jesus, a lawyer asks Him what the greatest commandment of the law is. Jesus answers that the first great commandment is to love God (see Matthew 22:33–38).

Nephi sees the same vision his father saw and understands that the tree of life represents the love of God, which is the most joyous thing to the human soul (see 1 Nephi 11:21–23).

After Jesus visited the Nephites, the people were all converted. They were blessed, happy, and experienced "no contention in the land, because of the love of God which did dwell in the hearts of the people" (4 Nephi 1:15) (see also 4 Nephi 1:1–18).

Gospel Art Pictures

- *Lehi's Dream* (#69)
- *Jesus Teaching in the Western Hemisphere* (#82)

Church History

President Ezra Taft Benson was sustained as the President of the Church in November 1985 and served as such until his death on May 30, 1994. Among other things, he preached putting God first in our lives, the power of the Book of Mormon, and patriotism. As a member of United States President Eisenhower's cabinet, he started every meeting he conducted with prayer. He also made difficult decisions based on what was right, not what was popular. He regularly called people to repentance and humility. He was a powerful example of putting God first.

LDS.org video "Put God First" with President Benson
https://goo.gl/H9yFVG

Gordon B. Hinckley was ordained and set apart as the fifteenth President of the Church on March 12, 1995. His life is a great example of going forward with complete faith in the Lord. His wife, Marjorie, sensed his devotion to the Lord when they were dating. She said, "As we got closer to marriage, I felt completely confident that Gordon loved me. But I also knew somehow that I would never come first with him. I knew I was going to be second in his life and that the Lord was going to be first. And that was okay. . . . It seemed to me that if you understood the gospel and the purpose of our being here, you would want a husband who put the Lord first." (Sheri L. Dew, *Go Forward with Faith: The Biography of Gordon B. Hinckley*, 114–15)

Gordon B. Hinckley: Documentary
https://goo.gl/7WNV2h

Adaptations for Younger Children

Quote

"I am a child of God. I know Heavenly Father loves me, and I love Him. I can pray to Heavenly Father anytime, anywhere. I am trying to remember and follow Jesus Christ" ("My Gospel Standards").

Lesson from *Behold Your Little Ones*

"Heavenly Father and Jesus Christ Love Me" (Lesson 4, pp. 20–23).

Faith in God

Read and discuss the "My Gospel Standards" quote (above) and the First Presidency letter in the *Faith in God* booklet (p. 1).

Activity ☺

Get two blank pieces of paper for each family member. Fold each set of two papers lengthwise to make a simple book. Staple the folded sides of the book. Write "Heavenly Father Loves Me and I Love Him" on the cover. Have everyone draw things in their books that show that God loves them. Write a description under the drawing. For example, "When I pray, I feel God's love for me. When I look at beautiful things like birds, butterflies, flowers, and the sky, I feel God's love for me. When I hug my family and friends, I feel God's love for me. I know God loves me because He gave me my family." Then have them draw things they do to show God that they love Him. For example, "I love Heavenly Father because He gives me many blessings and helps me feel His love." If you have babies, show them a picture book of beautiful creations like flowers or animals, and tell them that God loves them.

Adaptations for Older Children and Teens

Quotes

"God the Eternal Father did not give that first great commandment because He needs us to love Him. His power and glory are not diminished should we disregard, deny, or even defile His name. His influence and dominion extend through time and space independent of our acceptance, approval, or admiration. No, God does not need us to love Him. But oh, how we need to love God! For what we love determines what we seek. What we seek determines what we think and do. What we think and do determines who we are—and who we will become" (Dieter F. Uchtdorf, "The Love of God," *Ensign*, November 2009).

"How might we fulfill today the first part of the divine commandment to love the Lord our God? The Lord declared: 'He that hath my commandments, and keepeth them, he it is that loveth me'; 'Come, follow me'; 'I have set an example for you'; 'I am the light which ye shall hold up—that which ye have seen me do.' What, indeed, did He do? . . . The Savior's entire ministry exemplified love of neighbor, the second part of that lesson given to the inquiring lawyer—spoken of as the 'royal law' [James 2:8]" (Thomas S. Monson, "The Way of the Master," *Ensign*, May 1996).

Preach My Gospel

"Pray Often," p. 73; Chapter 5: "What Is the Role of the Book of Mormon?," 103–14; "The Book of Mormon Draws People Nearer to God," p. 108.‐

Personal Progress

Review your *Personal Progress* book. Read "What Do I Do When I Complete Personal Progress?" (pp. 83–84). Write in your journal about how Personal Progress has helped you love God more.

Duty to God

"The purpose of this book is to help you strengthen your testimony and your relationship with God" (p. 7). Review the "Spiritual Strength" section for your age group. See how you are doing in developing habits and studying doctrinal topics that increase your love for God (see pp. 13–21, 37–45, 61–69)

Activity ⏲

Get a clear jar, water, sand (optional), small rocks, and larger rocks. Show that if you put the water, sand, and smaller rocks in first, there will not be room for the largest rocks. Then, show that by putting the largest things in first and then the smaller things (in order of largest to smallest), you are able to fit more in the jar. Talk about priorities. When we put the most important things first, like prayer, scripture study, and family time, then the less important things mostly still fit. You will always have to decide what is most important and what you don't really need to fit into your life. Have everyone think about the things they are trying to fit into their lives. Are you putting God and the most important things first? Are there things that would be good to let go of for a while?

Daily Scriptures

The First Great Commandment: Love God

Sunday

"I know that [God] loveth his children. . . . The love of God . . . is the most desirable above of all things. . . . Yea, and the most joyous to the soul." (1 Nephi 11:17, 22–23)

Monday

"No man can serve two masters: for either he will hate the one, and love the other; or else he will hold to the one, and despise the other. Ye cannot serve God and mammon." (Matthew 6:24)

Tuesday

"Learn of me, and listen to my words; walk in the meekness of my Spirit, and you shall have peace in me. I am Jesus Christ; I came by the will of the Father, and I do his will. . . . I command thee that thou shalt pray vocally as well as in thy heart; yea, before the world as well as in secret, in public as well as in private. Pray always, and I will pour out my Spirit upon you, and great shall be your blessing." (D&C 19:23–24, 28, 38)

Wednesday 📖

"Trust in the Lord with all thine heart; and lean not unto thine own understanding. In all thy ways acknowledge him, and he shall direct thy paths." (Proverbs 3:5–6)

Thursday 📖

"If ye love me, keep my commandments. And I will pray the Father, and he shall give you another Comforter, that he may abide with you for ever; Even the Spirit of truth. . . . He that hath my commandments, and keepeth them, he it is that loveth me: and he that loveth me shall be loved of my Father, and I will love him, and will manifest myself to him." (John 14:15–17, 21)

Friday

"We know that there is a God in heaven, who is infinite and eternal, from everlasting to everlasting the same unchangeable God, the framer of heaven and earth, and all things which are in them; And that he created man, male and female, after his own image and in his own likeness, created he them; And gave unto them commandments that they should love and serve him, the only living and true God, and that he should be the only being whom they should worship." (D&C 20:17–19)

Saturday

"O love the Lord, all ye his saints: for the Lord preserveth the faithful, and plentifully rewardeth the proud doer. Be of good courage, and he shall strengthen your heart, all ye that hope in the Lord." (Psalm 31:23–24)

The Second Great Commandment: Love Others

"A lawyer, asked [Jesus] a question, tempting him, and saying, Master, which is the great commandment in the law? Jesus said unto him, Thou shalt love the Lord thy God with all thy heart, and with all thy soul, and with all thy mind. This is the first and great commandment. And the second is like unto it, Thou shalt love thy neighbour as thyself." (Matthew 22:35–39) 🔲

Music from Children's Songbook & Hymns

- I'm Trying to Be like Jesus (*CS*, 78)
- I'll Walk with You (*CS*, 140)
- Lord, I Would Follow Thee (*Hymns*, 220)
- Love One Another (*Hymns*, 308)

Short LDS.org video of Elder Nelson. Titled "Love Your Neighbor." https://goo.gl/YYoaZH

Quote

"Because love is the great commandment, it ought to be at the *center* of all and everything we do in our own family, in our Church callings, and in our livelihood. Love is the healing balm that repairs rifts in personal and family relationships. It is the bond that unites families, communities, and nations. Love is the power that initiates friendship, tolerance, civility, and respect. It is the source that overcomes divisiveness and hate. Love is the fire that warms our lives with unparalleled joy and divine hope. Love should be our walk and our talk" (Dieter F. Uchtdorf, "The Love of God," *Ensign*, November 2009).

Scripture Stories

Jesus tells the story of the good Samaritan who helps a man on the road that had been robbed and left for dead. The Samaritan treats his wounds, takes him to an inn, pays for his stay and doctoring, and promises to pay any other expenses. Through this story, Jesus tells the listening Jews (who hate Samaritans) to serve people regardless of their nationality (see Luke 10:25–37).

Jesus washes His disciples' feet prior to the Last Supper. Peter objects, but Jesus tells Him he does not understand. He says, "Ye call me Master and Lord: and ye say well; for so I am. If I then, your Lord and Master, have washed your feet; ye also ought to wash one another's feet. For I have given you an example, that ye should do as I have done to you" (John 13:13–15).

Gospel Art Pictures

- *The Good Samaritan* (#44)
- *Jesus Washing the Apostles' Feet* (#55)

Church History

George Albert Smith became President of the Church on May 21, 1945, just months after World War II ended. Thousands of people were homeless, starving, and suffering in Europe in the aftermath of the war. Of this time, Gordon B. Hinckley said,

LDS.org video "Ministry of George Albert Smith: Love for His Fellowmen" http://goo.gl/YHfUfR

> President Smith went to see the president of the United States, Harry Truman. He asked for transportation to get foodstuffs and clothing to those in need. President Truman asked President Smith where he would get these resources. President Smith replied that the Church operated production projects under a welfare program and that women of the Relief Society had saved wheat. The shelves of our storehouses were well stocked and our granaries were filled. This had come of the prophetic foresight of Church leaders. . . . I was among those who worked nights at Welfare Square here in Salt Lake City loading commodities onto railcars which moved the food to the port from which it was shipped across the sea. During the time of the Swiss Temple dedication [in 1955], when many of the Saints of Germany came to the temple, I heard some of them, with tears running down their cheeks, speak with appreciation for that food which had saved their lives. ("Believe His Prophets," *Ensign*, May 1992)

George Albert Smith: Documentary http://goo.gl/kq9fcr

Adaptations for Younger Children

Quote

"I will seek good friends and treat others kindly" ("My Gospel Standards").

Lesson from *Behold Your Little Ones*

"I Will Love Others" (Lesson 18, pp. 76–79).

Faith in God

"Plan or complete your own activity to serve others" (p. 9). Sing or read the lyrics to the song "I'll Walk With You" (*Children's Songbook*, 140). Talk about people you know that may need extra love and attention, like people who just moved in, people who have a sick family member, people with physical or mental challenges, or people who feel left out. Talk about how you can appropriately reach out to these people. Parents, encourage your children to pray for their classmates or friends who need help. Ask your children about these friends occasionally.

Activity ⊕

Get some paper and scissors. Have everyone cut out at least one heart. Brainstorm ways to show love for other people. Write one idea on each paper heart, and tape the hearts in a visible place. Then have each person pick someone they would like to show love for, and write that person's name and some ideas for how to show love for that person on a separate piece of paper. Ask if anyone would like help achieving their ideas. If desired, cut out more paper hearts and tape them around your house as a reminder to show love to each other. (Adapted from *Family Home Evening Resource Book*, Lesson 23: Loving Our Neighbors, pp. 98–101.)

Adaptations for Older Children and Teens

Quotes

"What a happy world it would be if men everywhere recognized their fellowmen as brothers and sisters, and then followed that up by loving their neighbors as themselves" (George Albert Smith, *Teachings of Presidents of the Church: George Albert Smith*, "Love Thy Neighbor As Thyself," p. 14).

"Jesus declared that a day of judgment would come. All individuals will give an account of their mortal lives and of how they have treated other people. The commandments to love God and neighbor are interrelated. We cannot fully love God without loving our neighbor. We cannot fully love our neighbor without loving God. Men really are brothers because God really is our Father. (Russell M. Nelson, "Blessed are the Peacemakers," *Ensign*, November 2002).

"In a hundred small ways, all of you wear the mantle of charity. Life is perfect for none of us. Rather than being judgmental and critical of each other, may we have the pure love of Christ for our fellow travelers in this journey through life. May we recognize that each one is doing her best to deal with the challenges which come her way, and may we strive to do *our* best to help out" (Thomas S. Monson, "Charity Never Faileth," Ensign, November 2010; italics in original).

Preach My Gospel

Chapter 2: "How Do I Study Effectively and Prepare to Teach?," pp. 17–28; "Service," p. 87; "Charity and Love," p. 118.

Personal Progress

Good Works #6—"Spend at least three hours giving service outside your family. Ask your ward or branch Relief Society president or a community leader for suggestions for service. . . . Record in your journal the reactions of the person you served and possible goals for future service opportunities" (p. 55).

Duty to God

"Write your answers to the following questions, and share them with your parents or quorum members: 1. How is your priesthood service different when you love those you serve? 2. What experiences have you had in which someone showed Christlike love for you? 3. How can you show your love for family members and others?" (pp. 79–80).

Activity ☺

Get some paper, scissors, and crayons. Have everyone color the paper different colors and then cut several hearts out of each sheet of paper. Put the colored hearts in a bowl. Tell everyone that throughout the week, when they do some secret act of service for someone else to get a heart from the bowl and put it on or nearby the place of service. For example, if you make someone's bed, put a heart on the pillow. If you do someone's vacuuming job, tape a heart to the vacuum.

Daily Scriptures

The Second Great Commandment: Love Others

Sunday 📖

"A lawyer, asked [Jesus] a question, tempting him, and saying, Master, which is the great commandment in the law? Jesus said unto him, Thou shalt love the Lord thy God with all thy heart, and with all thy soul, and with all thy mind. This is the first and great commandment. And the second is like unto it, Thou shalt love thy neighbour as thyself." (Matthew 22:35–39)

Monday

"As the Father hath loved me, so have I loved you: continue ye in my love. If ye keep my commandments, ye shall abide in my love; even as I have kept my Father's commandments, and abide in his love. These things have I spoken unto you, that my joy might remain in you, and that your joy might be full. This is my commandment, That ye love one another, as I have loved you." (John 15:9–12)

Tuesday 📖

"And behold, I tell you these things that ye may learn wisdom; that ye may learn that when ye are in the service of your fellow beings ye are only in the service of your God." (Mosiah 2:17)

Wednesday 📖

"And charity suffereth long, and is kind, and envieth not, and is not puffed up, seeketh not her own, is not easily provoked, thinketh no evil, and rejoiceth not in iniquity but rejoiceth in the truth, beareth all things, believeth all things, hopeth all things, endureth all things. . . . Charity never faileth. Wherefore, cleave unto charity, which is the greatest of all." (Moroni 7:45–46)

Thursday 📖

"All things must fail—But charity is the pure love of Christ, and it endureth forever; and whoso is found possessed of it at the last day, it shall be well with him. Wherefore, my beloved brethren, pray unto the Father with all the energy of heart, that ye may be filled with this love, which he hath bestowed upon all who are true followers of his Son, Jesus Christ; that ye may become the sons of God; that when he shall appear we shall be like him, for we shall see him as he is; that we may have this hope; that we may be purified even as he is pure. Amen." (Moroni 7:46–48)

Friday

"Thou shalt not hate thy brother in thine heart. . . . Thou shalt not avenge, nor bear any grudge against the children of thy people, but thou shalt love thy neighbour as thyself." (Leviticus 19:17–18)

Saturday

"Ye have been called unto liberty; only use not liberty for an occasion to the flesh, but by love serve one another. For all the law is fulfilled in one word, even in this; Thou shalt love thy neighbour as thyself." (Galatians 5:13–14)

The Ten Commandments

"I will go and do the things which the Lord hath commanded." (1 Nephi 3:7)

Music from *Children's Songbook* & *Hymns*

- The Commandments (*CS*, 112)
- Nephi's Courage (*CS*, 120)
- Keep the Commandments (*CS*, 146 or *Hymns*, 303)
- How Gentle God's Commands (*Hymns*, 125)

Quote

LDS.org video of President Monson's conference talk "Stand in Holy Places". Confirms that the Ten Commandments are still God's commandments, not "creative suggestions" http://goo.gl/AYRory

"Although the world has changed, the laws of God remain constant. They have not changed; they will not change. The Ten Commandments are just that—commandments. They are *not* suggestions. They are every bit as requisite today as they were when God gave them to the children of Israel" (Thomas S. Monson, "Stand in Holy Places," *Ensign*, November 2011, italics in original).

Scripture Stories

Moses receives the Ten Commandments (see Exodus 19–20).

Elijah teaches people to worship Jehovah and not the false god Baal. He invites the priests of Baal to pray to their god to show forth his power by sending fire to an altar prepared with an animal sacrifice. They accept the challenge, but when they pray to the false god, Baal is silent. Elijah then prepares an altar with an animal sacrifice, douses it with water three times and fills a moat around the altar with water. He then calls on Jehovah to send fire. Jehovah does and there is no animal sacrifice or water left when the fire goes out (see 1 Kings 18:17–39).

Abinadi reviews the Ten Commandments while in chains before King Noah and his wicked priests. They try to stop him after the second commandment, but he defies them and says his mission is not complete. He finishes preaching to them about the Ten Commandments (see Mosiah 12:31–13:24).

The Lord reviews the commandments in Doctrine and Covenants 42:18–28.

Gospel Art Pictures

- *The Ten Commandments* (#14)
- *Elijah Contends against the Priests of Baal* (#20)
- *Abinadi before King Noah* (#75)

Church History

On December 30, 1973, Spencer W. Kimball became the President of the Church. In the '60s and '70s (during the hippie era), "free love" became a popular idea, with people preaching that chastity was out-of-date and unnecessary. The media began portraying more and more people being immoral, yet enjoying positive consequences for their immoral actions. President Kimball spoke out against breaking the Lord's law of chastity as given in the eighth commandment.

LDS.org video "Obedience to the Ten Commandments" with Elder Perry
https://goo.gl/7sceUg

President Kimball also plainly taught the second commandment, "Thou shalt have no other gods before me," and the fourth commandment, "Thou shalt keep the Sabbath day holy." People were starting to turn away from religion to pursue power, pleasure, and wealth at the expense of their families and spiritual lives, which concerned President Kimball greatly. To learn more about his teachings on these subjects, see *Teachings of Presidents of the Church: Spencer W. Kimball*, 145–54, 165–88. To hear L. Tom Perry talk about the importance of keeping the Ten Commandments, go to https://goo.gl/7sceUg.

Adaptations for Younger Children

Quote

"I will choose the right" ("My Gospel Standards").

Lesson from *Behold Your Little Ones*

"I Will Obey" (Lesson 14, pp. 60–63).

Faith in God

"Keep the commandments and live 'My Gospel Standards'" (4).

"Read a recent conference address given by the prophet. Decide what you can do to follow the prophet, and do it" (p. 6). President Monson gave a conference talk in October 2011 called "Stand in Holy Places" that reviews the Ten Commandments.

Activity ⏲

Teach memory tricks to help your children remember each of the Ten Commandments. For ideas, see "Memory Tips and Tricks for The Ten Commandments" in the appendix (p. 231).

Explain the blessings of having boundaries. Draw a fenced field with some animals in it, or get out some animal toys and something for a fence. As long as the animals are in the fence, they are safe and can be fed and watered. If they get out, they can get hurt or hungry. Some might even die. Having good moral boundaries such as the Ten Commandments is a great blessing.

God gives us boundaries called commandments to strengthen and protect us spiritually. When we are obedient and stay within those boundaries, we can be safer and happier. If you have a fenced yard or playground nearby, go outside, point out the fence, and then play inside the fenced area.

Adaptations for Older Children and Teens

Quotes

"I recently read in the *Wall Street Journal* an article by Jonathan Sacks, Britain's chief rabbi. Among other things, he writes: 'In virtually every Western society in the 1960s there was a moral revolution, an abandonment of its entire traditional ethic of self-restraint. All you need, sang the Beatles, is love. The Judeo-Christian moral code was jettisoned. In its place came [the adage]: *[Do] whatever works for you.* The Ten Commandments were rewritten as the Ten Creative Suggestions.' . . . Although the world has changed, the laws of God remain constant. They have not changed; they will not change. The Ten Commandments are just that—commandments. They are *not* suggestions. They are every bit as requisite today as they were when God gave them to the children of Israel" (Thomas S. Monson, "Stand in Holy Places," *Ensign*, November 2011; italics in original).

"My message to you tonight is straightforward. It is this: *keep the commandments.* God's commandments are not given to frustrate us or to become obstacles to our happiness. Just the opposite is true. He who created us and who loves us perfectly knows just how we need to live our lives in order to obtain the greatest happiness possible. He has provided us with guidelines which, if we follow them, will see us safely through this often treacherous mortal journey" (Thomas S. Monson, "Keep the Commandments," *Ensign*, November 2015; italics in original).

Preach My Gospel

Lesson 4: "The Commandments," pp. 71–81; "Keep the Ten Commandments," pp. 76–77.

Personal Progress

Integrity #1—Living the Ten Commandments requires integrity. Notice how the Ten Commandments are highlighted and interwoven in *For the Strength of Youth* (p. 62).

Duty to God

The word *commandments* is used three times in your *Duty to God* pamphlet. Look up each instance of the word *commandments* (see pp. 5, 62, 103). What blessings go along with keeping the commandments?

Activity

Ask your kids to brainstorm different things that exemplify people living by the Ten Commandments as well as other things that show the opposite. For example, the prophets support living the Ten Commandments. LDS educational institutions like BYU, LDS Business College, institute, seminary, and church all teach living the Ten Commandments. Many "popular" songs and shows do *not* exemplify living the Ten Commandments, but rather sensationalize breaking them and falsify the consequences that go along with breaking them; however, some shows do model faithful living. What are they? Is it a good idea to watch shows or read magazines that portray breaking the Ten Commandments as fun or popular?

Daily Scriptures

The Ten Commandments

Sunday 📖ᴹ

"I will go and do the things which the Lord hath commanded, for I know that the Lord giveth no commandments unto the children of men, save he shall prepare a way for them that they may accomplish the thing which he commandeth them." (1 Nephi 3:7)

Monday 📖ᴹ

"If ye will obey my voice indeed, and keep my covenant, then ye shall be a peculiar treasure unto me above all people: for all the earth is mine: And ye shall be unto me a kingdom of priests, and an holy nation." (Exodus 19:5–6)

Tuesday 📖ᴹ

"I am the Lord thy God. . . . Thou shalt have no other gods before me. Thou shalt not make unto thee any graven image, or any likeness of any thing that is in heaven above, or that is in the earth beneath, or that is in the water under the earth: Thou shalt not bow down thyself to them, nor serve them. . . . Thou shalt not take the name of the Lord thy God in vain; for the Lord will not hold him guiltless that taketh his name in vain." (Exodus 20:2–5, 7)

Wednesday 📖ᴹ

"Remember the sabbath day, to keep it holy. Six days shalt thou labour, and do all thy work: But the seventh day is the sabbath of the Lord thy God: in it thou shalt not do any work. . . . For in six days the Lord made heaven and earth, the sea, and all that in them is, and rested the seventh day: wherefore the Lord blessed the sabbath day, and hallowed it." (Exodus 20:8–11)

Thursday 📖ᴹ

"Honour thy father and thy mother: that thy days may be long upon the land which the Lord thy God giveth thee. Thou shalt not kill. Thou shalt not commit adultery. Thou shalt not steal. Thou shalt not bear false witness against thy neighbour. Thou shalt not covet thy neighbour's house, thou shalt not covet thy neighbour's wife, nor his manservant, nor his maidservant, nor his ox, nor his ass, nor any thing that is thy neighbour's." (Exodus 20:12–17)

Friday

"O, remember, my son, and learn wisdom in thy youth; yea, learn in thy youth to keep the commandments of God." (Alma 37:35)

Saturday

"Keep the commandments which the Lord delivered, . . . saying: Thou shalt have no other God before me. Thou shalt not make unto thee any graven image. . . . Thou shalt not take the name of the Lord thy God in vain. . . . Remember the sabbath day, to keep it holy. Honor thy father and thy mother. . . . Thou shalt not kill. Thou shalt not commit adultery. Thou shalt not steal. Thou shalt not bear false witness against thy neighbor. Thou shalt not covet . . . anything that is thy neighbor's." (Mosiah 12:33, 35–36, 13:15–16, 20–24)

Spring Conference

"Blessed are ye if ye shall give heed unto the words of these twelve whom I have chosen from among you to minister unto you, and to be your servants." (3 Nephi 12:1)

LDS.org General Conference page
http://goo.gl/MYtB9P

LDS.org general conference
"Activities for Children"
https://goo.gl/mjiRjf

Music from Children's Songbook & Hymns

- Latter-day Prophets (*CS*, 134)
- Come, Listen to a Prophet's Voice (*Hymns*, 21)
- Joseph Smith's First Prayer (*Hymns*, 26)
- Praise to the Man (*Hymns*, 27)

Quote

"Conferences have always been part of the true Church of Jesus Christ. Adam gathered his posterity and prophesied of things to come. Moses gathered the children of Israel and taught them the commandments he had received. The Savior taught multitudes gathered both in the Holy Land and on the American continent. Peter gathered believers in Jerusalem. The first general conference in these latter days was convened just two months after the Church was organized, and conferences have continued to this very day" (Robert D. Hales, "General Conference: Strengthening Faith and Testimony," *Ensign*, November 2013).

Scripture Stories

Jesus appears to the Nephites at the temple in Bountiful. He invites the multitude to come to Him one by one to see, feel, and know He is the Christ. He calls and ordains His twelve disciples, gives them the power to baptize, teaches about baptism and the Holy Ghost, and tells the people they will be blessed if they follow the words of the twelve servants He has called (see 3 Nephi 11–12:1).

The latter-day elders wanted instructions from God. Joseph Smith asked the Lord about their desires and received the revelation recorded in Doctrine and Covenants 133, which includes the Lord telling them to prepare themselves, sanctify themselves, gather together, go out from Babylon, be clean, and call their solemn assemblies (see D&C 133 heading and D&C 133:1–6).

Gospel Art Pictures

- *Jesus Teaching in the Western Hemisphere* (#82)
- *Brother Joseph* (#87)
- *Latter-day Prophets* (#122–37)

Church History

When and where was the Church officially and legally organized? *On April 6, 1830, in Fayette, New York, the Church was organized and called The Church of Christ* (see D&C 20). To watch a short video of this event, go to https://goo.gl/yZzeHu.

What other names did the Church go by before receiving the revelation to call it The Church of Jesus Christ of Latter-day Saints? *The Church of Christ, The Church of Jesus Christ, The Church of God, and The Church of the Latter-day Saints.* The revelation providing the Church's official name was received on April 26, 1838 (D&C 115:4) (see also FairMormon's page "Why did the Church change its name twice during its history?," at http://goo.gl/qfwESo for details).

When was the first general conference of the latter-day Church? *On June 9, 1830, twenty-seven members attended the first conference of the Church in the latter days.* When did the Church begin the semi-annual schedule we now use? *1840.* This was also the year the Church held its first conference outside of the United States, and published conference talks (see an article on LDS. org titled "A Brief History of General Conference" at https://goo.gl /ftWbNj)

When did the *Ensign* magazine start publishing conference talks? *1971.* When was the new conference center first used? *April 1–2, 2000* (see the Church History timeline at http://goo.gl/wzamg1).

LDS.org video "Organization of the Church"
https://goo.gl/yZzeHu

LDS.org video page "Joseph Smith"
https://goo.gl/8o9mbr

Adaptations for Younger Children

Quote

"As the time for conference arrives, . . . we gather our families to hear the word of the Lord, as King Benjamin's people did. Children and youth love to be included. We make a serious mistake if we assume that the conference is above their intellect and spiritual sensitivity. To the young members of the Church, I promise that if you will listen, you will feel the Spirit" (Robert D. Hales, "General Conference: Strengthening Faith and Testimony," *Ensign*, November 2013).

Lesson from *Behold Your Little Ones*

"I Belong to the Church of Jesus Christ of Latter-day Saints" (Lesson 25, pp. 104–107).

Faith in God

"Read [or watch] a recent conference address given by the prophet. Decide what you can do to follow the prophet, and do it" (p. 6).

Activity

Act out King Benjamin building a tower and everyone bringing their families to the temple to hear him. Set up tents and make sure they face the tower. Have everyone settle in to listen to King Benjamin. Have someone climb up and talk to the people about Jesus, his birth, life, and mission, and how He wants people to act and treat each other.

Adaptations for Older Children and Teens

Quote

"In preparation for general conference, let me suggest three basic concepts that may help us to better receive, remember, and apply the words spoken by the Lord's servants. . . . As you prepare for general conference, I invite you to ponder questions you need to have answered. . . . Answers to your specific prayers may come directly from a particular talk or from a specific phrase. At other times answers may come in a seemingly unrelated word, phrase, or song. . . . Don't discount a message merely because it sounds familiar. Prophets have always taught by repetition; it is a law of learning. . . . The words spoken at general conference should be a compass that points the way for us during the coming months. . . . What a marvelous privilege it is to hear God's messages for each of us during general conference! Let us prepare well for this great blessing of divine guidance delivered by His chosen servants. For this is no ordinary blessing" (Dieter F. Uchtdorf, "General Conference—No Ordinary Blessing," *Ensign*, September 2011).

Preach My Gospel

Lesson 1: "The Message of the Restoration of the Gospel of Jesus Christ," pp. 31–46.

Personal Progress

A few value experiences and value projects say to study general conference talks (see pp. 14, 22, 30, 66). Consider using conference talks as cornerstones for personalized value experiences or value projects. Select a conference talk that stands out to you and study it, along with related scriptures and other talks on the same topic. Give a family home evening about it, and write about it in your journal.

Duty to God

"What specific things did you learn from the living prophets in the most recent general conference? How has following this counsel blessed you?" (p. 62).

Activity ⏱

Get several small pieces of paper that can be blown off a table and a good-sized rock that cannot be blown off a table. Put the papers on a table and invite someone to try to blow them off the table. The papers should blow off quickly and easily. Put the rock on the table and invite someone to blow it off the table. It should not budge. Tell the family that our testimonies should be strong and built on the rock of our Redeemer (see Helaman 5:12) and His servants so we are not "tossed to and fro, and carried about by every wind of doctrine" (Ephesians 4:14). One blessing we are given to help us strengthen our testimonies and learn what our leaders feel inspired to share is general conference. Encourage everyone to read, watch, or listen to conference talks online on LDS.org.

Daily Scriptures

Spring Conference

Sunday

Jesus said, "Blessed are ye if ye shall give heed unto the words of these twelve whom I have chosen from among you to minister unto you, and to be your servants." (3 Nephi 12:1)

Monday 📖

"The word of the Lord came unto me [Ezekial], saying, Son of man, I have made thee a watchman unto the house of Israel: therefore hear the word at my mouth, and give them warning from me." (Ezekiel 3:16–17)

Tuesday 📖

Jesus told His twelve disciples, "Greater love hath no man than this, that a man lay down his life for his friends. Ye have not chosen me, but I have chosen you, and ordained you, that ye should go and bring forth fruit, and that your fruit should remain: that whatsoever ye shall ask of the Father in my name, he may give it you. These things I command you, that ye love one another. If the world hate you, ye know that it hated me before it hated you." (John 15:13, 16–18)

Wednesday

"When ye are assembled together ye shall instruct and edify each other, that ye may know how to act and direct my church, how to act upon the points of my law and commandments, which I have given. And thus ye shall become instructed in the law of my church, and be sanctified by that which ye have received, and ye shall bind yourselves to act in all holiness before me." (D&C 43:8–9)

Thursday 📖

"Also those to whom these commandments were given, [were given] power to lay the foundation of this church, and to bring it forth out of obscurity and out of darkness, the only true and living church upon the face of the whole earth, with which I, the Lord, am well pleased, speaking unto the church collectively and not individually." (D&C 1:30)

Friday

Peter said to the elders of his day, "Feed the flock of God which is among you, taking the oversight thereof, not by constraint, but willingly; not for filthy lucre, but of a ready mind; Neither as being lords over God's heritage, but being ensamples to the flock." (1 Peter 5:2–3)

Saturday

Paul said to the elders of his day, "Take heed therefore unto yourselves, and to all the flock, over the which the Holy Ghost hath made you overseers, to feed the church of God, which he hath purchased with his own blood." (Acts 20:28)

Fall Conference

"What I the Lord have spoken, I have spoken, and I excuse not myself; and though the heavens and the earth pass away, my word shall not pass away, but shall all be fulfilled, whether by mine own voice or by the voice of my servants, it is the same." (D&C 1:38) ▢DM

A *New Era* May 2012 article titled, "General Conference Is for You." https://goo.gl/KQzY3T

LDS.org general conference "Games and Activities" for young children https://goo.gl/MNdmPf

Music from Children's Songbook & Hymns

- The Church of Jesus Christ (*CS*, 77)
- Follow the Prophet (*CS*, 110)
- Latter-day Prophets (*CS*, 134)
- We Thank, Thee, O God, for a Prophet (*Hymns*, 19)

Quotes

"Not every statement made by a Church leader, past or present, . . . constitutes doctrine. It is commonly understood in the Church that a statement made by one leader on a single occasion often represents a personal, though well-considered, opinion, not meant to be official or binding for the whole Church" (D. Todd Christofferson, "The Doctrine of Christ," *Ensign*, May 2012).

"When the First Presidency and the Quorum of the Twelve speak with a united voice, it is the voice of the Lord for that time" (M. Russell Ballard, "Stay in the Boat and Hold On!," *Ensign*, November 2014).

Scripture Stories

Many Israelites are bitten and killed by poisonous snakes. Moses makes a brass serpent that symbolizes Jesus Christ and His power to heal. Anyone who looks at the serpent lives. Conference is a time when our modern-day leaders help us "look to God and live" (Alma 37:47) (see also Exodus 3:1–4:17; Numbers 21:4–9; John 3:14–15; Alma 33:19–21).

King Benjamin calls his people to the temple to offer sacrifice, talk about Jesus, and share counsel. His words are written for those who cannot hear. He declares that he is no more than a mortal man. He experiences physical and mental challenges, but he has been called to serve them with all the strength the Lord gave him (see Mosiah 2:1–11, 31; 3–5).

Gospel Art Pictures

- *Moses and the Brass Serpent* (#16)
- *King Benjamin Addresses His People* (#74)
- *Latter-day Prophets* (#122–37)

Church History

When did the Church start broadcasting general conference locally? *The first radio broadcast was on October 3–5, 1924.* Heber J. Grant was the President of the Church then (*Teachings of Presidents of the Church: Heber J. Grant*, ix). The first television broadcast was in 1949. Satellite broadcasts began in 1975, and broadcasting using the Internet began in 1999. The oldest video of President Monson's conference talks on LDS.org is called "Lost Battalions," given in the April 1971 conference. To watch it, go https://goo.gl/XgtfiD.

In 1831, Joseph Smith received the revelation recorded in Doctrine and Covenants 1. In verse 38 it says, "My word shall not pass away, but shall be fulfilled, whether by mine own voice or by the voice of my servants, it is the same." Some people interpret this to mean that everything spoken at general conference is the word of God as if from His own mouth and is equivalent to official scripture. This belief has been countered by leaders of the Church. See the quotes in the first section of this lesson for examples. See also the FairMormon page, "Are Prophets Infallible?" at http://goo.gl/ey3Aou.

By the definition in Elder Ballard's quote at the beginning of this lesson, doctrine includes canonized scriptures and official proclamations such "The Family: A Proclamation to the World," and "The Living Christ." Technically speaking, it may exclude inspired and appreciated sermons given at general conference.

LDS.org video of President Monson's oldest conference talk available online, "Lost Battalions" https://goo.gl/XgtfiD

FairMormon article (Mormonism and doctrine/ Official or core doctrine/ What is it?) that answers the question, "What's official or core doctrine?" http://goo.gl/jBdfeh

Adaptations for Younger Children

Quote

"I promise that if you will listen [to General Conference], you will feel the Spirit. . . . Through conferences our faith is fortified and our testimonies deepened" (Robert D. Hales, "General Conference: Strengthening Faith and Testimony," *Ensign*, November 2013).

Lesson from *Behold Your Little Ones*

"I Will Follow the Prophet" (Lesson 24, pp. 100–103).

Faith in God

"Read [or watch] a recent conference address given by the prophet. Decide what you can do to follow the prophet, and do it" (p. 6).

Activity

Discuss how your family would like to approach general conference this year. Plan and prepare activities for the children to help them be somehow engaged, but relatively quiet. Blocks, coloring, and cutting activities may be appropriate for younger children, while making a conference notebook or making a conference bingo card may be appropriate for older children.

Adaptations for Older Children and Teens

Quotes

"We should be careful not to claim for Joseph Smith perfections he did not claim for himself. He need not have been superhuman to be the instrument in God's hands that we know him to be. . . . Joseph Smith was a mortal man striving to fulfill an overwhelming divinely appointed mission against all odds. The wonder is not that he ever displayed human failings, but that he succeeded in his mission. His fruits are both undeniable and undeniably good" (D. Todd Christofferson, "The Prophet Joseph Smith," [Devotional, Brigham Young University–Idaho, September 24, 2013]).

"There have been times when members or leaders in the Church have simply made mistakes. There may have been things said or done that were not in harmony with our values, principles, or doctrine. I suppose the Church would be perfect only if it were run by perfect beings. God is perfect, and His doctrine is pure. But He works through us—His imperfect children—and imperfect people make mistakes. . . . This is the way it has always been and will be until the perfect day when Christ Himself reigns personally upon the earth. It is unfortunate that some have stumbled because of mistakes made by men" (Dieter F. Uchtdorf, "Come, Join with Us," *Ensign*, November 2013).

Preach My Gospel

"Heavenly Father Reveals His Gospel in Every Dispensation," pp. 32–34; Lesson 3: "The Gospel of Jesus Christ," pp. 60–70.

Personal Progress

A couple of the value experiences and value projects say to study the words of living prophets (see pp. 14, 22, 30, 66). Review what you've done in Personal Progress and consider creating personalized value experiences or value projects around conference talks that stand out to you.

Duty to God

The *Duty to God* booklet encourages young men to develop and strengthen the daily habit of reading the scriptures and the words of living prophets. Evaluate your personal study habits and see if you would like to improve or change them in any way (see pp. 10, 13–14, 37–38, 61–62).

Activity

Get a pitcher filled with water and enough empty cups for everyone in the family. Have everyone pour themselves a drink of water and drink it. Why is water important? *Our bodies require water to survive. Plants require water to grow, and many plants provide food to sustain our bodies.* In essence, water is life. Jesus said, "Whosoever drinketh of this water shall thirst again: But whosoever drinketh of the water that I shall give him shall never thirst; but the water that I shall give him shall be in him a well of water springing up into everlasting life" (John 4:13–14). General conferences can nourish us spiritually by pointing us to Jesus Christ and His living water. Encourage everyone to read, watch, or listen to conference talks online on LDS.org.

Daily Scriptures

Fall Conference

Sunday 📖

"What I the Lord have spoken, I have spoken, and I excuse not myself; and though the heavens and the earth pass away, my word shall not pass away, but shall all be fulfilled, whether by mine own voice or by the voice of my servants, it is the same." (D&C 1:38)

Monday

Mosiah "made a proclamation throughout all the land, that the people gathered themselves together throughout all the land, that they might go up to the temple to hear the words which king Benjamin should speak unto them. And there were a great number, even so many that they did not number them. . . . And also that they might give thanks to the Lord their God." (Mosiah 2:1–2, 4)

Tuesday

"Verily, verily, I say unto thee [Oliver Cowdery], . . . if thou art led at any time by the Comforter to speak or teach, . . . thou mayest do it. But thou shalt not write by way of commandment, but by wisdom; And thou shalt not command him who is at thy head, and at the head of the church." (D&C 28:2, 4–6)

Wednesday 📖

"The church . . . shalt give heed unto all [the prophet and president's] words and commandments which he shall give unto you as he receiveth them, walking in all holiness before me; For his word ye shall

receive, as if from mine own mouth, in all patience and faith. For by doing these things the gates of hell shall not prevail against you; yea, and the Lord God will disperse the powers of darkness from before you, and cause the heavens to shake for your good, and his name's glory. For thus saith the Lord God: Him have I inspired to move the cause of Zion in mighty power for good, and his diligence I know, and his prayers I have heard." (D&C 21:4–7)

Thursday

"Behold, I give unto you a commandment, that when ye are assembled together ye shall instruct and edify each other, that ye may know how to act and direct my church, how to act upon the points of my law and commandments, which I have given." (D&C 43:8)

Friday

Jesus said, "Blessed are ye if ye shall give heed unto the words of these twelve whom I have chosen from among you to minister unto you, and to be your servants; and unto them I have given power that they may baptize you with water; and after that ye are baptized with water, behold, I will baptize you with fire and with the Holy Ghost." (3 Nephi 12:1)

Saturday

"Ye shall meet together oft. . . . Therefore, hold up your light that it may shine unto the world. Behold I am the light which ye shall hold up." (3 Nephi 18:22, 24)

New Year's Day
(Baptism)

"If any man be in Christ, he is a new creature: old things are passed away; behold, all things are become new." (2 Corinthians 5:17)

LDS.org video "The Baptism of Jesus"
http://goo.gl/XBZSrx

Music from Children's Songbook & Hymns

- When I Am Baptized (*CS*, 103)
- *Children's Songbook* songs about baptism (*CS*, 100–104)
- Father in Heaven, We Do Believe (*Hymns*, 180, v. 5–6)
- Ring Out, Wild Bells (*Hymns*, 215)

Quotes

"Let us resolve to spend more time with those we love. Resolve to strive more earnestly to become the person God wants us to be. Resolve to find happiness, regardless of our circumstances" (Dieter F. Uchtdorf, "Of Regrets and Resolutions," *Ensign*, November 2012).

"Our covenants will strengthen us to resist temptation. Keeping our covenants will steady us on the path of virtue. . . . Elder Jeffrey R. Holland reminds us: 'Beginning with our baptism, we make covenants as we follow this path to eternal life, and we stay on the path by keeping them'" (Elaine S. Dalton, "Stay on the Path," *Ensign*, May 2007).

Scripture Stories

Alma baptizes people in the Waters of Mormon, and talks about the promises they make by being baptized. They are "buried in the water" (Mosiah 18:14) (see also Mosiah 18:7–17).

Joseph Smith writes a letter to the Saints on how to do baptisms for the dead (see D&C 127).

Jesus is baptized by John the Baptist, and the Holy Ghost descends upon Him (see Matthew 3:13–17, Joseph Smith Translation, Matthew 3:43–46, [in the Bible appendix]).

Jesus will come again in glory and He will reign on this earth. The earth will be made new and be a paradise (see Joseph Smith—Matthew 1:1, 36–40; Articles of Faith 1:10).

Gospel Art Pictures

- *John the Baptist Baptizing Jesus* (#35)
- *Alma Baptizes in the Waters of Mormon* (#76)
- *Young Man Being Baptized* (#103)
- *Girl Being Baptized* (#104)
- *Temple Baptismal Font* (#121)

Church History

In 1829, Joseph Smith and Oliver Cowdery were translating the Book of Mormon and came across a passage about baptism by authority. On May 15, 1829, they went into the woods to pray about baptism. John the Baptist appeared to them and ordained them to the Aaronic Priesthood, and they then baptized each other. To read more about this experience see Joseph Smith—History 1:66–75 and the LDS.org's gospel topic "Aaronic Priesthood" at https://goo.gl/jcm98F.

LDS.org video "Glad Tidings: The History of Baptisms for the Dead" https://goo.gl/Eawuzg

When was baptism for the dead announced? *August 15, 1840* (see LDS.org's gospel topic "Baptisms for the Dead" at https://goo.gl/nHhXih). See Doctrine and Covenants 138 to read a revelation on the salvation of the dead. To see a short video on the history of Joseph Smith's receiving the revelation about baptisms for the dead, go to https://goo.gl/Eawuzg.

On January 1, 2000, the First Presidency and Quorum of the Twelve Apostles published "The Living Christ," their testimony to the world about the reality of the Son of God and His role as Savior of the world (see "The Living Christ: The Testimony of the Apostles," *Ensign*, April 2000 or http://goo.gl/tPj8cG).

Adaptations for Younger Children

Quote

"I will remember my baptismal covenant and listen to the Holy Ghost" ("My Gospel Standards").

Lesson from *Behold Your Little Ones*

"I Will Be Baptized and Confirmed" (Lesson 26, pp. 108–111).

Faith in God

Read and discuss the section "My Baptismal Covenant" (pp. 2–3).

Activity

Brainstorm! First let everyone share their favorite things about the past year. Then, brainstorm about what they would like to do in the New Year. Select a few things, and plan when you can do them.

Tell your children that "immersion" means being completely surrounded by water. Baptism by immersion symbolizes the death and burial of Jesus Christ, as well as the end of the spiritual life of the person who is being baptized. Being brought up out of the water symbolizes Christ's Resurrection, as well as the beginning of a new spiritual life for the person being baptized (see Romans 6). Get a container and fill it most of the way with water. Get a pencil or crayon and put it halfway in the water standing up. Ask if it is immersed. Then put it mostly in the water, but with one end up. Ask if it is immersed. Then put it all the way under the water and ask again. For fun, gather several random objects and see which ones sink (become immersed) and which ones float.

Adaptations for Older Children and Teens

Quote

"The Church is the creation of Him in whom our spirituality is centered—Jesus Christ. It is worth pausing to consider why He chooses to use a church, His Church, The Church of Jesus Christ of Latter-day Saints, to carry out His and His Father's work 'to bring to pass the immortality and eternal life of man.' Beginning with Adam, the gospel of Jesus Christ was preached, and the essential ordinances of salvation, such as baptism, were administered . . . It is important to recognize that God's ultimate purpose is our progress. His desire is that we continue 'from grace to grace, until [we receive] a fulness' of all He can give. That requires more than simply being nice or feeling spiritual. It requires faith in Jesus Christ, repentance, baptism of water and of the Spirit, and enduring in faith to the end. One cannot fully achieve this in isolation, so a major reason the Lord has a church is to create a community of Saints that will sustain one another in the 'strait and narrow path which leads to eternal life.'" (D. Todd Christofferson, "Why the Church," *Ensign*, November 2015)

Preach My Gospel

Chapter 8: "How Do I Use Time Wisely?," pp. 137–54; "How to Set Goals," pp. 146–47. "Baptism and Confirmation," pp. 9–10; "Baptism, Our First Covenant," pp. 63–65; "The Gift of the Holy Ghost," pp. 65–66; Chapter 12: "How Do I Prepare People for Baptism and Confirmation?," pp. 203–12.

Personal Progress

Divine Nature #4—"Memorize the sacrament prayers. . . . Practice keeping your baptismal covenants" (p. 23).

Virtue #2—"When you are baptized and confirmed, you are given the gift of the Holy Ghost to guide all aspects of your life. . . . A virtuous life is a prerequisite to having the companionship of the Holy Ghost" (p. 70).

Duty to God

Study the doctrinal topic of "Baptism" and "Covenants and Ordinances." Record what you learn and share what you learned with your parents or a priesthood leader (see pp. 18–21, 42–45, 66–69).

Also, read "Performing a Baptism" (p. 104).

Activity

Ask your family members to think of ways to remember the Savior on a day-to-day basis. Include ideas that incorporate thoughts, words, and actions. Put a piece of paper on the wall near the dinner table. During family meals or scripture time this week, talk about the ways each person showed that he or she remembered the Savior each day, and write what people did on the paper. (Adapted from *Family Home Evening Resource Book*, (Church of Jesus Christ of Latter-day Saints, 1983), pp. 56–63. Found online at LDS.org.)

Daily Scriptures

New Year's Day (Baptism)

Sunday

"If any man be in Christ, he is a new creature: old things are passed away; behold, all things are become new." (2 Corinthians 5:17)

Monday 📖

"We believe that the first principles and ordinances of the Gospel are: first, Faith in the Lord Jesus Christ; second, Repentance; third, Baptism by immersion for the remission of sins; fourth, Laying on of hands for the gift of the Holy Ghost." (Articles of Faith 1:4)

Tuesday 📖

"Jesus answered and said unto him, Verily, verily, I say unto thee, Except a man be born again, he cannot see the kingdom of God. Nicodemus saith unto him, How can a man be born when he is old? can he enter the second time into his mother's womb, and be born? Jesus answered, Verily, verily, I say unto thee, Except a man be born of water and of the Spirit, he cannot enter into the kingdom of God." (John 3:3–5)

Wednesday

"Jesus, when he was baptized, went up straightway out of the water: and . . . he saw the Spirit of God descending like a dove, and lighting upon him: And lo a voice from heaven, saying, This is my beloved Son, in whom I am well pleased." (Matthew 3:16–17)

Thursday

Jesus said, "He that is baptized in my name, to him will the Father give the Holy Ghost, like unto me; wherefore, follow me, and do the things which ye have seen me do." (2 Nephi 31:12)

Friday

"Go ye therefore, and teach all nations, baptizing them in the name of the Father, and of the Son, and of the Holy Ghost: Teaching them to observe all things whatsoever I have commanded you: and, lo, I am with you alway." (Matthew 28:19–20)

Saturday 📖

"Now this is the commandment: Repent, all ye ends of the earth, and come unto me and be baptized in my name, that ye may be sanctified by the reception of the Holy Ghost, that ye may stand spotless before me at the last day." (3 Nephi 27:20)

Martin Luther King Jr. Day
(Cultural Diversity)

"[The Lord] inviteth . . . all to come unto him and partake of his goodness; and he denieth none that come unto him, black and white, bond and free, male and female . . . all are alike unto God." (2 Nephi 26:33) 🔖

LDS.org video "Good Samaritan" with Elder Ballard
https://goo.gl/DMyqqm

Music from Children's Songbook & Hymns

- Children All Over the World (*CS*, 16)
- Jesus Said Love Everyone (*CS*, 61)
- We Are Different (*CS*, 263)
- Love One Another (*CS*, 136 or *Hymns*, 308)

Quote

"Even with diversity of languages and beautiful, uplifting cultural traditions, we must have hearts knit in unity and love. . . . While we treasure appropriate cultural diversities, our goal is to be united in the culture, customs, and traditions of the gospel of Jesus Christ in every respect" (Quentin L. Cook, "The Lord Is My Light," *Ensign*, May 2015).

Scripture Stories

Jesus visits Samaria, which is unheard of in his culture since the Jews and the Samaritans hate each other. He talks with a Samaritan woman, who believes Him when He tells her He is the Christ. She goes to get others to come and meet Jesus. He stays with them for two days (see John 4:3–30, 39–43).

Ammon goes to the land of Ishmael to serve and preach the gospel. The Lamanites hate the Nephites and immediately tie Ammon up and take him to the king. Ammon asks to become the king's servant. He teaches King Lamoni the gospel, and he teaches it to his people (see Alma 17–20:30).

Gospel Art Pictures

- *Jesus and the Samaritan Woman* (#36)
- *Go Ye Therefore* (#61)
- *Ammon Defends the Flocks of King Lamoni* (#78)
- *Christ and Children from around the World* (#116)

Church History

On September 30, 1978, President Spencer W. Kimball received the revelation that all worthy males could receive the priesthood (see Official Declaration 2 in the Doctrine and Covenants). Leaders of the Church had prayed for years about the matter and were very grateful that the time had come to remove the dictate that African-American men were not allowed to hold the priesthood (see *Teachings of Presidents of the Church: Spencer W. Kimball*, 238). Of this experience, President Kimball said,

Spencer W. Kimball: Documentary
https://goo.gl/bN7gU4

> "We had the glorious experience of having the Lord indicate clearly that the time had come when all worthy men and women everywhere can be fellowheirs and partakers of the full blessings of the gospel. . . . We do not expect the people of the world to understand such things, for they will always be quick to assign their own reasons or to discount the divine process of revelation." (*Teachings of Presidents of the Church: Spencer W. Kimball*, 239)

LDS.org video "Roll Up Our Sleeves." A woman shares her positive experience as a member of the Church in a biracial marriage. https://goo.gl/Q8BSGm

To learn more about race and the priesthood, see LDS.org's gospel topic "Race and the Priesthood" at https://goo.gl/3LE5Jp, and FairMormon's post titled "Mormonism and Racial Issues" at http://goo.gl/YTYAG3. To see a video documentary of the life of Spencer W. Kimball, go to https://goo.gl/bN7gU4.

Adaptations for Younger Children

Quote

"I will seek good friends and treat others kindly" ("My Gospel Standards").

Lesson from *Behold Your Little Ones*

"Jesus Christ Showed Us How to Love Others" (Lesson 5, pp. 24–27). Martin Luther King Jr. dreamt of different races of people accepting each other and living together harmoniously.

Faith in God

"Visit an art museum or attend a concert, play, or other cultural event. Share your experience with your family or activity day group" (p. 10).

Activity

Look at pictures of people from various countries and cultures. You can use pictures #111–16 in the *Gospel Art Book* to show a variety of cultures. Share things you know about people from other countries such as how they live, what they eat, and how they talk. Teach your children phrases in another language. The song, "Children All over the World" (*Children's Songbook*, p. 16) teaches the words "thank you" in several languages. Also, you can share that in Japanese, adding "chan" to the end of a child's name is a term of endearment. We call our daughters Leia-chan, Hana-chan, and Avvy-chan. In Spanish, adding -ita or -ito to a child's name is a term of endearment. My girls would be Le-ita, Han-ita, and Av-ita. Boys names end in -ito. Add "chan" and "-ita" or "-ito" to your children's names and see how they like it.

Adaptations for Older Children and Teens

Quote

"Good neighbors should put forth every effort to understand each other and to be kind to one another regardless of religion, nationality, race, or culture. . . . I believe it would be good if we eliminated a couple of phrases from our vocabulary: 'nonmember' and 'non-Mormon.' Such phrases can be demeaning and even belittling. Personally, I don't consider myself to be a 'non-Catholic' or a 'non-Jew.' I am a Christian. I am a member of The Church of Jesus Christ of Latter-day Saints. That is how I prefer to be identified—for who and what I am, as opposed to being identified for what I am not. Let us extend that same courtesy to those who live among us. If a collective description is needed, then 'neighbors' seems to work well in most cases. . . . Love one another. Be kind to one another despite our deepest differences. Treat one another with respect and civility" (M. Russell Ballard, "Doctrine of Inclusion," *Ensign*, November 2001).

Preach My Gospel

Chapter 7: "How Can I Better Learn My Mission Language?," pp. 127–36; "Culture and Language Learning," 132–33; "The Gift of Tongues," p. 133; "Cultural Views of Scriptures," p. 181; "Teach the Restored Gospel to Those without a Christian Background," pp. 190–91.

Personal Progress

Knowledge #4—Research a gospel principle you would like to understand better, for example, the doctrine of inclusion in Elder Ballard's quote above (p. 39).

Duty to God

Study the doctrinal topic "The Plan of Salvation." Write down what you learn, and share it with a parent or leader (see pp. 18–21, 42–45, 66–69).

Activity ⏲

Get several rocks that are fairly easy to differentiate with your eyes closed. Have everyone choose a rock, observe it closely, and try to memorize it. Then have everyone put the rocks in a pile and close their eyes. Mix up the rocks. With their eyes closed, tell them to feel through the pile and find their rock. When everyone is through, have them open their eyes and see if they got the right rock. Ask them why they thought they could identify their rock with their eyes closed. Tell them that God made each of us and He knows us very well, even better than we know ourselves. And just like God made rocks look and feel different, he made people—and whole cultures—different with distinctive qualities. Despite religious, cultural, and ethnic differences, we are all children of God and can connect, accept, and enjoy each other as such.

Daily Scriptures

Martin Luther King Jr. Day (Cultural Diversity)

Sunday

"The Lord . . . doeth that which is good among the children of men; and he doeth nothing save it be plain unto the children of men; and he inviteth them all to come unto him and partake of his goodness; and he denieth none that come unto him, black and white, bond and free, male and female; and he remembereth the heathen; and all are alike unto God, both Jew and Gentile." (2 Nephi 26:33)

Monday

"A new commandment I give unto you, That ye love one another; as I have loved you, that ye also love one another. By this shall all men know that ye are my disciples, if ye have love one to another." (John 13:34–35)

Tuesday

May "the Lord make you to increase and abound in love one toward another, and toward all men." (1 Thessalonians 3:12)

Wednesday

"Look not on his countenance, or on the height of his stature; because I have refused him: for the Lord seeth not as man seeth; for man looketh on the outward appearance, but the Lord looketh on the heart." (1 Samuel 16:7)

Thursday

"And now, my beloved brethren, after ye have gotten into this strait and narrow path, I would ask if all is done? Behold, I say unto you, Nay; for ye have not come thus far save it were by the word of Christ with unshaken faith in him, relying wholly upon the merits of him who is mighty to save. Wherefore, ye must press forward with a steadfastness in Christ, having a perfect brightness of hope, and a love of God and of all men. Wherefore, if ye shall press forward, feasting upon the word of Christ, and endure to the end, behold, thus saith the Father: Ye shall have eternal life." (2 Nephi 31:19–20)

Friday

"See that ye love one another; cease to be covetous; learn to impart one to another as the gospel requires. Cease to be idle; cease to be unclean; cease to find fault one with another; cease to sleep longer than is needful; retire to thy bed early, that ye may not be weary; arise early, that your bodies and your minds may be invigorated. And above all things, clothe yourselves with the bond of charity, as with a mantle, which is the bond of perfectness and peace." (D&C 88:123–25)

Saturday

"Let thy bowels also be full of charity towards all men." (D&C 121:45)

Valentine's Day

"Charity is the pure love of Christ. . . . Wherefore, my beloved brethren, pray unto the Father with all the energy of heart, that ye may be filled with this love . . . that ye may become the sons of God; that when he shall appear we shall be like him." (Moroni 7:47–48) 🔖

Mormonad—Be a Smart Cookie
https://goo.gl/vZjoug

Music from Children's Songbook & Hymns

- Love Is Spoken Here (*CS*, 190)
- A Happy Family (*CS*, 198)
- Love One Another (*CS*, 136 or *Hymns*, 308)
- Love at Home (*Hymns*, 294)

Quotes

"Whatever problems your family is facing, whatever you must do to solve them, the beginning and the end of the solution is charity, the pure love of Christ. Without this love, even seemingly perfect families struggle. With it, even families with great challenges succeed" (Dieter F. Uchtdorf, "In Praise of Those Who Save," *Ensign*, May 2016).

"[Love] ought to be at the *center* of all and everything we do in our own family, in our Church callings, and in our livelihood. . . . Love should be our walk and our talk. . . . Love is the defining characteristic of a disciple of Christ" (Dieter F. Uchtdorf, "The Love of God," *Ensign*, November 2009; italics in original).

Scripture Stories

On the Passover evening, Jesus eats His last supper with His apostles before His crucifixion. After the supper, He washes the feet of His disciples and teaches His apostles to love each other as He loves them. He teaches them that all people will know they are His apostles because they love each other (see John 13:1–35).

King Benjamin teaches his people to keep the commandments, to love God and each other, and to teach their children to love and serve each other (see Mosiah 2:4, 3:19, 4:12–16).

Jesus visits the Nephites and exemplifies pure love. He invites each person to come to Him individually. He calls His twelve disciples to lead the Nephites. He teaches them. He heals them. He prays for and blesses their children. He institutes the sacrament (see 3 Nephi 11–20).

Gospel Art Pictures

- *Jesus Washes the Apostles' Feet* (#55)
- *King Benjamin Addresses His People* (#74)
- *Jesus Blesses the Nephite Children* (#84)

Church History

The first Quorum of the Twelve Apostles in the latter days was organized on February 14, 1835. The members of that quorum were Lyman E. Johnson, Brigham Young, Heber C. Kimball, Orson Hyde, David W. Patten, Luke S. Johnson, William E. McLellin, John F. Boynton, Orson Pratt, William B. Smith, Thomas B. Marsh, and Parley P. Pratt. For more information about this Quorum of the Twelve Apostles, see chapter thirteen of *Church History in the Fulness of Times Student Manual*, pp. 153–68 or at https://goo.gl/RQfXPQ.

LDS.org video "Zion's Camp"
https://goo.gl/uC6DZY

Each of the of the Twelve Apostles listed above were part of Zion's Camp—a group of members who were going to Missouri to help fellow members recover lands confiscated by locals who were infringing on their property rights. Their trek did not go as they thought it would, but there were many valuable lessons learned. Many early Church leaders came from men who faithfully served with Joseph Smith in Zion's Camp. For more information, read the article "Joseph Smith and Zion's Camp" (Alexander L. Baugh, *Ensign*, June 2005 or https://goo.gl/66eRyq) and watch a video on Zion's Camp at https://goo.gl/uC6DZY.

Adaptations for Younger Children

Quote

"Your family can be the best friends you have. . . . If you build your family friendships now, they can bring you joy for the rest of your life and into eternity" (Bonnie Brown, "How to Be Friends with Your Family," *New Era*, February 2015).

Lesson from *Behold Your Little Ones*

"I Will Love Others" (Lesson 18, pp. 76–79).

Faith in God

"Make an item from wood, metal, fabric, or other material, or draw, paint, or sculpt a piece of art. Display your finished work for others to see" (p. 10). Make something that relates to Valentine's Day, like a project that represents love or includes hearts. Or you could make a gift for someone you care about.

Activity ☺

Choose one or more of these activities to do in celebration of Valentine's Day:

- Make heart-shaped cookies for friends, family, or missionaries.

- Cut out paper hearts and decorate the house.

- Make paper hearts and tape them to the door of a special neighbor, teacher, or friend.

- Have each person decorate an envelope and write their name on it. Then have everyone write a note, draw a picture, or choose a small gift to put in the envelopes of each family member. You could tape the envelopes on the fridge and have this activity continue throughout the week.

Adaptations for Older Children and Teens

Quotes

"True love elevates, protects, respects, and enriches another. It motivates you to make sacrifices. . . . Satan would promote counterfeit love, which is really lust. That is driven by hunger to satisfy personal appetite. Protect the one you love by controlling your emotions to the limits set by the Lord" (Richard G. Scott, "Making the Right Choices," *Ensign*, November 1994).

"I wish to speak to you about Christlike love and what I think it can and should mean in your friendships, in your dating, in serious courtship, and, ultimately, in your marriage. . . . In a dating and courtship relationship, I would not have you spend five minutes with someone who belittles you, who is constantly critical of you, who is cruel at your expense and may even call it humor. Life is tough enough without having the person who is supposed to love you leading the assault on your self-esteem, your sense of dignity, your confidence, and your joy. In this person's care you deserve to feel physically safe and emotionally secure. . . . Do you want capability, safety, and security in dating and romance, in married life and eternity? Be a true disciple of Jesus. Be a genuine, committed, word-and-deed Latter-day Saint. Believe that your faith has everything to do with your romance, because it does. You separate dating from discipleship at your peril. . . . How should I love thee? As He does, for that way 'never faileth'" (Jeffrey R. Holland, "How Do I Love Thee?," *New Era*, October 2003).

Preach My Gospel

"Charity and Love," p. 118.

Personal Progress

Divine Nature #3—"For two weeks make a special effort to strengthen your relationship with a family member by showing love through your actions" (p. 23).

Duty to God

Ponder these questions from the *For the Strength of Youth* sections "Family" and "Friends." "How is your priesthood service different when you love those you serve? [When has] someone showed Christlike love for you? How can you show your love for family members and others?" (p. 80).

Activity

Ask everyone: who is tallest, who has the longest hair, the longest fingers, the biggest feet, the most weight, the longest legs, the biggest eyes, and so on. Be selective about what you measure and make sure you don't focus on anything someone is sensitive about. Measure, weigh, and write down everyone's statistics. Then ask, "Who has the most love?" Can you measure how much love someone has? How can you tell if you have charity, or the pure love Christ? How do you feel? What kinds of things do you think, do, and say? Talk about something each person has recently done that shows their immeasurable love.

Daily Scriptures

Valentine's Day

Sunday 📖

"And charity suffereth long, and is kind, and envieth not, and is not puffed up, seeketh not her own, is not easily provoked, thinketh no evil, and rejoiceth not in iniquity but rejoiceth in the truth, beareth all things, believeth all things, hopeth all things, endureth all things. . . . Charity never faileth. . . . Charity is the pure love of Christ, and it endureth forever; and whoso is found possessed of it at the last day, it shall be well with him. Wherefore, my beloved brethren, pray unto the Father with all the energy of heart, that ye may be filled with this love, which he hath bestowed upon all who are true followers of his Son, Jesus Christ; that ye may become the sons of God; that when he shall appear we shall be like him." (Moroni 7:45–48)

Monday

"As the Father hath loved me, so have I loved you: continue ye in my love. If ye keep my commandments, ye shall abide in my love. . . . These things have I spoken unto you, that my joy might remain in you, and that your joy might be full. This is my commandment, That ye love one another, as I have loved you." (John 15:9–12)

Tuesday

"There was no contention in the land, because of the love of God which did dwell in the hearts of the people." (4 Nephi 1:15)

Wednesday

"Ye will not suffer your children that they go hungry, or naked; neither will ye suffer that they transgress the laws of God, and fight and quarrel one with another, and serve the devil, who is the master of sin, . . . he being an enemy to all righteousness. . . . Ye will teach them to love one another, and to serve one another." (Mosiah 4:14–15)

Thursday

"The love of God . . . is the most desirable above all things. . . . Yea, and the most joyous to the soul." (1 Nephi 11:22–23)

Friday

"As ye have come to the knowledge of the glory of God, or if ye have known of his goodness and have tasted of his love, and have received a remission of your sins, which causeth such exceedingly great joy in your souls, . . . remember, and always retain in remembrance, the greatness of God . . . and humble yourselves even in the depths of humility, calling on the name of the Lord daily, and standing steadfastly in the faith of that which is to come. . . . If ye do this ye shall always rejoice, and be filled with the love of God." (Mosiah 4:11–12)

Saturday

"Beloved, let us love one another: for love is of God; and every one that loveth is born of God, and knoweth God. . . . For God is love." (1 John 4:7–8)

St. Patrick's Day
(We're Lucky We're So Blessed)

"Pray always, and I will pour out my Spirit upon you,
and great shall be your blessing." (D&C 19:38)

LDS.org short video clip of part
of President Monson's conference
talk "Consider the Blessings"
http://goo.gl/rkpxDY

Music from Children's Songbook & Hymns

- A Song of Thanks (*CS*, 20)
- My Heavenly Father Loves Me (*CS*, 228)
- The World Is So Big (*CS*, 235)
- Popcorn Popping (*CS*, 242)
- *Children's Songbook* songs about nature and seasons (*CS*, 228–49)
- All Creatures of Our God and King (*Hymns*, 62)
- Count Your Blessings (*Hymns*, 241)

Quotes

"If we will take a step back and consider the blessings in our lives, including seemingly small, sometimes overlooked blessings, we can find greater happiness" (Thomas S. Monson, "Consider the Blessings," *Ensign*, November 2012).

Speaking of the Relief Society, which was organized on March 17, 1842, Joseph Smith said, "The Church was never perfectly organized until the women were thus organized" (*Teachings of Presidents of the Church: Joseph Smith*, 448).

Scripture Stories

The Lord tells us that He created the earth and all things in it for our benefit, use, and pleasure (see D&C 59:16–19).

Jesus heals ten lepers and only one returns to thank Him for healing him (see Luke 17:11–19).

Gospel Art Pictures

- *The Lord Created All Things* (#2)
- *The Earth* (#3)
- *The Ten Lepers* (#46)

Church History

On March 17, 1842, the Relief Society was officially organized (see https://goo.gl/Fscvgu). To see a conference talk on the sacred work of Relief Society, go to https://goo.gl/kvQvZ6 (Julie B. Beck, "Relief Society: A Sacred Work," *Ensign*, November 2009). To see a video about Relief Society sisters worldwide, go to https://goo.gl/d2ZypF.

In the middle of March 1898, the First Presidency started talking about sending sister missionaries into the mission field. During the April 1898 general conference, it was officially announced that sisters would be regularly called into the mission field and Amanda Inez Knight and Lucy Jane Brimhall were set apart to be the first single, proselyting sister missionaries of the Church (see https://goo.gl/UycTvo for a related video).

LDS.org video "Relief Society: A Sacred Work" https://goo.gl/kvQvZ6

LDS.org video "Noble Women, Righteous Lives". This video shares what it's like to be a woman in our world-wide Church today in our world-wide Church: https://goo.gl/d2ZypF

Adaptations for Younger Children

Quote

"Take an inventory of your life and look specifically for the blessings, large and small, you have received" (Thomas S. Monson, "Consider the Blessings," *Ensign*, November 2012).

Lesson from *Behold Your Little Ones*

"Jesus Christ Created the World for Me" (Lesson 7, pp. 32–35).

Faith in God

"Write a poem, story, or short play that teaches a principle of the gospel or is about Heavenly Father's creations" (p. 10). You can focus on gratitude, the Creation, or another gospel principle.

Activity ☺

Talk about the Creation and the beauty of nature. One of God's creations is a clover. It is easy to overlook regular three-leafed clovers because they are more common than four-leafed clovers. Draw or print off some paper three- and four-leaf clovers. Write blessings on each clover. Talk about how blessed and lucky each person is and how lucky your family is. Also, you can tell your children that, according to legend, Saint Patrick, the Catholic saint, used the three-leafed shamrock as a teaching tool to explain his understanding of the Godhead. We might use it to explain our understanding of how the Father, the Son, and the Holy Ghost are separate and distinct beings who work together. (http://en.wikipedia.org/wiki/Shamrock)

Have everyone go outside for just a few minutes and collect a few things in nature that God created. Come back together and share what you collected. Talk about the natural blessings we are surrounded by and how nature testifies of God—the Creator of all things in heaven and in earth.

LDS.org video "This Grand Opportunity: Elizabeth McCune and the First Sister Missionaries" https://goo.gl/UycTvo

Adaptations for Older Children and Teens

Quotes

"Sincerely giving thanks not only helps us recognize our blessings, but it also unlocks the doors of heaven and helps us feel God's love. . . . This requires conscious effort—at least until we have truly learned and cultivated an attitude of gratitude. . . . When we encounter challenges and problems in our lives, it is often difficult for us to focus on our blessings. However, if we reach deep enough and look hard enough, we will be able to feel and recognize just how much we have been given" (Thomas S. Monson, "The Divine Gift of Gratitude," *Ensign*, November 2010).

"You could have an experience with the gift of the Holy Ghost today. You could begin a private prayer with thanks. You could start to count your blessings, and then pause for a moment. If you exercise faith, and with the gift of the Holy Ghost, you will find that memories of other blessings will flood into your mind. If you begin to express gratitude for each of them, your prayer may take a little longer than usual. Remembrance will come. And so will gratitude" (Henry B. Eyring, "Remembrance and Gratitude," *Ensign*, November 1989).

Preach My Gospel

"Promise People Blessings," pp. 197–98.

Personal Progress

Good Works #1—Notice the blessings you receive because others serve you. "Others often give service you may not notice. . . . For two weeks record in your journal the quiet acts of service your family members and other perform. Acknowledge their service in some meaningful way" (p. 54).

Duty to God

Study, discuss, and personally apply the section on "Gratitude" in the *For the Strength of Youth* pamphlet (*For the Strength of Youth*, p. 18). This will help you do part of each section titled "Live Worthily" (see pp. 16–17, 40–41, 64–65).

Activity

Look at your hand. It can help you remember lots of blessings. The thumb represents the things closest to you that are easy to see and be grateful for. The second finger is the pointer finger and it represents teachers, coaches, and leaders who "point the way." The tallest finger represents God, Christ, and the Holy Ghost, who are highest in wisdom, love, and truth. The fourth finger is the ring finger; it represents all the loving family and friend relationships in your life. The fifth finger is the littlest one, and it reminds you to notice and be grateful for even the "littlest" blessings you receive. When you look at your hand, spend some time thinking about each thing and give thanks for all your many blessings in detail.

Daily Scriptures

St. Patrick's Day (We're Lucky We're So Blessed)

Sunday

"Pray always, and I will pour out my Spirit upon you, and great shall be your blessing." (D&C 19:38)

Monday

"Ye are commanded in all things to ask of God, who giveth liberally; and that which the Spirit testifies unto you even so I would that ye should do in all holiness of heart, walking uprightly before me, considering the end of your salvation, doing all things with prayer and thanksgiving, that ye may not be seduced by evil spirits, or doctrines of devils, or the commandments of men. . . . And ye must give thanks unto God in the Spirit for whatsoever blessing ye are blessed with." (D&C 46:7, 32)

Tuesday

"All that [God] requires of you is to keep his commandments; and he has promised you that if ye would keep his commandments ye should prosper in the land; and he never doth vary from that which he hath said; therefore, if ye do keep his commandments he doth bless you and prosper you. And now, in the first place, he hath created you, and granted unto you your lives, for which ye are indebted unto him. And secondly, he doth require that ye should do as he hath commanded you; for which if ye do, he doth immediately bless you." (Mosiah 2:22–24)

Wednesday 📖

"Consider on the blessed and happy state of those that keep the commandments of God. For behold, they are blessed in all things, both temporal and spiritual; and if they hold out faithful to the end they are received into heaven, that thereby they may dwell with God in a state of never-ending happiness." (Mosiah 2:41)

Thursday

"I [God] delight to bless [my people] with the greatest of all blessings." (D&C 41:1)

Friday 📖

"Bring ye all the tithes into the storehouse, that there may be meat in mine house, and prove me now herewith, saith the Lord of hosts, if I will not open you the windows of heaven, and pour you out a blessing, that there shall not be room enough to receive it. And I will rebuke the devourer for your sakes, and he shall not destroy the fruits of your ground; neither shall your vine cast her fruit before the time in the field, saith the Lord of hosts. And all nations shall call you blessed." (Malachi 3:10–12)

Saturday

"Blessed be the Lord, who daily loadeth us with benefits." (Psalm 68:19)

Easter

"And now, after the many testimonies which have been given of him, this is the testimony, last of all, which we give of him: That he lives! For we saw him, even on the right hand of God; and we heard the voice bearing record that he is the Only Begotten of the Father." (D&C 76:22–23) 📖M

Gospel Topic: Easter
https://goo.gl/aspBzC

Music from Children's Songbook & Hymns

- Did Jesus Really Live Again? (*CS*, 64)
- *Children's Songbook* songs about Easter(*CS*, 34, 64–70, 88)
- I Believe in Christ (*Hymns*, 134)
- He Is Risen! (*Hymns*, 199)
- Easter hymns (*Hymns*, 197–220)

Quote

"I am a witness of the Resurrection of the Lord as surely as if I had been there. . . . I know that He lives as surely as did Joseph Smith when he saw the Father and the Son" (Henry B. Eyring, "Come Unto Me," *Ensign*, May 2013).

Scripture Stories

LDS.org video "His Sacred Name— An Easter Declaration." This is a non-graphic review of Jesus's Atonement, arrest, crucifixion, and resurrection. https://goo.gl/ZXEeQY

Jesus is told that his friend Lazarus is on his deathbed. Lazarus's sisters ask Him to come. Jesus waits two days, and then goes to visit. When He arrives, Lazarus has been dead for four days already. Jesus calls Lazarus back from the dead (see John 11:1–46).

Jesus enters Jerusalem on a donkey, cleanses the temple of moneychangers, eats His Last Supper with His friends, institutes the sacrament, and washes His disciples' feet. Later that night, He prays in Gethsemane and is betrayed and arrested. He is crucified, buried, and resurrected. He visits several of His friends and tells them to spread the gospel before He ascends into heaven (see Matthew 21–28; Mark 11–16; Luke 19:29–Luke 24; John 13, 18–20; Acts 1:1–11).

Jesus dies and his body is put in a sepulchre nearby. Mary Magdalene and Jesus's Apostles visit the sepulchre only to find Jesus's body gone. The Apostles go home, but Mary stays there and cries. Jesus comes and speaks to Mary. Later He appears to ten of His apostles. Later still, He shows Himself to Thomas, one of His apostles (see John 19:30–John 20).

Gospel Art Pictures

- *Jesus Raising Lazarus from the Dead* (#49)
- *Triumphal Entry* (#50)
- *Jesus Cleansing the Temple* (#51)
- *Easter-related pictures* (#54–62)

Church History

Joseph Smith was visited by the resurrected Lord several times. Other leaders have also shared that they have seen the resurrected Lord. On several occasions, George Q. Cannon, a member of the First Presidency, shared that he had seen and spoken to Jesus Christ face-to-face. Three people have verified that President Lorenzo Snow told them that Jesus came to him in the Salt Lake City temple shortly after Wilford Woodruff died, making him (Lorenzo Snow) the next prophet and President of the Church. (For more details of this experience, see a FairMormon.org post titled "Why have so few revelations after Joseph Smith been added to the Doctrine and Covenants?" dated September 13, 2014 at http://goo .gl/GY4zR7). To see a video on the life and experiences of Lorenzo Snow, including an account of this visitation, go to https://goo.gl/duh2Zn.

Lorenzo Snow: Documentary
https://goo.gl/duh2Zn

LDS.org video "He Lives: Testimonies of Jesus Christ." In this video, modern-day Apostles testify of Jesus Christ.
http://goo.gl/M3PKZk

Ezra Taft Benson declared, "He lives! He lives with resurrected body. There is no truth or fact of which I am more assured, or know better by personal experience, than the truth of the literal Resurrection of our Lord" ("Five Marks of the Divinity of Jesus Christ," *Ensign*, December 2001). Hugh B. Brown shared with his nephew Harold B. Lee that the Lord had come to see him and speak with him. John Taylor said, "I know that Jesus Christ lives for I have seen him" (Stephen K. Iba, "A Cloud of Witnesses," *Ensign*, December 2002) Henry B. Eyring said, "I know as surely as did the Apostles Peter, James, and John that Jesus is the Christ, our risen Lord" (Henry B. Eyring, "Witnesses for God," *Ensign*, November 1996).

Adaptations for Younger Children

Quote

"This is Easter morning. This is the Lord's day, when we celebrate the greatest victory of all time, the victory over death. . . . He is our King, our Lord, our Master, the living Christ, who stands on the right hand of His Father. He lives! He lives, resplendent and wonderful, the living Son of the living God. Of this we bear solemn testimony this day of rejoicing, this Easter morning, when we commemorate the miracle of the empty tomb" (Gordon B. Hinckley, "This Glorious Easter Morn," *Ensign*, May 1996).

Lesson from Behold Your Little Ones

"Jesus Christ Was Resurrected (Easter)" (Lesson 29, pp. 120–23).

Faith in God

Write your testimony of Jesus Christ (pp. 14–15).

Activity ⊙

Have an Easter egg hunt. Use plastic Easter eggs if you have them, or color and cut out some paper eggs. Write Easter-related words on strips of paper and put them in the plastic eggs, or if you're using paper eggs write them directly on the eggs. Hide the eggs and let the kids hunt for them. Then see which words are in or on the eggs and talk about how they relate to Jesus's Resurrection. You could use words like *Jesus Christ*, *tomb*, *angels*, *death*, *resurrection*, *great stone*, *linen clothes*, *Joseph of Arimathea*, and *Mary Magdalene*.

Adaptations for Older Children and Teens

Quote

"As one of His ordained witnesses, I declare this Easter morning that Jesus of Nazareth was and is that Savior of the world. . . . Today we celebrate the gift of victory over every fall we have ever experienced, every sorrow we have ever known, every discouragement we have ever had, every fear we have ever faced—to say nothing of our resurrection from death and forgiveness for our sins. . . . That first Easter sequence of Atonement and Resurrection constitutes the most consequential moment, the most generous gift, the most excruciating pain, and the most majestic manifestation of pure love ever to be demonstrated in the history of this world. Jesus Christ, the Only Begotten Son of God, suffered, died, and rose from death in order that He could . . . grasp us as we fall, hold us with His might, and through our obedience to His commandments, lift us to eternal life" (Jeffrey R. Holland, "Where Justice, Love, and Mercy Meet," *Ensign*, May 2015).

Preach My Gospel

Lesson 2: "The Plan of Salvation," pp. 47–59; "The Resurrection, Judgment, and Immortality," p. 53; "Key Definitions: Resurrection," p. 59.

Personal Progress

Review all of the "Faith" value experiences and value project ideas (pp. 13–20). Read "The Living Christ" (p. 102). Memorizing "The Living Christ" is one idea for your *Faith* value project (p. 18).

Duty to God

Select a doctrinal topic to study that relates to Christ's Resurrection, such as "The Plan of Salvation," "The Atonement of Jesus Christ," or "Faith" (see pp. 18–21, 42–45, 66–69).

Activity ☉

Get some money, treats, and small food items together. Put them in piles and tell the family that all the adults get the money, all the girls get the treats, and all the boys get food. Ask if any of the girls would like any money or food. If so, tell them that's too bad, they only get treats. Ask the boys if they would like money or treats. If so, tell them they can't have anything besides food. Ask if this seems fair. While there are lots of things we don't understand about why some people have different things and situations than others, there is one thing that is 100 percent fair for everyone. Because of the Atonement of Jesus Christ and His Resurrection, every person ever born will be resurrected. This is what a lot of members of other churches mean when they say they are saved and ask if members of our Church believe they are saved.

Daily Scriptures

Easter

Sunday

"And now, after the many testimonies which have been given of him, this is the testimony, last of all, which we give of him: That he lives! For we saw him, even on the right hand of God; and we heard the voice bearing record that he is the Only Begotten of the Father." (D&C 76:22–23)

Monday

"In the end of the sabbath, . . . came Mary Magdalene and the other Mary to see the sepulchre. And, behold, . . . two angels of the Lord descended from heaven, and came and rolled back the stone from the door, and sat upon it. And their countenance was like lightning, and their raiment white as snow: And for fear of him the keepers did shake, and became as dead men. And the angels answered and said unto the women, Fear not ye; for we know that ye seek Jesus, which was crucified. He is not here: for he is risen." (Matthew 28:1–6, footnotes 2a, 3a, 5a; from Joseph Smith Translation)

Tuesday

"And as they thus spake, Jesus himself stood in the midst of them, and saith unto them, Peace be unto you. But they were terrified and affrighted, and supposed that they had seen a spirit. And he said unto them, Why are ye troubled? and why do thoughts arise in your hearts? Behold my hands and my feet, that it is I myself: handle me, and see; for a spirit hath not flesh and bones, as ye see me have." (Luke 24:36–39)

Wednesday

"Jesus said . . . I am the resurrection, and the life: he that believeth in me, though he were dead, yet shall he live." (John 11:25)

Thursday

"There is a resurrection, therefore the grave hath no victory, and the sting of death is swallowed up in Christ." (Mosiah 16:8)

Friday

"Now, there is a death which is called a temporal death; and the death of Christ shall loose the bands of this temporal death, that all shall be raised from this temporal death. The spirit and the body shall be reunited again in its perfect form; both limb and joint shall be restored to its proper frame, even as we now are at this time." (Alma 11:42–43)

Saturday

"But now is Christ risen from the dead, and become the firstfruits of them that slept. For since by man came death, by man came also the resurrection of the dead. For as in Adam all die, even so in Christ shall all be made alive." (1 Corinthians 15:20–22)

Mother's Day

"Honour thy father and thy mother: that thy days may be long upon the land which the Lord thy God giveth thee." (Exodus 20:12) 🔲🔲

LDS.org video "To Every Mother"
https://goo.gl/E6se4h

LDS.org Bible video, scriptures, and images "Mary, the Mother of Jesus." https://goo.gl/yq4YCm

Music from *Children's Songbook* & *Hymns*

- Grandmother (*CS*, 200)
- I Often Go Walking (*CS*, 202)
- *Children's Songbook* songs about Mother's Day (202–8)
- Home Can Be a Heaven on Earth (*Hymns*, 298)

Quote

"To all of our mothers everywhere, past, present, or future, I say, 'Thank you. Thank you for giving birth, for shaping souls, for forming character, and for demonstrating the pure love of Christ.' To Mother Eve, to Sarah, Rebekah, and Rachel, to Mary of Nazareth, and to a Mother in Heaven, I say, 'Thank you for your crucial role in fulfilling the purposes of eternity.' To all mothers in every circumstance, including those who struggle—and all will—I say, 'Be peaceful. Believe in God and yourself. You are doing better than you think you are. . . . Your love "never faileth."' I can pay no higher tribute to anyone" (Jeffrey R. Holland, "Behold Thy Mother," *Ensign*, November 2015).

Scripture Stories

Mary is visited by an angel who tells her she will be the mother of the Son of God. She expresses humility and trust. She visits her cousin Elizabeth and praises the Lord (see Luke 1:26–56).

Eve expresses gratitude that she and Adam ate the fruit of the knowledge of good and evil and in consequence, can now experience joy and have children. They teach their children the plan of redemption (see Moses 5:10–12).

LDS.org video and article "Motherhood: An Eternal Partnership with God" https://goo.gl/v7mwso

The two thousand young Anti-Nephi-Lehi warriors faithfully defend their families. Their mothers taught them that if they had faith and did not doubt, God would keep them safe. All of them end up being injured, but none of them are killed (see Alma 53:10–22, Alma 56, and Alma 57:19–27).

Gospel Art Pictures

- *Adam and Eve Teaching Their Children* (#5)
- *The Annunciation: The Angel Gabriel Appears to Mary* (#28)
- *Jesus Praying with His Mother* (#33)
- *Two Thousand Young Warriors* (#80)

Church History

Over the years, leaders of the Church have honored Mother Eve for her courage and wisdom:

> Some Christians condemn Eve for her act, concluding that she and her daughters are somehow flawed by it. Not the Latter-day Saints! Informed by revelation, we celebrate Eve's act and honor her wisdom and courage in the great episode called the Fall. Joseph Smith taught that it was not a "sin," because God had decreed it. Brigham Young declared, "We should never blame Mother Eve, not the least." Elder Joseph Fielding Smith said: "I never speak of the part Eve took in this fall as a sin, nor do I accuse Adam of a sin. . . . This was a transgression of the law, but not a sin . . . for it was something that Adam and Eve had to do!" (Dallin H. Oaks, "The Great Plan of Happiness," *Ensign*, November 1993; ellipses in original. To see this talk, go to https://goo.gl/y2DZQk; ellipses in original)

Joseph Smith's mother, Lucy Mack Smith, was a great source of support for Joseph. She was the first to hear of his relief after the witnesses of the Book of Mormon had their marvelous experiences. While Joseph and Hyrum were very sick with cholera (and far from home in Zion's Camp), Hyrum told Joseph that he had a vision of their mother praying under an apple tree for their safety and that the Spirit confirmed to him that they would return home (see M. Russell Ballard, "The Family of the Prophet Joseph Smith," *Ensign*, November 1991. To see this talk, go to at http://goo.gl/AtQsid).

LDS.org image depicting
Adam and Eve: "Similitude"
http://goo.gl/EFWS5A

"Adam and Eve"
http://goo.gl/8RwXHE

"Adam and Eve Teaching
Their Children"
http://goo.gl/jyze8E

Adaptations for Younger Children

Quote

"I will honor my parents and do my part to strengthen my family" ("My Gospel Standards").

Lesson from *Behold Your Little Ones*

"I Love My Family" (Lesson 11, pp. 48–51).

Faith in God

"Entertain young children with songs or games you have learned or made yourself. Show that you know how to care for and protect a young child" (p. 9).

Activity

Make Mother's Day cards. You can make a card for the mother in your family, your grandmothers, or female teachers and leaders your kids particularly like.

Write the letters M-O-T-H-E-R on a large paper and have the children think of things mothers like that begin with each letter. Write their answers on the paper. See the example on the right.

M	Music
O	Otters
T	Talking to her friends
H	Help with chores
E	Essential oils
R	Reading to her kids

Adaptations for Older Children and Teens

Quotes

"Do we also teach our sons and daughters there is no greater honor, no more elevated title, and no more important role in this life than that of mother or father? I would hope that as we encourage our children to reach for the very best in this life that we also teach them to honor and exalt the roles that mothers and fathers play in Heavenly Father's plan" (Bonnie L. Oscarson, "Defenders of the Family Proclamation," *Ensign*, May 2015).

"Let us speak about our worthy and wonderful sisters, particularly our mothers, and consider our sacred duty to honor them. . . . My opinion [is] that the highest and noblest work in this life is that of a mother. . . . Because mothers are essential to God's great plan of happiness, their sacred work is opposed by Satan, who would destroy the family and demean the worth of women. . . . Show respect and gratitude [to women]. Remember that your mother is your *mother*. She should not need to issue orders. . . . Thank her and express your love for her. And if she is struggling to rear you without your father, you have a double duty to honor her" (Russell M. Nelson, "Our Sacred Duty to Honor Women," *Ensign*, May 1999; italics in original).

Preach My Gospel

Chapter 10: "How Can I Improve My Teaching Skills?," pp. 175–94.

Personal Progress

Faith #2—Read "The Family: A Proclamation to the World" (*Personal Progress,* p. 101), and study the role of mothers. Study and discuss how mothers can help their children develop faith in God (p. 14).

Review the section on "Divine Nature." See what you've done and what you haven't done. Look over the project ideas and see if any appeal to you. Think up some ideas for value experiences and project ideas (pp. 21–28).

Duty to God

"Interview a mother, grandmother, sister, or other woman to learn about how to show proper respect to women. Make a plan to apply what you learn" (p. 81). Focus on general respect for women.

Activity

You can adapt the Father's Day activity idea (p. 206), so you can use it for Mother's Day.

Hold up your hands and show how similar they are to each other. Are they exactly the same? No, but they are very similar. Can you work better with one hand or with both? Both, of course! Read the following quote: "Our two hands are similar to each other but not exactly the same. In fact, they are exact opposites, but they complement each other and are suited to each other. Working together, they are stronger. . . . 'The nature of male and female spirits is such that they complete each other.' Please note that it does not say 'compete with each other' but 'complete each other'! We are here to help, lift, and rejoice with each other as we try to become our very best selves" (Linda K. Burton, "We'll Ascend Together," *Ensign*, May 2015).

Daily Scriptures

Mother's Day

Sunday 📖

"Honour thy father and thy mother: that thy days may be long upon the land which the Lord thy God giveth thee." (Exodus 20:12)

Monday 📖

"God created man in his own image, in the image of God created he him; male and female created he them. And God blessed them, and God said unto them, Be fruitful, and multiply, and replenish the earth." (Genesis 1:27–28)

Tuesday

"Among the great and mighty ones who were assembled in this vast congregation of the righteous were Father Adam, the Ancient of Days and father of all, And our glorious Mother Eve, with many of her faithful daughters who had lived through the ages and worshiped the true and living God." (D&C 138:38–39)

Wednesday

"Behold, one came and said unto [Jesus], Good Master, what good thing shall I do, that I may have eternal life? . . . If thou wilt enter into life, keep the commandments. He saith unto him, Which? Jesus said, Thou shalt do no murder, Thou shalt not commit adultery, Thou shalt not steal, Thou shalt not bear false witness, Honour thy father and thy mother: and, Thou shalt love thy neighbour as thyself." (Matthew 19:16–19)

Thursday

"Now they [the stripling warriors] never had fought, yet they did not fear death; and they did think more upon the liberty of their fathers than they did upon their lives; yea, they had been taught by their mothers, that if they did not doubt, God would deliver them. And they rehearsed unto me the words of their mothers, saying: We do not doubt our mothers knew it." (Alma 56:47–48)

Friday

"Yea, and [the stripling warriors] did obey and observe to perform every word of command with exactness; yea, and even according to their faith it was done unto them; and I did remember the words which they said unto me that their mothers had taught them." (Alma 57:21)

Saturday

"Children, obey your parents in the Lord: for this is right. Honour thy father and mother; (which is the first commandment with promise;) That it may be well with thee, and thou mayest live long on the earth. . . . Provoke not your children to wrath: but bring them up in the nurture and admonition of the Lord." (Ephesians 6:1–4)

Memorial Day

"Greater love hath no man than this, that a man lay down his life for his friends." (John 15:13)

Gospel Topic: Family History Work
http://goo.gl/KxQP2i

LDS.org "Joseph Smith
Birthplace Memorial"
http://goo.gl/gAZYMi

Music from Children's Songbook & Hymns

- Truth from Elijah (*CS*, 90)
- I Love to See the Temple (*CS*, 95)
- I Stand All Amazed (*Hymns*, 193)
- Turn Your Hearts (*Hymns*, 291)

Quote

"May we acknowledge gratitude for our *country*—the land of our birth. When we ponder that vast throng who have died honorably defending home and hearth, we contemplate those immortal words, 'Greater love hath no man than this, that a man lay down his life for his friends' (John 15:13). The feelings of heartfelt gratitude for the supreme sacrifice made by so many cannot be confined to a Memorial Day, a military parade, or a decorated grave" (Thomas S. Monson, "An Attitude of Gratitude," *Ensign*, May 1992; italics in original).

Scripture Stories

Teancum works with Captain Moroni and dies for his country (see Alma 62:31–37).

Jesus died for all people. Every Sunday the sacrament is offered as a memorial to His sacrifice. He said, "Greater love hath no man than this, that a man lay down his life for his friends" (John 15:13) (see also D&C 20:77, 79; D&C 35:2).

Malachi and Joseph Smith are told that Elijah will return to turn the hearts of children to their ancestors (see Malachi 4:5–6; D&C 2). Elijah appears to Joseph Smith and Oliver Cowdery in the Kirtland Temple and restores the sealing power (see D&C 110:13–15). Each day, as temple work is done for ancestors, it is like a memorial day for that family because they are remembering, honoring, and serving those who have gone before them. 🅓🅜

Gospel Art Pictures

- *The Last Supper* (#54)
- *The Crucifixion* (#57)
- *Captain Moroni Raises the Title of Liberty* (#79)
- *Elman Appearing in the Kirtland Temple* (#95)

Church History

On January 2, 1945, Joseph Fielding Smith received a telegram that his son Lewis had been killed while serving in the military (*Teachings of Presidents of the Church: Joseph Fielding Smith,* 25). Joseph Fielding Smith was ninety-three when he became the President of the Church, making him the oldest man to become president in the latter days. To see a documentary of Joseph Fielding Smith, go to https://goo.gl/p6xy5E.

Joseph Fielding Smith: Documentary
https://goo.gl/p6xy5E

Out of love for family members who have died, latter-day Saints do temple work and seal families together. When were the sealing keys given to Joseph Smith? *On April 3, 1836.* On this day, in the Kirtland Temple, Jesus Christ, Moses, Elias, and Elijah appeared to Joseph Smith and Oliver Cowdery. They received the keys of each dispensation and the sealing power (see *Teachings of Presidents of the Church: Joseph Smith*, 308 or https://goo.gl/v4gKNm).

LDS.org video ("Your Fingers Have Been Trained") of Elder Bednar inviting the youth to do family history work.
https://goo.gl/E6pZQN

When was the revelation given to Joseph F. Smith on the redemption of the dead? *October 3, 1918.* The vision is recorded in Doctrine and Covenants 138.

When did Elder Bednar invite the youth of the Church to become seriously involved in doing family history research and temple work? *October 2011* (see "The Hearts of the Children Shall Turn," *Ensign,* November 2011).

Adaptations for Younger Children

Quote

"I am trying to remember and follow Jesus Christ" ("My Gospel Standards").

Lesson from *Behold Your Little Ones*

"The Sacrament Helps Me Think about Jesus Christ" (Lesson 27, pp. 112–15). Every Sunday we memorialize Jesus's atoning sacrifice by participating in the sacrament ordinance.

Faith in God

"Prepare a pedigree chart with your name and your parents' and grandparents' names. Prepare a family group record for your family and share a family story. Discuss how performing temple work blesses families" (p. 7). See https://goo.gl/5qeeFD for a pedigree chart from LDS.org, and https://goo.gl/kkf8zG for a family group record from LDS.org. Both are also found in "Keeping Family History Records," in *Young Women Manual 2* (1993), 60–62.

Activity

Memorial Day is traditionally a day to remember people who have died serving their country in the armed forces. Tell stories about people who have served their country.

Many people use this day to remember friends and family members who have died. Tell inspiring stories of loved ones who have died. You can also tell stories about your parents and grandparents, whether living or dead. Share what you admire about them. Show pictures of your parents, grandparents, and any other ancestors whose pictures you have.

Adaptations for Older Children and Teens

Quotes

"God bless the memory of those who have given their lives in the service of their country, and God bless those who languish in prison camps. May he sustain and bless them, those of every faith, and hasten the day of their release. God bless those whose bodies have been broken and whose minds have been injured, and particularly may he bless those who have fallen casualties of the moral ugliness that abounds when men will not live in peace. May he sustain those of you who have been bereft of a loved one, and speak to you of peace—that peace which surpasseth understanding" (Boyd K. Packer, "Our Honored Brethren," *New Era*, August 1971).

"It is no coincidence that FamilySearch and other tools have come forth at a time when young people are so familiar with a wide range of information and communication technologies. Your fingers have been trained to text and tweet to accelerate and advance the work of the Lord—not just to communicate quickly with your friends. The skills and aptitude evident among many young people today are a preparation to contribute to the work of salvation. . . . Elijah returned to the earth and restored the sacred sealing authority. I witness that what is bound on earth can be bound in heaven. And I know the youth of the rising generation have a key role to play in this great endeavor" (David A. Bednar, "The Hearts of the Children Shall Turn," Ensign, November 2011).

Preach My Gospel

Lesson 5: "Laws and Ordinances," pp. 82–88; "Temples and Family History," pp. 86–87; "Family History," pp. 163–65.

Personal Progress

Individual Worth #6—Participate in family history work. Visit with family members and learn about your family history. Complete a pedigree chart of your family (p. 31). (Go to https://goo.gl/5qeeFD for a printable pedigree chart from LDS.org).

Duty to God

Study doctrinal topics of "Eternal Families and Family History Work" and "Service." The scriptures have many war stories and tell of people who died while fighting for their country. Study those stories and learn about soldiers who were faithful during wartimes. Record what you learn and share what you learned with your parents or a priesthood leader (see pp. 18–21, 42–45, 66–69).

Activity

Have two people stand on opposite sides of the room. One person represents the people on earth and the other person represents the people who have died. Tell your family they need to connect the two people, but neither person can move. Brainstorm ideas until you decide to make a human chain by having the rest of the family hold hands to connect the two people on the ends. Talk about the importance of doing temple work to connect and seal families together on both sides of the veil. (Adapted from Richard R. Eubank, *Is There an Object to Your Lesson?*, 74.)

Daily Scriptures

Memorial Day

Sunday

"Greater love hath no man than this, that a man lay down his life for his friends." (John 15:13)

Monday 📖

"Behold, I will send you Elijah the prophet before the coming of the great and dreadful day of the Lord: And he shall turn the heart of the fathers to the children, and the heart of the children to their fathers, lest I come and smite the earth with a curse." (Malachi 4:5–6)

Tuesday

Helaman's stripling warriors "fought most desperately; yea, they were firm before the Lamanites, and did administer death unto all those who opposed them. And as the remainder of our army were about to give way before the Lamanites, behold, those two thousand and sixty were firm and undaunted. Yea, and they did obey and observe to perform every word of command with exactness; yea, and even according to their faith it was done unto them; and I did remember the words which they said unto me that their mothers had taught them." (Alma 57:19–21)

Wednesday

"My beloved brethren, I would speak unto you concerning hope. How is it that ye can attain unto faith, save ye shall have hope? And what is it that ye shall hope for? Behold I say unto you that ye shall have hope through the atonement of Christ and the power of his resurrection, to be raised unto life eternal, and this because of your faith in him according to the promise." (Moroni 7:40–41)

Thursday

"The Lord has said that: Ye shall defend your families even unto bloodshed. Therefore for this cause were the Nephites contending with the Lamanites, to defend themselves, and their families, and their lands, their country, and their rights, and their religion." (Alma 43:47)

Friday

"My beloved brethren, I say unto you that the Lord God worketh not in darkness. He doeth not anything save it be for the benefit of the world; for he loveth the world, even that he layeth down his own life that he may draw all men unto him." (2 Nephi 26:23–24)

Saturday

The stripling warriors "did not fear death; and they did think more upon the liberty of their fathers than they did upon their lives. . . . And they . . . fought as if with the strength of God; yea, never were men known to have fought with such miraculous strength; and with such mighty power." (Alma 56:47, 56)

Father's Day

"Verily, verily, I say unto you, ye must watch and pray always, lest ye be tempted by the devil, and ye be led away captive by him. Pray in your families unto the Father, always in my name, that your wives and your children may be blessed." (3 Nephi 18:15, 21) 🅳🅼

LDS.org video "Today's Family: Fathers"
https://goo.gl/Tku6ky

LDS.org video "All the Reasons We Love Dad"
https://goo.gl/qkBnaa

Music from Children's Songbook & Hymns

- When Grandpa Comes (*CS*, 201)
- Daddy's Homecoming (*CS*, 210)
- *Children's Songbook* songs about fathers (*CS*, 208–11)
- Teach Me to Walk in the Light (*Hymns*, 304)

Quotes

"Every father in the Church should function as the patriarch of his home. He should take the lead in spiritually guiding the family. He ought not to delegate nor abrogate his responsibilities to the mother" (F. Melvin Hammond, "Dad, Are You Awake?," *Ensign*, November 2002).

"As a Church, we believe in fathers. We believe in 'the ideal of the man who puts his family first.' We believe that 'by divine design, fathers are to preside over their families in love and righteousness and are responsible to provide the necessities of life and protection for their families.' We believe that in their complementary family duties, 'fathers and mothers are obligated to help one another as equal partners.' We believe that far from being superfluous, fathers are unique and irreplaceable" (D. Todd Christofferson, "Fathers," *Ensign*, May 2016).

Scripture Stories

Lehi explains that Adam, the father of mankind, could not have had children in the Garden of Eden. Because of his and Eve's choice to eat the forbidden fruit, they were able to have children and experience joy in this life (see 2 Nephi 2:19–25).

An angel appears to Alma the Younger and his friends. He says God has heard Alma's father's prayers and sent him, the angel, in response to his faith and prayers. He calls Alma the Younger to repentance (see Mosiah 27:8–14).

Gospel Art Pictures

- *Adam and Eve Teaching Their Children* (#5)
- *Conversion of Alma the Younger* (#77)

Church History

The Lord covenanted with the childless *Abram* (whose name means "exalted father" in Hebrew) that he would have a son. The Lord changed Abram's name to *Abraham*, meaning "the father of a multitude" (see Bible Dictionary "Abraham"). In 1835, Joseph Smith came across some Egyptian papyri and translated them. The translation was first published in 1842 and was later published as "The Book of Abraham" in the Pearl of Great Price in 1880. On LDS.org, it says,

> "This book . . . recounts how Abraham sought the blessings of the priesthood, rejected the idolatry of his father, covenanted with Jehovah, married Sarai, moved to Canaan and Egypt, and received knowledge about the Creation. The book of Abraham largely follows the biblical narrative but adds important information regarding Abraham's life and teachings." (LDS.org gospel topic on the Book of Abraham, https://goo.gl/573ZE9. To learn more, go to FairMormon's page "Book of Abraham" at http://goo.gl/TC9FYv. For videos, go to https://goo.gl/cf7tWm and https://goo.gl/fV7WzE).

LDS.org video "Abrahamic Covenant" https://goo.gl/fV7WzE

LDS.org video "Seed of Abraham" https://goo.gl/cf7tWm

Adaptations for Younger Children

Quote

"I will honor my parents and do my part to strengthen my family" ("My Gospel Standards").

Lesson from *Behold Your Little Ones*

"My Family Can Be Together Forever" (Lesson 13, pp. 56–59).

Faith in God

"List five things you can do to help around your home. Discuss the importance of obeying and honoring your parents and learning how to work" (p. 11).

Activity

Make Father's Day cards. You can make a card for the father in your family, your grandfathers, or male teachers and leaders your kids particularly like.

Write the letters F-A-T-H-E-R on a large paper and have the children think of things that describe their father that begin with each letter. Write their answers on the paper. See the example on the right.

F	Funny
A	Active
T	Tall
H	Happy
E	Energetic
R	Reader

Adaptations for Older Children and Teens

Quotes

"Fathers, yours is an eternal calling from which you are never released. Callings in the Church, as important as they are, by their very nature are only for a period of time, and then an appropriate release takes place. But a father's calling is eternal, and its importance transcends time. It is a calling for both time and eternity. . . . [Fathers,] you have a sacred responsibility to provide spiritual leadership in your family" (Ezra Taft Benson, *Teachings of Presidents of the Church: Ezra Taft Benson*, 194; brackets in original).

"Husbands and fathers in Israel, you can do so much for the salvation and exaltation of your families! Your responsibilities are so important. . . . Your homes should be havens of peace and joy for your family. Surely no child should fear his own father—especially a priesthood father. A father's duty is to make his home a place of happiness and joy. . . . The powerful effect of righteous fathers in setting an example, disciplining and training, nurturing and loving is vital to the spiritual welfare of [their] children" (Ezra Taft Benson, *Teachings of Presidents of the Church: Ezra Taft Benson*, 195–96).

Preach My Gospel

Chapter 12: "How Do I Prepare People for Baptism and Confirmation?," pp. 203–12.

Personal Progress

Divine Nature #5—"Obedience is an attribute of the Savior. Strive to be more obedient to your parents. . . . Treat your parents with respect and kindness" (p. 24).

Divine Nature #8 or #9: Personalized Value Experience—Complete Divine Nature value experiences 1 and 2. Then do parallel activities focusing on studying divine qualities of a *son* of God, learning about divine masculine qualities, and increasing in your appreciation for righteous manhood. (pp. 22, 25).

Duty to God

"Read: 'The Family: A Proclamation to the World,' [see *Duty to God*, p. 107] and identify your role as a future husband and father" (p. 55).

Activity

Have everyone quickly write down their five favorite characteristics about their dad, their grandpa, or a favorite male teacher or friend. Then have everyone quickly write down five memories of their dad (or other chosen man). Finally, have everyone list five things they've learned from their dad (or whoever they've chosen). Make a poster that includes some or all of what everyone wrote down. Invite everyone to write a letter to their dad (or other chosen man), and include some or all of what they wrote down in the activity.

Daily Scriptures

Father's Day

Sunday

"Verily, verily, I say unto you, ye must watch and pray always, lest ye be tempted by the devil, and ye be led away captive by him. Pray in your families unto the Father, always in my name, that your wives and your children may be blessed." (3 Nephi 18:15, 21)

Monday

"Honour thy father and thy mother: that thy days may be long upon the land which the Lord thy God giveth thee." (Exodus 20:12)

Tuesday

"God created man in his own image, in the image of God created he him; male and female created he them. And God blessed them, and God said unto them, Be fruitful, and multiply, and replenish the earth." (Genesis 1:27–28)

Wednesday

"My son, despise not thou the chastening of the Lord. . . . For whom the Lord loveth he chasteneth. . . . If ye endure chastening, God dealeth with you as with sons; for what son is he whom the father chasteneth not? Furthermore we have had fathers of our flesh which corrected us, and we gave them reverence: shall we not much rather be in subjection unto the Father of spirits? . . . He [chasteneth us] for our profit, that we might be partakers of his holiness." (Hebrews 12:5–7, 9–10. Footnote *b* in verse 7 provides the Greek translation for the word "chastening." It says "correction, instruction." Reread these verses, replacing the words "chastening" and "chastenth" with "correction" and "corrects," or "instruction" and "instructs.")

Thursday

"The angel said [to Alma the Younger]: Behold, the Lord hath heard the prayers of his people, and also the prayers of his servant, Alma, who is thy father; for he has prayed with much faith concerning thee that thou mightest be brought to the knowledge of the truth; therefore, for this purpose have I come to convince thee of the power and authority of God, that the prayers of his servants might be answered according to their faith." (Mosiah 27:14)

Friday

"Children, obey your parents in the Lord: for this is right. And, ye fathers, provoke not your children to wrath: but bring them up in the nurture and admonition of the Lord." (Ephesians 6:1, 4)

Saturday

"I give unto you a commandment, to teach [the gospel] freely unto your children." (Moses 6:58)

Independence Day

"The Spirit of God . . . is also the spirit of freedom." (Alma 61:15)

LDS.org image "The Statue of Liberty" https://goo.gl/ySaVy8

Music from Children's Songbook & Hymns

- My Country (*CS*, 224)
- My Flag, My Flag (*CS*, 225)
- The Star-Spangled Banner, or your national anthem (*Hymns*, 340)
- Patriotic hymns (*Hymns*, 338–41)

Quote

"We must put our trust in Him who has promised us His protection—and pray that he will intervene to preserve our freedom just as He intervened in our obtaining it in the first place" (Ezra Taft Benson, "A Witness and a Warning," *Ensign*, November 1979).

Scripture Stories

LDS.org image "Tabernacle Interior in July" https://goo.gl/rRs8aQ

Moses comes across a bush that is covered in flames, but is not burning. In that place, the Lord speaks to him and calls him to free Israel from the Egyptians. Moses courageously follows God's direction and the Israelites are led out of bondage. The Sabbath is to be used as a memorial for their deliverance (see Exodus 3–14).

David fights Goliath and wins the battle with the Philistines (see 1 Samuel 17).

After Lehi dies, the Lord tells Nephi to take those who believe in Him and separate themselves from Laman and Lemuel, so they can be safe and free to worship Him (see 2 Nephi 4:12–14; 2 Nephi 5).

Captain Moroni makes the title of liberty, dresses in his armor, prays mightily for God to bless his people with freedom, and raises the title of liberty. Everyone runs toward him and pledges that they will fight for their freedom and be faithful to God (see Alma 46:10–21)

Gospel Art Pictures

- *Moses and the Burning Bush* (#13)
- *David Slays Goliath* (#19)
- *Nephi Subdues His Rebellious Brothers* (#70)
- *Captain Moroni Raises the Title of Liberty* (#79)
- *Family Prayer* (#112)

Church History

The *Journal of Discourses* is a twenty-six volume set of sermons delivered by early Church leaders between 1854 and 1866. These volumes were published privately (not as an official publication of the Church) by George Watt. There are several talks in the *Journal of Discourses* that were given on July 4 during Independence Day celebrations. On July 4, 1854, George A. Smith said, "I love American Independence: the principle is dear to my heart. When I have been in foreign countries, I have felt proud of the American flag, and have desired that they could have the enjoyment of as much liberty as the American people" (*Journal of Discourses*, vol 6, 366).

Ezra Taft Benson Documentary
https://goo.gl/JsLzam

Some people wonder if the *Journal of Discourses* are considered canonical and if the teachings therein are considered doctrinal and binding. On LDS.org it says, "The Journal of Discourses includes interesting and insightful teachings by early Church leaders; however, by itself it is not an authoritative source of Church doctrine" (see the gospel topic "Journal of Discourses" at http://goo .gl/CFyrrc. See also the FairMormon page "Was the Journal of Discourses one of the 'standard works' of the Church?" at http://goo.gl/kT37J3). One obviously nondoctrinal topic published in the *Journal of Discourses* that has gotten a lot of attention is something called the "Adam-God" theory, a belief of Brigham Young's that was not well understood, and which modern leaders have clearly explained is not doctrine. To learn more about the Adam-God theory, go to FairMormon's page "What is the Adam-God Theory?" at http://goo.gl/JpnnDN.

Ezra Taft Benson had an unparalleled zeal for patriotism and served for years as the United States Secretary of Agriculture under President Eisenhower. To see a video documentary of his life, go to https://goo.gl/JsLzam.

Adaptations for Younger Children

Quote

"Love the country in which you live. Be a good citizen. Be patriotic. Fly your country's flag on special holidays. Pray for your country's leaders" (Ezra Taft Benson, "To the Children of the Church," *Ensign*, May 1989).

Lesson from *Behold Your Little Ones*

"I Can Pray with My Family" (Lesson 12, pp. 52–55). Talk about the importance of praying for your country and its leaders, and to know how you can support your country.

Faith in God

"Read the twelfth article of faith. Discuss what it means to be a good citizen and how your actions can affect others" (p. 9).

Activity ☺

Sing patriotic songs, tell patriotic stories, or read patriotic poems. Draw or color a picture of your nation's flag. You can bake a cake and decorate it to look like your country's flag. For example, you can make it look like the Unites States flag by using whipped cream or white frosting, blueberries for the blue between the stars, and strawberries for the red stripes.

Adaptations for Older Children and Teens

Quotes

"Those men who laid the foundation of this American government and signed the Declaration of Independence were the best spirits the God of heaven could find on the face of the earth. . . . General Washington and all the men who labored for the purpose were inspired of the Lord" ("President Wilford Woodruff," *Conference Report,* April 1898, 89).

"If we truly cherish the heritage we have received, we must maintain the same virtues and the same character of our stalwart forebears—faith in God, courage, industry, frugality, self-reliance, and integrity. We have the obligation to maintain what those who pledged their lives, their fortunes, and sacred honor gave to future generations. . . . May we begin to repay this debt by preserving and strengthening this heritage in our own lives, in the lives of our children, their children, and generations yet unborn" (Ezra Taft Benson, "Our Priceless Heritage," *Ensign*, November 1976).

Preach My Gospel

"Obedience," pp. 72, 122; "Obey and Honor the Law," p. 80–81; Chapter 11: "How Do I Help People Make and Keep Commitments?," pp. 195–202. Making and keeping commitments can lead to personal freedom.

Personal Progress

Integrity #8 or #9: Personalized Value Experience—Read conference talks on citizenship, such as the ones quoted in this FHE lesson. Talk to your parents and other respected adults about how to be an excellent and contributing citizen. Write about what you learn in your journal, as well as what you plan to do now and in the future to be a good citizen. (p. 65).

Duty to God

Study the doctrinal topic of "Agency," focusing on how the use of agency can bring personal as well as national freedom and independence. Record what you learn and share what you learned with your parents or a priesthood leader (see pp. 18–21, 42–45, 66–69).

Activity

Whether or not you live in the United States, the United States Independence Day is part of your heritage as a member of the Church. The Church could not have been restored without the freedom to worship as one chooses. The best-known symbol for the United States is its flag. A flag is a banner that stands for something; it usually has symbolic colors and designs to convey information about the thing it stands for. The United States flag has thirteen alternating red and white stripes and a blue rectangle in the top left corner with fifty small, white stars. The common understanding is that red stands for courage, white stands for purity, and blue stands for justice. On a piece of paper, design a flag for your family. Include things that represent your family, such as your family's talents, values, and character. Decide what colors to use, and what you want them to stand for. Display it somewhere where the family will see it often, such as on a wall near the dinner table or by the front door.

Daily Scriptures

Independence Day

Sunday

"The Spirit of God . . . is also the spirit of freedom." (Alma 61:15)

Monday

"I, the Lord God, make you free, therefore ye are free indeed; and the law also maketh you free. Nevertheless, when the wicked rule the people mourn. Wherefore, honest men and wise men should be sought for diligently, and good men and wise men ye should observe to uphold." (D&C 98:8–10)

Tuesday

"The sins of many people have been caused by the iniquities of their kings. . . . And now I [King Mosiah] desire that this inequality should be no more in this land, especially among this my people; but I desire that this land be a land of liberty, and every man may enjoy his rights and privileges alike. . . . [and] that the burden should come upon all the people, that every man might bear his part." (Mosiah 29:31–32, 34)

Wednesday

"The laws and constitution of the people, which I have suffered to be established . . . should be maintained for the rights and protection of all flesh. . . . And for this purpose have I established the Constitution of this land, by the hands of wise men whom I raised up unto this very purpose." (D&C 101:77, 80)

Thursday

"I, Lehi, prophesy according to the workings of the Spirit which is in me, that there shall none come into this land save they shall be brought by the hand of the Lord. Wherefore, this land is consecrated unto him whom he shall bring. And if it so be that they shall serve him according to the commandments which he hath given, it shall be a land of liberty." (2 Nephi 1:6–7)

Friday

"This land, said God, shall be a land of thine inheritance, and the Gentiles shall be blessed upon the land. And this land shall be a land of liberty unto the Gentiles, and there shall be no kings upon the land." (2 Nephi 10:10–11)

Saturday

"That law of the land which is constitutional, supporting that principle of freedom in maintaining rights and privileges, belongs to all mankind, and is justifiable before me. Therefore, I, the Lord, justify you, and your brethren of my church, in befriending that law which is the constitutional law of the land." (D&C 98:5–6)

Pioneer Day
(Faith and Fasting)

The Nephites "did fast and pray oft, and did wax stronger and stronger in their humility, and firmer and firmer in the faith of Christ, unto the filling their souls with joy." (Helaman 3:35)

Music from Children's Songbook & Hymns

Gospel Topic: Fasting and Fast Offerings
https://goo.gl/4HV1CC

- Pioneer Children Sang As They Walked (*CS*, 214)
- *Children's Songbook* songs about pioneers (*CS*, 214–22)
- Come, Come, Ye Saints (*Hymns*, 30)
- Pioneer hymns (*Hymns*, 34–37, 255)
- Fasting hymns (*Hymns*, 138–39, 219)

Quote

"Is there a lesson in the pioneer experience for us today? I believe there is. The faith that motivated the pioneers of 1847 as well as pioneers in other lands was a simple faith centered in the basic doctrines of the restored gospel, which they knew to be true" (M. Russell Ballard, "You Have Nothing to Fear from the Journey," *Ensign*, May 1997).

Scripture Stories

LDS.org video "Caring for the Poor and Needy"
https://goo.gl/877rjV

The Jews are condemned to death by a decree. Queen Esther asks the Jews to fast and pray with her for three days. She risks her life to save her people, and the king reverses the decree (see Esther 3:8–15, 4:16, 8:17).

After being chastised by an angel, the sons of Mosiah bring an immobile Alma the Younger to his father. Alma's father and some priests fast and pray for Alma the Younger. He receives strength and tells everyone he has repented and has been forgiven (see Mosiah 27:19–24).

Gospel Art Pictures

LDS.org video "Pioneers." Elder Oaks honors modern-day pioneers.
https://goo.gl/2SYgzy

- *Esther* (#21)
- *Conversion of Alma the Younger* (#77)
- *Exodus from Nauvoo, February–May 1846* (#99)
- *Mary Fielding Smith and Joseph F. Smith Crossing the Plains* (#101)
- *Handcart Pioneers Approaching the Salt Lake Valley* (#102)

Church History

On July 24, 1847, President Brigham Young declared that the Salt Lake Valley would be the Saints' new home. The pioneers planted a lot of seeds in hopes that there would be a great harvest for themselves and for those who were still coming. However, as the food grew and began to ripen, thousands of crickets began eating the crops. The people tried everything they could to stop the crickets, but were unsuccessful for three weeks. They held a special fast, and prayed that the Lord would stop the crickets and save the crops. Amazingly, seagulls came and ate the crickets. They'd eat the crickets, go to get a drink, spit out the crickets they had eaten, then come back for more. After about three weeks, the crickets were gone and the crops were saved. When Utah

LDS.org image "Coming of the Gulls" https://goo.gl/bmqgw5

became a state, the pioneers named the seagull the state bird in gratitude for the Lord saving their crops fifty years earlier. There is even a monument, titled the Seagull Monument, on Temple Square in Salt Lake City, Utah. (*Primary 5 Manual*, "Lesson 41: The Saints Settle the Salt Lake Valley," 238–44)

One hundred years later, on July 24, 1947, President George Albert Smith dedicated the This is the Place Monument. Membership that year reached one million members (*Teachings of Presidents of the Church: George Albert Smith*, x). To learn more about the pioneer's arrival and the monument to their success, see Thomas Toone's article, "Mahonri Young: Sculptor of His Heritage," from the October 1985 *Ensign*.

Adaptations for Younger Children

Quote

"Parents, teach your children the joys of a proper fast. And how do you do that? The same as with any gospel principle—let them see you live it by your example. Then help them live the law of the fast themselves, little by little. They can fast and they can also pay a fast offering if they choose. As we teach our children to fast, it can give them the power to resist temptations along their life's journey" (Joseph B. Wirthlin, "The Law of the Fast," *Ensign*, May 2001).

Lesson from *Behold Your Little Ones*

"I Am a Child of God" (Lesson 1, pp. 8–11). The pioneers believed they were God's children and had faith that He was helping them.

Faith in God

"Plan and complete your own activity that will help you learn and live the gospel" (p. 7). Read and discuss Isaiah 58:5–11 about fasting. If you would like to fast, tell your parents how they can support you in doing so.

Activity

Talk about fasting, how you do it, and why it is important to you. Many people think about what they want to fast about, open and close their fasting with prayer, and write down impressions they receive while fasting. Share some personal stories of fasting and its power in your life.

Adaptations for Older Children and Teens

Quotes

"[Our Mormon forebears came west] with indomitable faith and courage, following incredible suffering and adversity. . . . Today we live in a choice land, yes, a land choice above all other lands. We live amid unbounded prosperity—this because of the heritage bequeathed to us by our forebears, a heritage of self-reliance, initiative, personal industry, and faith in God, all in an atmosphere of freedom" (Ezra Taft Benson, "Our Priceless Heritage," *Ensign*, November 1976).

"We haven't really called on the Lord so that we can reach him intimately if we don't fast occasionally, and pray often. Many of our personal problems can be solved by so doing" (Marion G. Romney, "The Blessings of the Fast," *Ensign*, July 1982).

Preach My Gospel

"Observe the Law of the Fast," pp. 79–80; "How to Donate Tithes and Offerings," p. 80.

Personal Progress

Integrity #6—"Living the law of the fast is an opportunity to practice integrity. On a designated fast Sunday, [fast] and contribute to your family's fast offering. Have a specific purpose in mind as you fast. . . . Begin and close your fast with a prayer" (p. 64).

Duty to God

"Read Alma 17:2–3, 9, and write what the sons of Mosiah did to prepare themselves for missionary service. Consider ways you can follow their example" (p. 52). One of the things they did was fast. Study "fasting" and decide what you will do to fast with more sincerity and purpose.

Activity ☺

Get a screw, a screwdriver, and a drill (optional). Show your family the screw, but keep the screwdriver (or drill) hidden away. Talk about what the screw is and what it can be used for. Ask if one screw is useful by itself. What does it need to be useful? A screwdriver or a drill! (Show only the screwdriver.) Talk about fasting. What's the difference between fasting and just going hungry? How can you make your fasts more meaningful? By coupling it with prayer. If the screw represents going hungry, the prayer represents the screwdriver because prayer makes the fasting more meaningful. There are other things you can focus on during a fast to make it even more meaningful. You can give fast offerings, share food or money, invite people into your home, and spend special time with your family (see Isaiah 58:3–7). Adding these things to your fast is like using a drill instead of screwdriver (show the drill, if you have it). It's much more powerful. Imagine you are building a temple. Will just one screw—even if it's screwed in with a drill—be enough for your project? Of course not. Just as you need many screws to help build a temple, many experiences with fasting, prayer, and inspired actions help build your testimony. (Adapted from *Aaronic Priesthood Manual 1*, (2002), 109.)

Daily Scriptures

Pioneer Day (Faith and Fasting)

Sunday

"They did fast and pray oft, and did wax stronger and stronger in their humility, and firmer and firmer in the faith of Christ, unto the filling their souls with joy." (Helaman 3:35)

Monday

"Organize yourselves; prepare every needful thing; and establish a house, even a house of prayer, a house of fasting, a house of faith, a house of learning, a house of glory, a house of order, a house of God." (D&C 88:119)

Tuesday 🔖

"Wherefore have we fasted, say they, and thou seest not? wherefore have we afflicted our soul, and thou takest no knowledge? Behold, in the day of your fast ye find pleasure, and exact all your labours. Behold, ye fast for strife and debate, and to smite with the fist of wickedness: ye shall not fast as ye do this day, to make your voice to be heard on high. Is it such a fast that I have chosen? a day for a man to afflict his soul? is it to bow down his head as a bulrush, and to spread sackcloth and ashes under him? wilt thou call this a fast, and an acceptable day to the Lord?" (Isaiah 58:3–5)

Wednesday 🔖

"Is not this the fast that I have chosen? to loose the bands of wickedness, to undo the heavy burdens, and to let the oppressed go free, and that ye break every yoke? Is it not to deal thy bread to the hungry, and that thou bring the poor that are cast out to thy house? when thou seest the naked, that thou cover him; and that thou hide not thyself from thine own flesh? Then shall thy light break forth as the morning, and thine health shall spring forth speedily: and thy righteousness shall go before thee; the glory of the Lord shall be thy rearward. Then shalt thou call, and the Lord shall answer; thou shalt cry, and he shall say, Here I am." (Isaiah 58:6–9)

Thursday

"The church did meet together oft, to fast and to pray, and to speak one with another concerning the welfare of their souls." (Moroni 6:5)

Friday

"When ye fast be not as the hypocrites, of a sad countenance, for they disfigure their faces that they may appear unto men to fast. . . . But thou, when thou fastest, anoint thy head, and wash thy face; That thou appear not unto men to fast, but unto thy Father, who is in secret; and thy Father, who seeth in secret, shall reward thee openly." (3 Nephi 13:16–18)

Saturday

"They did fast much and pray much, and they did worship God with exceedingly great joy." (Alma 45:1)

Veterans Day

"We believe that all men are justified in defending themselves, their friends, and property, and the government." (D&C 134:11)

LDS.org video "Dare to Stand Alone." President Monson tells of how he had to stand up for his beliefs while he was in the US Navy. https://goo.gl/iJJAsz

Music from Children's Songbook & Hymns

- I Will Be Valiant (*CS*, 162)
- We'll Bring the World His Truth (*CS*, 172)
- Onward, Christian Soldiers (*Hymns*, 246)
- We Are All Enlisted (*Hymns*, 250)
- Behold! A Royal Army (*Hymns*, 251)
- The Star-Spangled Banner, or your national anthem (*Hymns*, 340)

Quote

"World peace, though a lofty goal, is but an outgrowth of the personal peace each individual seeks to attain. I speak not of the peace promoted by man, but peace as promised of God. I speak of peace in our homes, peace in our hearts, even peace in our lives. Peace after the way of man is perishable. Peace after the manner of God will prevail" (Thomas S. Monson, "The Path to Peace," *Ensign*, May 1994).

Gospel Topics: War https://goo.gl/XzrAV9

Scripture Stories

Gideon is called to lead the Israelites out of bondage. God tells him to only take three hundred men with him to Midian. They frighten the Midianites and conquer them (see Judges 6–7).

David faces and kills Goliath. He ends the war between Israel and the Philistines (see 1 Samuel 17).

Captain Moroni makes the title of liberty, prays for freedom for his people, and calls everyone together to protect themselves (see Alma 46:10–37).

LDS.org video "Spiritual Vertigo." A veteran World War II fighter pilot shares the importance of obedience. https://goo.gl/EBht6c

Two thousand young sons of the people of Ammon vow to defend their liberty. They become veterans at a very young age (see Alma 53:16–22; Alma 56; Alma 57:19–27).

Gospel Art Pictures

- *David Slays Goliath* (#19)
- *Captain Moroni Raises the Title of Liberty* (#79)
- *Two Thousand Young Warriors* (#80)

Church History

On July 21, 1846, the Mormon Battalion left their homes to help fight in the Mexican War. After marching 2,030 miles, they reached California on January 29, 1847. By that time, the war was won. To learn more about the Mormon Battalion, see chapter twenty-six of *Church History in the Fulness of Times Student Manual* (2003), 323–36 at https://goo.gl/JbY9Fj.

On September 11, 1857, a tragic event occurred when some members of the Church massacred almost everyone in a wagon train heading west. This was done without the knowledge or consent of the leaders of the Church. Those who planned and executed the massacre were legally tried and punished, as well as excommunicated from the Church. To learn more, go to LDS.org's gospel topic "Mountain Meadows Massacre" at https://goo.gl/fcJ2mr and Richard E. Turley Jr.'s September 2007 *Ensign* article, "The Mountain Meadows Massacre" (https://goo.gl/FbwAJj).

LDS.org images "San Diego Mormon Battalion Historic Site" https://goo.gl/8Pxq6f

LDS.org image "Mountain Meadows Massacre Site" https://goo.gl/TGJKMT

Adaptations for Younger Children

Quote

"I will keep my mind and body sacred and pure, and I will not partake of things that are harmful to me" ("My Gospel Standards").

Lesson from *Behold Your Little Ones*

"I Have a Body like Heavenly Father's" (Lesson 9, pp. 40–43) and "I Will Take Care of My Body" (Lesson 10, pp. 44–47). Explain that veterans are people who have served their country. They take good care of their bodies so they can serve, and we are grateful for their service.

Faith in God

"Plan a physical fitness program for yourself that may include learning to play a sport or game. Participate in the program for one month" (p. 11). Physical fitness is important for people serving in the military. Those in the Lord's army—missionaries—set aside time each day to exercise.

Activity ☺

Invite a veteran to come talk to your family about their service, how they feel about their country, and what they do to strengthen the country. Prepare a package for someone who is serving in the armed forces, and sing patriotic songs.

If you have a chess or checkers game, get it out. If not, talk about any team sport your family likes. Designate one team as "Christ's side" and one as "Satan's side." Satan and his followers always try to get Christ's disciples to help them, or at least to "sit the game out" so they can't be a positive influence on others. Talk about some of Satan's obvious, and less obvious, strategies for inviting people to follow him, or at least sit out the game. Blatant things like addictions, greed, and immorality entice some people away. Less obvious things include encouraging people not to cooperate and to fight with their siblings. We have the chance to be active soldiers for the cause of Christ. Read Revelation 12:7–11 (Monday's scripture below), and talk about ways to keep your testimony strong, follow the Spirit, and be a righteous influence on others.

Adaptations for Older Children and Teens

Quote

"On this evening we meet to do honor to those who have given their lives in the service of their country. . . . There are many things in mortal life difficult [to] understand, many things that tear at the heartstrings and test the temper of the human soul. These are the perplexities of life. We live in perplexing days. And yet, there comes promise that if we will be faithful to Him and teach his word, we can come to know peace. . . . God bless the memory of those who have given their lives in the service of their country" (Boyd K. Packer, "Our Honored Brethren," *New Era*, August 1971).

Preach My Gospel

Chapter 1: "What Is My Purpose as a Missionary?" pp. 1–16. Just as veterans are people who have actively served in their nation's army, full-time missionaries are active servants in the Lord's army.

Personal Progress

Good Works #8: Personalized Value Experience—Talk to your parents and identify any veterans you know. Determine a way to serve one or more veterans (p. 57).

Duty to God

"List some specific things your quorum will do to give service. Also plan several things you will do on your own to give service" (pp. 26–27, 50–51, 74–75). Talk to several veterans about their service to their country, and ask them what they feel makes a good citizen. Ask them what they think you could to be doing to contribute to the country's strength and purity. Commit to doing your part to strengthen your county. Offer to serve the veterans you talk to.

Activity

If you have a chess or checkers game, get it out. If not, talk about any team sport your family likes. Designate one team as "Christ's side" and one as "Satan's side." Imagine that Satan's pieces could talk and reason with Christ's pieces and get some of them to convert to their side. Imagine that they could persuade some of them to sit the game out. Would that change the odds of who would win if many of Christ's original followers sat out or started helping the other team? Satan and his followers are diligent in trying to convert Christ's disciples to help them, or at least to "sit the game out" so they can't be a positive influence on others. Talk about some of Satan's obvious, and less obvious, strategies for inviting people to follow him, or at least sit out the game. Blatant things like addictions, greed, and immorality entice some people away. Less obvious things like encouraging people to be too busy, to be proud, or to neglect personal prayers and scripture study help disable some Christians and their positive influence. We have the chance to be active soldiers for the cause of Christ. Read Revelation 12:7–11 (Monday's scripture below), and talk about ways to keep your testimony strong, follow the Spirit, and be a righteous influence on others.

Daily Scriptures

Veterans Day

Sunday

"We believe that all men are justified in defending themselves, their friends, and property, and the government." (D&C 134:11)

Monday

"And there was war in heaven: Michael and his angels fought against the dragon; and the dragon fought and his angels, And prevailed not; neither was their place found any more in heaven. And the great dragon was cast out, that old serpent, called the Devil, and Satan, which deceiveth the whole world: he was cast out into the earth, and his angels were cast out with him. And I heard a loud voice saying in heaven, Now is come salvation, and strength, and the kingdom of our God, and the power of his Christ: for the accuser of our brethren is cast down, which accused them before our God day and night. And they overcame him by the blood of the Lamb, and by the word of their testimony." (Revelation 12:7–11)

Tuesday

Moroni "inspired [the Nephites'] hearts with . . . the thoughts of their lands, their liberty, yea, their freedom from bondage. And it came to pass that [the Nephites] turned upon the Lamanites, and they cried with one voice unto the Lord their God, for their liberty and their freedom from bondage. And they began to stand against the Lamanites with power." (Alma 43:48–50)

Wednesday

"When Moroni, who was the chief commander of the armies of the Nephites, had heard of these dissensions, he was angry with Amalickiah. And it came to pass that he rent his coat; and he took a piece thereof, and wrote upon it—In memory of our God, our religion, and freedom, and our peace, our wives, and our children." (Alma 46:11–12)

Thursday

Moroni said to Zerahemnah: "We have gained power over you, by our faith, by our religion, and by our rites of worship, and by our church, and by the sacred support which we owe to our wives and our children, by that liberty which binds us to our lands and our country; yea, and also by the maintenance of the sacred word of God, to which we owe all our happiness; and by all that is most dear unto us." (Alma 44:5)

Friday

"[The two thousand stripling warriors] entered into a covenant to fight for the liberty of the Nephites, yea, to protect the land unto the laying down of their lives; yea, even they covenanted that they never would give up their liberty, but they would fight in all cases to protect the Nephites and themselves from bondage." (Alma 53:17)

Saturday

"Greater love hath no man than this, that a man lay down his life for his friends." (John 15:13)

Thanksgiving Day

"Live in thanksgiving daily, for the many mercies and blessings which [God] doth bestow upon you." (Alma 34:38)

Mormonads—Gratitude
https://goo.gl/i8miMD

LDS.org video "Thanksgiving Daily"
https://goo.gl/Pjxx9f

Music from *Children's Songbook* & *Hymns*

- A Song of Thanks (*CS*, 20)
- For the Beauty of the Earth (*Hymns*, 92)
- Prayer of Thanksgiving (*Hymns*, 93)
- Come, Ye Thankful People (*Hymns*, 94)

Quote

"I would like to mention three instances where I believe a sincere 'thank you' could lift a heavy heart, inspire a good deed, and bring heaven's blessings closer to the challenges of our day. First, may I ask that we express thanks to our parents for life, for caring, for sacrificing, for laboring to provide a knowledge of our Heavenly Father's plan for happiness. . . . Next, have we thought on occasion of a certain teacher at school or at church who seemed to quicken our desire to learn, who instilled in us a commitment to live with honor? . . . Third, I mention an expression of 'thank you' to one's peers" (Thomas S. Monson, "Think to Thank," *Ensign*, November 1998).

Scripture Stories

Jesus healed ten lepers and only one came back to thank Him (see Luke 17:11–19).

Before Jesus miraculously fed the multitude with only five loaves of bread and two small fish, He gave thanks. After everyone had eaten till they were full, the leftovers were gathered and they totaled twelve baskets of food (see John 6:9–13).

Jesus's friend Lazarus dies. After four days, Jesus arrives to great grieving among his friends. He goes to the cave where Lazarus's body is, looks to heaven, and says, "Father, I thank thee that thou hast heard me" (John 11:41). Then he calls Lazarus from the dead (see John 11:14–45).

Amulek teaches the Zoramites to pray over everything in their lives, care for the needs of others, and "live in thanksgiving daily" (Alma 34:38) (see Alma 34:17–28, 38).

Gospel Art Pictures

- *The Ten Lepers* (#46)
- *Jesus Raising Lazarus from the Dead* (#49)
- *Thomas S. Monson* (#137)

Church History

In 1863, United States President Abraham Lincoln declared the last Thursday in November as a federal holiday for thanksgiving. To see his declaration, go to AbrahamLincolnOnline.org's page "Proclamation of Thanksgiving" at http://goo.gl/ru2uk3. To read a PBS.org article titled "Thanksgiving, Lincoln, and Pumpkin Pudding," which includes a recipe for pumpkin pudding adapted from one made in the 1800s, see http://goo.gl/dK6YmU.

The same year President Lincoln declared Thanksgiving Day to be an official holiday, the Saints started planning to build the Salt Lake City Tabernacle. It was first used in October of 1867, and it served as the location for general conferences until the Conference Center opened in the year 2000. To read or watch a conference talk about it, see Gordon B. Hinckley's talk "Good-bye to This Wonderful Old Tabernacle" (*Ensign*, November 1999).

Throughout the Church's history, several things happened around Thanksgiving Day. On November 28, 1869, the Young Ladies' Retrenchment Association was organized; this was the forerunner to the Young Women program. On November 27, 1919, the Church dedicated the Laie Hawaii Temple, the first temple built outside of the continental United States. In November 1997, Church membership reached ten million members. In November 2004, *Preach My Gospel* was published. To see a timeline of these and other important events in Church history, go to https://goo.gl/fNKhvG.

LDS.org image "Construction of the Salt Lake Temple." This picture shows the tabernacle in the background and men working with large granite bricks in the foreground.
http://goo.gl/R3mab3

LDS.org images "Conference Center"
https://goo.gl/okqhXV

LDS.org image "Aerial View of Temple Square"
http://goo.gl/tYbgfd

Adaptations for Younger Children

Quote

"Why does God command us to be grateful? . . . Our loving Heavenly Father knows that choosing to develop a spirit of gratitude will bring us true joy and great happiness" (Dieter F. Uchtdorf, "Grateful in Any Circumstances," *Ensign*, May 2014).

Lesson from *Behold Your Little Ones*

"I Will Be Thankful" (Lesson 15, pp. 64–67).

Faith in God

"Write a letter to a teacher, your parents, or your grandparents telling them what you appreciate and respect about them" (p. 9).

Activity ⊕

Give three blank thank-you cards to each person in your family. Write a note or draw a picture in the thank-you cards for each of the three people mentioned in President Monson's quote on page 222: parents, a special teacher, and a friend.

Make a gratitude journal by listing and drawing things you are grateful for. Leave the journal out so your family can add to it during the week.

Adaptations for Older Children and Teens

Quotes

"Walk with gratitude in your hearts, my dear friends. Be thankful for the wonderful blessings which are yours. Be grateful for the tremendous opportunities that you have. Be thankful to your parents, who care so very much about you and who have worked so very hard to provide for you. Let them know that you are grateful. Say thank you to your mother and your father. Say thank you to your friends. Say thank you to your teachers. Express appreciation to everyone who does you a favor or assists you in any way. . . . Let a spirit of thanksgiving guide and bless your days and nights. Work at it. You will find it will yield wonderful results" (Gordon B. Hinckley, "A Prophet's Counsel and Prayer for Youth," *Ensign*, January 2001).

"To express gratitude is gracious and honorable, to enact gratitude is generous and noble, but to live with gratitude ever in our hearts is to touch heaven" (Thomas S. Monson, "The Divine Gift of Gratitude," *Ensign*, November 2010).

Preach My Gospel

"Pray with Faith," pp. 93–95.

Personal Progress

Good Works #1—Learn about service. Over the next two weeks, notice and do something to thank the many people who serve you (p. 54).

Duty to God

The *Duty to God* book focuses on serving others. As you serve others, also focus on how others are serving you. Make expressing thanks a daily habit (see pp. 23, 26, 47, 50, 71, 74, 87).

Activity ☉

Wrap a present or prepare a gift bag. You can put a gift for your family in it if you want to. Tell one person about this activity so they can help at the end by asking, "Are you going to give us the present?" Tell your family you are thankful for them and you love them all so much. Show them the present, but don't give it to them. Tell them it represents your gratitude. Then say that family home evening is over. (Do not give them the present.) Have the person you talked to ahead of time ask if you are planning to give everyone the present. Say, "No," and that everyone should go ahead with whatever they normally do. Act like you are leaving and then call everyone back and read them this quote: 'Often we feel grateful and *intend* to express our thanks but forget to do so or just don't get around to it. Someone has said that 'feeling gratitude and not expressing it is like wrapping a present and not giving it.'" (Thomas S. Monson, "The Divine Gift of Gratitude," *Ensign*, November 2010; italics in original).

Daily Scriptures

Thanksgiving Day

Sunday

"Live in thanksgiving daily, for the many mercies and blessings which [God] doth bestow upon you." (Alma 34:38)

Monday

"And now I would that ye should be . . . diligent in keeping the commandments of God at all times; asking for whatsoever things ye stand in need, both spiritual and temporal; always returning thanks unto God for whatsoever things ye do receive." (Alma 7:23)

Tuesday

"Be of good cheer, for I will lead you along. The kingdom is yours and the blessings thereof are yours, and the riches of eternity are yours. And he who receiveth all things with thankfulness shall be made glorious; and the things of this earth shall be added unto him, even an hundred fold, yea, more." (D&C 78:18–19)

Wednesday

"Pray without ceasing, and . . . give thanks in all things." (Mosiah 26:39)

Thursday

"O, remember, my son, and learn wisdom in thy youth; yea, learn in thy youth to keep the commandments of God. Yea, and cry unto God for all thy support; yea, let all thy doings be unto the Lord, and whithersoever thou goest let it be in the Lord; yea, let all thy thoughts be directed unto the Lord; yea, let the affections of thy heart be placed upon the Lord forever. Counsel with the Lord in all thy doings, and he will direct thee for good; yea, when thou liest down at night lie down unto the Lord, that he may watch over you in your sleep; and when thou risest in the morning let thy heart be full of thanks unto God; and if ye do these things, ye shall be lifted up at the last day." (Alma 37:35–37)

Friday

"And now, my beloved brethren, I desire that ye . . . worship God, in whatsoever place ye may be in, in spirit and in truth; and that ye live in thanksgiving daily, for the many mercies and blessings which he doth bestow upon you." (Alma 34:37–38)

Saturday

"Behold, my soul abhorreth sin, and my heart delighteth in righteousness; and I will praise the holy name of my God. Come, my brethren, every one that thirsteth, come ye to the waters; and he that hath no money, come buy and eat; yea, come buy wine and milk without money and without price. . . . Feast upon that which perisheth not, neither can be corrupted. . . . Behold, my beloved brethren, remember the words of your God; pray unto him continually by day, and give thanks unto his holy name by night. Let your hearts rejoice." (2 Nephi 9:49–52)

Christmas Day

"For God so loved the world, that he gave his only begotten Son, that whosoever believeth in him should not perish, but have everlasting life." (John 3:16)

Mormonads—Christmas
https://goo.gl/QuVVe7

Music from Children's Songbook & Hymns

- Stars Were Gleaming (*CS*, 37)
- The Nativity Song (*CS*, 52)
- When He Comes Again (*CS*, 82)
- *Children's Songbook* songs about Christmas (*CS*, 34–54)
- Silent Night (*Hymns*, 204)
- Christmas hymns (*Hymns*, 200–214)

Quote

"Let us make Christmas real. It isn't just tinsel and ribbon, unless we have made it so in our lives. Christmas is the spirit of giving without a thought of getting. It is happiness because we see joy in people. It is forgetting self and finding time for others. . . . It is peace because we have found peace in the Savior's teachings. It is the time we realize most deeply that the more love is expended, the more there is of it for others" (Thomas S. Monson, "Christmas is Love," in 2012 First Presidency Christmas Devotional).

Scripture Stories

An angel appears to Mary to tell her she will be Jesus's mother. The Lord comes to Joseph in a dream to tell him to marry Mary and that she will be the mother of the Savior (see Luke 1:26–38; Matthew 1:18–25).

Joseph and Mary travel to Bethlehem. Jesus is born. Angels appear to shepherds to announce His birth and encourage them to go see the baby (see Luke 2:1–21).

Samuel the Lamanite cries repentance to the Nephites and prophesies of Christ's birth. He tells them the signs that they will see when Christ is born. He also teaches of Christ's mission and the plan of redemption. (Helaman 13–16, especially 14:1–9)

Gospel Art Pictures

- *The Annunciation: The Angel Gabriel Appears to Mary* (#28)
- Christmas-related Pictures (#28–32)
- *Samuel the Lamanite on the Wall* (#81)

Church History

Two days before Christmas, on December 23, 1805, Joseph Smith Jr. was born to Joseph Smith Sr. and Lucy Mack Smith in Sharon, Vermont.

On April 6, 1830, Joseph received the revelation recorded in Doctrine and Covenants 20. In verse one it says, "The rise of the Church of Christ in these last days, being one thousand eight hundred and thirty years since the coming of our Lord and Savior Jesus Christ in the flesh, it being regularly organized and established agreeable to the laws of our country, by the will and commandments of God, in the fourth month, and on the sixth day of the month which is called April." Many members believe that this verse officially declares the birth of Jesus Christ as happening on April 6. However, the Church does not take an official position regarding the exact date of Christ's birth, though some leaders have expressed their personal belief that it is April 6. To learn more about this see the FairMormon post "Do Latter-day Saints believe Jesus was born on April 6th?" at http://goo.gl /vMz2xt. To see LDS.org's Christmas video page, go to http://goo.gl/rmhsM3.

LDS.org videos on Christmas
http://goo.gl/rmhsM3

Adaptations for Younger Children

Quote

"I hope that this Christmas and every day of the year we will consider, in particular, the many gifts we have been given by our loving Heavenly Father. I hope we will receive these gifts with the wonder, thankfulness, and excitement of a child" (Dieter F. Uchtdorf, "The Good and Grateful Receiver," in 2012 First Presidency Christmas Devotional).

Lesson from *Behold Your Little Ones*

"Jesus Christ Is the Son of Heavenly Father" (Lesson 30, pp. 124–27).

Faith in God

"Tell a story from the Book of Mormon that teaches about faith in Jesus Christ. Share your testimony of the Savior" (p. 6).

Activity

Teach your children some ways to see Christ in secular Christmas traditions. For example, the Christmas tree reminds us of the tree of life and of the cross, referred to in the New Testament as "the tree" (Acts 5:30; 1 Peter 2:24). Stars and angels on the tops of trees remind us of the star that led the Wise Men to Jesus and of the angels that told the shepherds of His birth. Candy canes symbolize the shepherd's crook, and Christ is the Good Shepherd. Gifts remind us of the gifts given by the Wise Men to Jesus, as well as Jesus's great gift of the Atonement. For more ideas on symbols, as well as some great ideas for enhancing Christmas for yourself and your family, see *Remembering Christ at Christmas* by Monte F. Shelley.

Adaptations for Older Children and Teens

Quote

"Christmas is a time for remembering the Son of God and renewing our determination to take upon us His name. It is a time to reassess our lives and examine our thoughts, feelings, and actions. Let this be a time of remembrance, of gratitude, and a time of forgiveness. Let it be a time to ponder the Atonement of Jesus Christ and its meaning for each of us personally. Let it especially be a time of renewal and recommitment to live by the word of God and to obey His commandments. By doing this, we honor Him far more than we ever could with lights, gifts, or parties. . . . I pray that during this season and always, we will see the purity of the story of the Savior's birth and feel sincere gratitude for His life, teachings, and saving sacrifice for us. May this gratitude cause us to renew our determination to follow Him. May it also lead us to draw closer to our family, our church, and our fellowmen. And may we look steadfastly forward to that blessed day when the resurrected Christ will walk the earth again as our Lord, our King, and our blessed Savior" (Dieter F. Uchtdorf, "Seeing Christmas through New Eyes," in 2010 First Presidency Christmas Devotional).

Preach My Gospel

"The Savior's Earthly Ministry and Atonement," pp. 34–35.

Personal Progress

Write your testimony on the note pages in the back of your book (pp. 103–6) or in your journal. If you have received your Young Womanhood Recognition, write your testimony on pages 79–80.

Duty to God

Study the doctrinal topic of "The Plan of Salvation" focusing on Christ's role as our Savior and His choice to come to earth as a baby. Record what you learn and share what you learned with your parents or a priesthood leader (see pp. 18–21, 42–45, 66–69).

Activity

When Jesus was young, the Wise Men brought him gifts. When he was older, Jesus *gave* many gifts. One of the greatest gifts Jesus gave people in his life was the gift of time. The scriptures tell stories of how he changed his plans to give others the gifts of his love and his time. Ask everyone what they would want if they could have the gift of one hour with Jesus. Ask them what they would like if they were given the gift of two hours of family time. Ask them what they would like to do if they were given an hour of one-on-one time with one person in the family. Decide how each of you can follow the Savior by giving the gift of time this Christmas season. If possible, start tonight and spend just a little extra time together as a family doing something fun.

Daily Scriptures

Christmas Day

Sunday

"For God so loved the world, that he gave his only begotten Son, that whosoever believeth in him should not perish, but have everlasting life." (John 3:16)

Monday

"Behold, a virgin shall be with child, and shall bring forth a son, and they shall call his name Emmanuel, which being interpreted is, God with us." (Matthew 1:23)

Tuesday 🅳🅼

"The Son of God . . . shall be born of Mary, at Jerusalem which is the land of our forefathers, she being a virgin, a precious and chosen vessel, who shall be overshadowed and conceive by the power of the Holy Ghost, and bring forth a son, yea, even the Son of God. And he shall go forth, suffering pains and afflictions and temptations of every kind. . . . And he will take upon him death, that he may loose the bands of death which bind his people; and he will take upon him their infirmities, that his bowels may be filled with mercy, according to the flesh, that he may know according to the flesh how to succor his people according to their infirmities." (Alma 7:9–12)

Wednesday

"And the angel came in unto [Mary], and said . . . thou shalt conceive in thy womb, and bring forth a son, and shalt call his name Jesus. He shall be great, and shall be called the Son of the Highest." (Luke 1:28, 31–32)

Thursday

An angel told Joseph, "[Mary] shall bring forth a son, and thou shalt call his name Jesus: for he shall save his people from their sins." (Matthew 1:21)

Friday

Mary "brought forth her firstborn son, and wrapped him in swaddling clothes, and laid him in a manger. . . . And there were in the same country shepherds abiding in the field, keeping watch over their flock by night. And, lo, the angel of the Lord came upon them, and the glory of the Lord shone round about them: and they were sore afraid. And the angel said unto them, Fear not: for, behold, I bring you good tidings of great joy, which shall be to all people. For unto you is born this day in the city of David a Saviour, which is Christ the Lord." (Luke 2:7–11)

Saturday

"Behold I have given unto you my gospel, and this is the gospel which I have given unto you—that I came into the world to do the will of my Father." (3 Nephi 27:13)

Lesson Helps,
Appendices & Index

Lesson Helps

Articles of Faith Memorization Tips and Tricks

Here are some memory tricks to help your children remember the topics of each article of faith. If you would like to share your own tips and tricks, please contact me at FHEasy.com.

1. Son. "We believe in God, the Eternal Father, and in His Son, Jesus Christ . . ."

2. Two, too. There are two people, Adam and Eve. When you make choices, you get consequences too.

3. Tree, Free, Obee. Tree refers to the Atonement; free refers to everyone being saved; and obee refers to the need to be obedient to the laws and ordinances of the gospel. "Through the Atonement [tree] . . . all mankind may be saved [free] by obedience . . ."

4. Four. This article of faith lists the first four principles and ordinances of the gospel: faith, repentance, baptism by immersion, and receiving the gift of the Holy Ghost.

5. Thrive. Men are called of God to thrive and spread the gospel so others can thrive too.

6. Ex-six-ted. "We believe in the same organization that ex-*six*-ted in the Primitive Church . . ."

7. Seven. Seven days are the gift of a week. The seventh day is Sunday, a gift from God for us to improve our relationships and relax. This article lists seven gifts we believe in.

8. Gate. Think of a gate made of iron rods. Nephi taught that the iron rod in his father's dream represented the word of God (1 Nephi 11:25). In this memory trick, "iron rods" refer to the scriptures: the Bible and Book of Mormon.

9. Line. There are two lines of revelation: personal and priesthood. (Dallin H. Oaks, "Two Lines of Communication," *Ensign*, November 2010)

10. Ten. Ten tribes. We believe in the restoration of the ten tribes.

11. Heaven. We worship the God of heaven and believe in letting all people worship in whatever way they want to.

12. Twelve, delve, shelve. Think of law books on shelves. Delve into the laws on the shelves.

13. Thirteen, fourteen, honest, true. The thirteenth article of faith lists fourteen things. Honest! It's true! "We believe in being honest, true, chaste, benevolent . . ."

Lesson Helps

Memory Tricks for the Ten Commandments

Here are some memory tricks to help your children remember the Ten Commandments. If you would like to share your own tips and tricks, please contact me at FHEasy.com.

1. One, none. Hold one index finger high over your head pointing toward heaven, pointing to God. Worship none other than the one true God.

2. Two, moo. Make two horns by putting your thumbs on your temples, curling in your middle three fingers, and sticking out your pinkie fingers. The Israelites made a golden calf to worship while Moses was receiving the Ten Commandments from God.

3. Three, blasphemy. Hold three fingers up and then cover your mouth with them to show you will not blaspheme, which, in part, means taking the Lord's name in vain.

4. Four, door. Hold up four fingers on both hands, palms out away from you. Keep one hand still and move the other hand toward you as if you were opening a door, specifically the door of the church. We go to church as part of honoring the Sabbath day.

5. Five, alive. Hold up two hands and spread all five fingers out as far as possible. Then extend your elbows and reach your hands up and out to show how alive you feel. This commandment says you will live longer if you honor your parents.

6. Six, sticks. Hold up six fingers, then act like you are picking up a big stick. Swing it like you are swinging a bat, then drop it showing you won't use sticks to hurt other people.

7. Seven, heaven. Hold up seven fingers, then open both hands palms up gesturing toward heaven. There are no adulterers in heaven.

8. Eight, gate. Hold up eight fingers (four on each hand), then turn your hands so your eight fingertips are touching and your palms are toward your body. Keep one hand still and move the other toward your body as if you were opening a gate. Imagine the gate is made of steel—"no steeling/stealing."

9. Nine, lion. Hold up nine fingers, then put your wrists on top of your head with one hand in front and one hand in back, depicting a lion's mane. "No lion/lyin'."

10. Ten, men. Hold up ten fingers, and then turn your palms up and gesture outward toward everyone else, symbolizing other people and their things. Don't covet other "men's" [people's] things.

Lesson Helps

Comparing Joseph Smith's Four Accounts of the First Vision

Joseph Smith's Written Accounts of the First Vision

All accounts include the following:

- Joseph has questions about religion.

- He searches the scriptures.

- The Lord comes to him and speaks to him.

1832 Account

(This account is the only one Joseph Smith wrote himself. The focus is on Joseph's concern over his sins, his concern over which church to join, and his joy in being forgiven.)

- Joseph is concerned for his soul.

- Jesus tells him his sins are forgiven, and Joseph feels great joy.

- In this account, Joseph does not specify that there were two personages; the wording makes readers wonder if there may have been only one.

1835 Account

(Told to Robert Matthews. It is the only one that mentions many angels.)

- Joseph is concerned for his soul. This overlaps with the 1832 account.

- Satan's presence is spoken of in this account.

- Jesus tells him his sins are forgiven. This overlaps with the 1832 account.

- Joseph sees many angels.

1838 Account

(Most members are familiar with this account because it is published in the Pearl of Great Price. The focus is on the beginning of the Restoration of the Church because no other church was correct.)

- Background information of religious excitement in the area is given.

- Satan's presence is spoken of in this account. This overlaps with the 1835 account.

- Heavenly Father introduces Joseph to Jesus.

- Jesus tells Joseph that all the churches are wrong.

1842 Account

(This account was written in the "Wentworth letter" where the articles of faith were first written. It is brief.)

• This account shares all the details bulleted in the 1838 account.

For access to the original texts of all twelve written accounts of the First Vision (along with a variety of other issues related to the First Vision), go to FairMormon's page "Joseph Smith's First Vision" at http://goo.gl /kQHKxC. To read responses to the differences between the accounts, read the article "Why Are There Differences Between Joseph Smith's 4 First Vision Accounts?" on LDS.net (http://goo.gl/JGnP86).

FairMormon page "Joseph Smith's different accounts of the First Vision"
http://goo.gl/ujzVXs

LDS.net blog post "Why Are There Differences Between Joseph Smith's 4 First Vision Accounts?" This includes an easy-to-understand graphic showing how different accounts overlap and differ.
http://goo.gl/JGnP86

Lesson Helps

The Boy Who Cried Wolf

Once upon a time, a boy was tending the sheep for his whole village. It was a beautiful day, and tending the sheep was getting boring. To spice things up, he decided to play a trick on the townspeople. "Wolf! Wolf!" he cried. All the townspeople dropped their tools and came running to help save the sheep. The boy laughed and laughed at the people's concerned faces. He had really tricked them! Irritated, the townspeople went back to work.

The boy thought his joke was so funny that a few hours later he decided to see if it would work again. "Wolf! Wolf!" he cried. Again, all the townspeople stopped their work and raced to help save the sheep, only to find the shepherd boy laughing at them again. Angry, they returned to their work.

Shortly thereafter, a real wolf came into the herd and started chasing the sheep. Alarmed, the boy cried, "Wolf! Wolf!" and started trying to save the sheep. The townspeople didn't even look up. They had been fooled twice before, and they didn't want to be fooled again. Because of the shepherd boy's dishonesty, many sheep were killed and carried off by a very happy wolf.

Lesson Helps

Walking through Paper

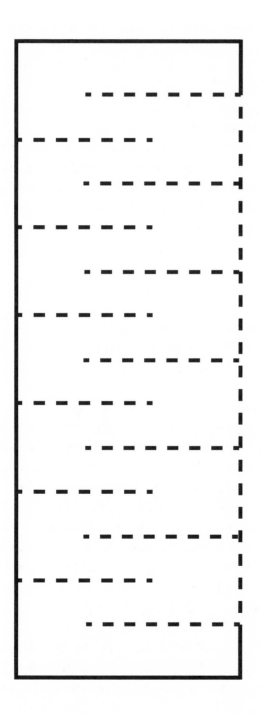

Fold an 8.5 × 11 piece of paper in half lengthwise. Cut the paper from both sides along the horizontal dotted lines. Don't cut all the way to the edge. Then cut along the dotted line on the fold, but *only* on the dotted line. Gently unfold your piece of paper and open it up. Let your family members walk through the paper.

Appendix A

When Did FHE Start?

Answer: Over one hundred years ago now. FHE was introduced as a Churchwide program in 1915. Here is the official letter from the presidency of the Church at the time.

To the Presidents of Stakes, Bishops and Parents in Zion:

Dear Brethren and Sisters: We counsel the Latter-day Saints to observe more closely the commandment of the Lord given in the 68th section of the Doctrine and Covenants:

"And again, inasmuch as parents have children in Zion, or in any of her stakes which are organized, that teach them not to understand the doctrine of repentance, faith in Christ the Son of the living God, and of baptism and the gift of the Holy Ghost by the laying on of hands when eight years old, the sin be upon the heads of the parents;

"For this shall be a law unto the inhabitants of Zion, or in any of her stakes which are organized;

"And their children shall be baptized for the remission of their sins when eight years old, and receive the laying on of hands,

"And they shall also teach their children to pray, and to walk uprightly before the Lord" [see D&C 68:25–28].

The children of Zion should also observe more fully the commandment of the Lord given to ancient Israel and reiterated to the Latter-day Saints: "Honor thy father and thy mother: that thy days may be long upon the land which the Lord thy God giveth thee" [see Ex. 20:12].

These revelations apply with great force to the Latter-day Saints, and it is required of fathers and mothers in this Church that these commandments shall be taught and applied in their homes.

To this end we advise and urge the inauguration of a "home evening" throughout the Church, at which time fathers and mothers may gather their boys and girls about them in the home and teach them the word of the Lord. They may thus learn more fully the needs and requirements of their families, at the same time familiarizing themselves and their children more thoroughly with the principles of the gospel of Jesus Christ. This home evening should be devoted to prayer, singing hymns, songs, instrumental music, scripture reading, family topics, and specific instruction on the principles of the gospel and on the ethical problems of life, as well as the duties and obligations of children to parents, the home, the Church, society, and the nation. For the smaller children, appropriate recitations, songs, stories, and games may be introduced. Light refreshments of such a nature as may be largely prepared in the home might be served.

Formality and stiffness should be studiously avoided, and all the family should participate in the exercises.

These gatherings will furnish opportunities for mutual confidence between parents and children, between brothers and sisters, as well as give opportunity for words of warning, counsel, and advice by parents to their boys and girls. They will provide opportunity for the boys and girls to honor father and mother and to show their appreciation of the blessings of home so that the promise of the Lord to them may be literally fulfilled and their lives be prolonged and made happy.

We request that the presidents of stakes and bishops throughout the Church set aside at least one evening each month for this purpose and that upon such evenings no other Church duties shall be required of the people.

We further request that all the officers of the auxiliary organizations throughout the Church support this movement and encourage the young people to remain at home that evening and use their energies in making it instructive, profitable, and interesting.

If the Saints obey this counsel, we promise that great blessings will result. Love at home and obedience to parents will increase. Faith will be developed in the hearts of the youth of Israel, and they will gain power to combat the evil influences and temptations which beset them.

Your brethren,
JOSEPH F. SMITH
ANTHON H. LUND
CHARLES W. PENROSE
First Presidency[1]

---

1 *Improvement Era*, June 1915, 733–34; reprinted in "Family Home Evening: Counsel and a Promise," *Ensign*, June 2003.

Appendix B

Customizing Family Home Evening for Your Family

Your Family Is Unique

This is *your* family, and these are *your* family traditions you are creating. What do *you* want to do? What would be fun, bonding, practical, and effective for *your* family? Just like *"the sabbath was made for man, and not man for the sabbath,"* family home evening and family scripture study were made for the family, not the other way around (Mark 2:27).

There is no right, wrong, or perfect way to do these things! The goals are clear: teach your kids the gospel and get closer as a family in the process.

Customizing FHE to Work for Your Family

Family home evening ends up being what you make it. If you are a stress case putting pressure on your family to act a certain way in order to make you feel successful, you are missing the boat. Family home evening is meant to bless and connect our families, not become just another weekly chore. So relax. You have a year's worth of low-prep FHE ideas in your hands. Now enjoy your family.

Perfectionism can be a problem for some people when it comes to FHE. Please know that it is not only okay for things to be different for your family than for other families, but that it is expected. Your family is truly unique. Why would you do FHE exactly the same as another family?

I know of families who have a serious, sit-down lesson every week for an hour. Others make treats, chase each other around the house, and end with a five-minute lesson. Some people hold their home evenings on Sunday afternoon or Monday morning or on a weekday afternoon. Do what works for you and don't worry about doing things differently than whomever you currently compare yourself with.

Here are some ideas my family has used that make our family home evenings work well.

1.   Put together a "Family Home Evening Activity Box." Fill it with fun things your family likes to do together. In our box, we have an animal joke book, cars, dinosaurs, bubbles, and toys that fly around the house. We don't get into it every week, but it's there as a quick place to go for something fun to do together.

2.   If you are short on time, discuss an FHE lesson while the family is eating dinner. Skip other activities completely, or plan on doing them another time during the week.

3.   If you get the Church magazines, you can always grab one and read something out of it for an alternative to the lessons in this book. The magazines are full of pictures and stories, and they are quick and easy resources for discussing gospel topics.

4.   The *Gospel Art Book* is a great resource. You can just choose a picture and talk about it.

5.   I've also used some of the suggestions offered on LDS.org. Start and end with a prayer; learn from the scriptures; add music; make it fun by playing games, acting out stories, or making treats; be consistent; and add variety, like helping a neighbor, going to the park, or going for a walk (see https://www.lds.org/topics/family-home-evening).

Appendix C

Customizing Family Scripture Study to Fit Your Family

Every time you have family scripture study, you are informally bearing your testimony to your family about how important Heavenly Father, Jesus Christ, the Holy Ghost, and the gospel are in your life.

When children are young, the main things most families are trying to do are establish the habit of family scripture study, model scripture reading, familiarize children with scriptural language and stories, teach basic principles of the gospel, and bond through wholesome and fun activities. This can be done by reading scripture stories as part of a regular story time as well as reading topical scriptures throughout the week.

Like family home evening, you get to do family scripture study however you want to, regardless of how you have seen it done in other families. Many families enjoy reading and discussing scripture stories together, and, in my opinion, this is always a good thing to keep going. The things to consider are when, where, and how to do it. In this book, daily scriptures are provided so you just need to decide when and where to read them with your family. I have found that the best times to read the scriptures together tend to be in the morning or evening along with prayers or meals. Since many families are already praying and eating together, it is easy to add in scripture time, especially when you are only discussing one short scripture, such as provided in this book.

In my family, our *FHEasy* book is kept by the kitchen table and someone reads the scripture for the day while everyone is eating breakfast. Sometimes we talk about it and sometimes we don't. If we miss reading our scripture for that day in the morning, I may read it when we have our family prayer at night, or I may wait until the next day and read two scriptures. Sometimes I just let it go and get back on track the next day. This routine is simple and doable for my family.

Some families like to have a parent read the scripture every day. Others like to whisper the scripture into a child's ear and have the child say the scripture. Older children can take turns reading the daily scripture. I like to read the reference before I read the scripture, so my kids get used to saying references in talks when they get older. My husband likes us to look up the daily scripture reference in the scriptures so we are modeling scripture reading that way as well.

Most mornings, we just read the scripture and have a short discussion about it. On occasion, we have a longer discussion. For example, one morning we read about baptism and discussed the method of baptism. My nephew had recently been baptized, so we talked about what he wore, what he and his dad did, and why it was important for him to be fully immersed in the water. Then we discussed how old children have to be to be baptized and sang a song about baptism—all around the breakfast table where we were sitting together anyway.

Faith and Flexibility

These are all just ideas for you to play with. My foremost recommendation is for you to believe that you can be successful at family home evening and family scripture study and that the Lord will help you. **The Lord wouldn't give this prophetic counsel if it were impossible to follow; there is always a way.** Find a pattern that will work for a while, and expect that you will occasionally need to change how you do things, but that your family will be blessed by those changes.

Also, please realize that it's okay to have weeks that flop, times when you forget, or days when no one's really into it. It's okay to go through periods when things are less organized or less exciting. If the way you are doing things doesn't seem to be serving your family, prayerfully ask for help in coming up with ideas that *will* work, and then experiment with those ideas. You will be inspired with ideas that work for your family that wouldn't work for other families. It's okay! Go with it!

Appendix D

Favorite Quotes on Family Home Evening and Family Scripture Study

"We call upon parents to devote their best efforts to the teaching and rearing of their children in gospel principles which will keep them close to the Church. The home is the basis of a righteous life, and no other instrumentality can take its place or fulfill its essential functions in carrying forward this God-given responsibility. We counsel parents and children to give highest priority to family prayer, family home evening, gospel study and instruction, and wholesome family activities. However worthy and appropriate other demands or activities may be, they must not be permitted to displace the divinely appointed duties that only parents and families can adequately perform" (Excerpt from February 27, 1999 Letter from the First Presidency; "News of the Church," *Ensign*, June 1999**).**

"The prophetic counsel to have daily personal and family prayer, daily personal and family scripture study, and weekly family home evening are the essential, weight-bearing beams in the construction of a Christ-centered home. Without these regular practices it will be difficult to find the desired and much needed peace and refuge from the world. . . . Simple, consistent, good habits lead to a life full of bountiful blessings" (Richard G. Scott, "For Peace at Home," *Ensign*, May 2013).

"Insisting that you have a picture-perfect family home evening each week—even though doing so makes you and everyone around you miserable—may not be the best choice. Instead, ask yourself, 'What could we do as a family that would be enjoyable and spiritual and bring us closer together?' That family home evening—though it may be modest in scope and execution—may have far more positive long-term results" (Dieter F. Uchtdorf, "Forget Me Not," *Ensign*, November 2011).

"Sometimes Sister Bednar and I wondered if our efforts to do these spiritually essential things were worthwhile. Now and then verses of scripture were read amid outbursts such as 'He's touching me!' 'Make him stop looking at me!' 'Mom, he's breathing my air!' Sincere prayers occasionally were interrupted with giggling and poking. And with active, rambunctious boys, family home evening lessons did not always produce high levels of edification. At times Sister Bednar and I were exasperated because the righteous habits we worked so hard to foster did not seem to yield immediately the spiritual results we wanted and expected. . . . Sister Bednar and I thought helping our sons understand the content of a particular lesson or a specific scripture was the ultimate outcome. But such a result does not occur each time we study or pray or learn together. The consistency of our intent and work was perhaps the greatest lesson—a lesson we did not fully appreciate at the time" (David A. Bednar, "More Diligent and Concerned at Home," *Ensign*, November 2009).

Index

A

Accountability 22, 26, 76, 78, 79
Agency 24, 26, 62, 74, 76, 77, 78, 79, 210
Apostles 40, 41, 42, 43, 136, 185, 193
Articles of Faith 12, 16–71, 233
    Memorization tips 230
    Scriptures 16, 19, 20, 23, 24, 27, 28,
    31, 32, 35, 36, 39, 40, 43, 44, 47, 48,
    51, 52, 55, 56, 59, 60, 63, 64, 67, 68,
    71, 95, 179
Atonement, the 24, 25, 26, 28, 30, 31, 34,
    104, 129, 192, 194, 226

B

Baptism 19, 35, 168, 175, 176, 177, 178, 179,
    206
Bible, the 16, 19, 40, 48, 49, 50, 51
Blessings 34, 74, 83, 104, 106, 144, 145, 146,
    188, 189, 190, 220, 222, 223, 241
    Patriarchal blessings 152, 153, 154
Book of Mormon 19, 25, 48, 49, 50, 51, 109,
    129, 137, 158, 225, 230
    History of 49, 125
Budgeting 146, 149

C

Church organization 40, 41, 169, 185, 188,
    189, 221, 225
    Quorum of the Twelve Apostles 185
    Relief Society 188, 189
Creation, the 24, 25, 77, 189, 205
Cultural diversity 105, 160, 180, 181, 182

D

Dancing 92, 93, 118
Dating 80, 81, 82, 142
    vs. Hanging out 82
Doctrinal Mastery 12
    Doctrinal Mastery scriptures 22,
    23, 25, 27, 31, 35, 39, 43, 47, 51, 55,
    59, 63, 71, 75, 79, 80, 83, 84, 87, 88,
    91, 92, 95, 99, 111, 115, 119, 123,
    124, 126, 127, 128, 131, 135, 136,
    139, 140, 143, 144, 147, 155, 159,
    160, 163, 164, 167, 171, 172, 175,
    179, 180, 183, 184, 187, 191, 192,
    195, 196, 199, 200, 203, 204, 207,
    215, 227
Doctrine and Covenants 49, 52, 53, 193
Dress and Appearance 38, 84, 85, 86, 121,
    141

E

Education 88, 89, 90
Entertainment 92, 93, 94. *See also* Dancing;
    Media; Music

F

Faith 19, 22, 32, 33, 34, 35, 106, 126, 152,
    154, 155, 179, 194, 198, 212, 213, 215, 222
Fall, the 24, 25, 26, 27, 62, 197
Family 97, 98, 198, 204, 238
Family: A Proclamation to the World, the 97,
    98, 198, 206
Family Home Evening 96, 98, 236, 240, 241
Fasting 212, 213, 214, 215

Online Support

Free Online Support at FHEasy.com

For additional information and resources, please visit my website at FHEasy.com.

There you will find

- Free family home evening tips and tricks.

- Quotes about families, family home evening, and family scripture study.

- Recipes to help make dinner and cleanup easy on family night.

- A free FHEasy lesson: "Seminary and Doctrinal Mastery Scriptures."

- Supplementary lesson and activity ideas.

- Information on speaking events and media topics related to strengthening families.

- My contact information so you can share feedback, suggestions, or activity ideas.

Also, if you have found this book to be helpful, please consider telling your friends or writing a review online.

Happy Home Evenings!

About the Author

Christina Shelley Albrecht graduated from BYU with a degree in linguistics and a master's certificate in Teaching English to Speakers of Other Languages (TESOL). In the course of getting married and having children, she realized the need for books to support parents in having practical, effective, and fun family home evenings and daily scripture study. She originally compiled this book for her family, but ended up sharing it with some friends. The feedback was so positive that she decided to publish it for all LDS families to enjoy. Tina invites you to visit her at FHEasy.com

SCAN to visit

www.FHEasy.com